Defending Public Education from Corporate Takeover

Edited by

Todd Alan Price

John Duffy

Tania Giordani

University Press of America,® Inc.
Lanham · Boulder · New York · Toronto · Plymouth, UK

Copyright © 2013 by
University Press of America,® Inc.
4501 Forbes Boulevard
Suite 200
Lanham, Maryland 20706
UPA Acquisitions Department (301) 459-3366

10 Thornbury Road
Plymouth PL6 7PP
United Kingdom

Library of Congress Control Number: 2012951106
ISBN: 978-0-7618-6049-5 (clothbound : alk. paper)
eISBN: 978-0-7618-6050-1

Contents

Foreword

It has never been more obvious than it is today, in the age of ever accelerating corporate and financial globalization, that we are all connected by our common humanity. Virtually every economic aspect of our lives is tied to the well-being of billions of fellow citizens across the continents. Yet shared prosperity remains elusive.

Under globalization, increasing opportunity and enhanced communication is expected to lift all boats; however the grim reality of human exploitation and natural resource degradation persists. For educators concerned about social justice, these matters are paramount. Because the *new managerialism* is spreading globally, our collective struggle becomes to preserve and expand human labor rights from the sweatshops of the Pacific Rim, to the agricultural plantations of Mexico and Latin America. A shared spirit of solidarity unites us across borders, reaching out from, for example, the occupation of a factory by striking industrial workers in Chicago, and stretching to Egypt where citizens assemble for democracy and the right to cast their ballot. We are interconnected by faith and solidarity as the popular, mass resistance to corporate and financial imposed austerity by citizens in Greece continues (a struggle which began, it should be noted, years past with student protest over exorbitant tuition). The political aftershocks and ripples return back across hemispheres in the form of threats to collective bargaining in Wisconsin and spirited talk concerning unionization in Chicago's charter schools. As citizens and educators alike we are joined in this shared struggle across continents, confronting similar global strategies which aim to subordinate workers and citizens to the narrow interests of multinational corporations and financial elites.

We have subsequently assembled the stories in this volume providing witness to and solidarity with the defense of public education, democracy and social justice here in the Midwest region, the heartland of the United States of America. We do so with the commitment that the work of citizens, teachers and students told in the chapters of this collection must be informed by, share common ground with and provide lessons for others involved in their own local struggles across the country in the defense of public education and democracy. We offer several reasons why this, the collection of narratives and critical analysis, focus largely on three key states of the Midwest.

Democratic Public Education Under Attack

One reason this book has a Midwestern focus is that, first and foremost, we have joined together with students, parents, teachers, and union leaders amidst Midwestern fights on behalf of public education. We clearly and openly understand that the struggle for fair, equitable and *a democratic public education* is constrained by a range of forces including: institutional racism and classism, the gendered nature of teaching, individual ability, and access and opportunity. We seek to demonstrate in these chapters that the overarching and dominant—but certainly not the only one—force attempting to redefine public education in the latest "education reform" effort, is the business community.

To be specific, it is the venture capitalist class—through educational philanthropy—that exerts inordinate influence over public policy; however, that influence has always been pre-eminent in Chicago, stretching back well over the last century. Thus we start with and focus on Chicago, in the Part I of the book.

Commercial Club Curriculum

In the first years of 20th century Chicago, businessmen sought to reform, reorganize and rationalize public education reform in a way that served their industrial and class interests. John Dewey, the great American philosopher and educator noted at that time that American political dominance was little more than "the shadow cast on society by big business" and that this undemocratic influence would persist as long as prevailing power continued to rest in "business for profit through the control of banking, land, industry, reinforced by command of the press, press agents, and other means of publicity and propaganda."[1]

We have conceptualized the influence of early 20th century Chicago, that Dewey so eloquently described above, as an era of "Commercial Club Curriculum." While the motives, values, and beliefs shared by commercial interests in shaping public schools then was localized, school reform today transcends states, regions and international borders. Yet Commercial Club Curriculum still underpins all school reform efforts, and retains some of the features of unique origin in Chicago's past. The most recent iteration of school reform across the United States, for example, has direct ties to Chicago's earlier designs; the captains of industry today aim to re-imagine, re-tool and re-introduce earlier school reform for a national stage via the Obama administration's *Blueprint for Reform* and Race to the Top (RTT) policies.

Communities Across the Heartland Push Back

Secondly, we focus our narratives and critical analysis in the Midwest because of its long commitment to labor and to public education. Historically the organization of workers and their resistance to the undemocratic social, political and economic designs of the captains of industry and finance found a unique, inspiring response in the cities and farm communities of the Midwest, especially in Chicago and Wisconsin. As was the case in the late nineteenth and early twentieth century, so it is in the 21st century: a challenge to undemocratic forces has grown in the streets, workplaces, and school communities of Illinois, Wisconsin and Ohio. In these places, citizens, union leaders, teachers and students are imagining and fighting for a public education that serves communities not corporations. The formulators and administrators of RTT with their Commercial Club sponsors emphasize repeatedly a narrow conception of education (student achievement as measured on standardized test scores) and economic opportunity (conflating school success with economic success, almost as if schools and teachers should be responsible for the economy and the literal creation of family sustaining jobs). Meanwhile, a renewed teacher and community based activism in Chicago and Wisconsin fully embrace the belief that education is intimately tied to issues of popular democracy and social justice. These citizens and teachers have directly challenged 21st century corporate school reforms that ignore and in fact deliberately gut any connections schools have to a vibrant and critical democracy. Instead, these so called reformers move to do everything possible to turn schools into a commodity to be pursued by consumers in the same manner that they might shop for and buy cars and home entertainment technology. A resistance movement is forming to fight back against that mentality.

We focus on the Midwest because this region has been a vital cauldron for resisting and challenging those who seek to excise the public and democratic heart of education. We tell the largely unknown charter school struggle waged by former Governor Ted Strickland in Ohio. Union leaders, teachers, parents and citizens—parallel to developments in Chicago—have joined the vanguard defense of public education and renewed popular school reform centered in and modeled for the rest of the country over a century ago. Wisconsin is the birthplace of the idea that the state should provide basic rights to both public and private workers through basic protections like workers disability, factory safety inspection, and collective bargaining. After decades of popular organizing, Wisconsin granted collective bargaining to public employees in 1959. The state's teacher collective bargaining law in the early 1980s preceded similar legislation that included teachers' right to strike in Illinois.

Yet, Wisconsin is also the birthplace of the first and most extensive voucher program in the country that shifted millions of public tax dollars to private school vouchers in Milwaukee almost 20 years ago. Robert Miranda relates the intense corporate support behind this movement in his chapter "Voucher Vultures Blueprint for Restructuring Milwaukee Public Schools."

The mass political mobilization of the 2011 Wisconsin Uprising to protect collective bargaining rights for public employees—despite its limited success and failure to recall Governor Scott Walker—added a major chapter to American labor history. Citizens in Wisconsin have inspired workers across the U.S. and the world. However, in the run up to these dramatic developments, most people are unaware of key events in Milwaukee, important to setting the stage for the Wisconsin Uprising. Todd Price tells this story that centered around the successful popular fight to stop the Milwaukee mayoral takeover of the public schools and the dissolution of an elected school board by Mayor Barrett with the backing of Arne Duncan and the then Democratic Governor Jim Doyle. T.J. Mertz extends the untold chapters of the Wisconsin resistance to Commercial Club Curriculum as he relates the successful effort to stop Governor Walker's attempt—paralleling the spirit of charter expansion advocated by RTT—to acquire the executive authority to sponsor the unlimited expansion of charters schools by bypassing local school board approval. We believe these yet untold stories of important Wisconsin victories against the forces out to destroy public education offer insights and lessons for organizers elsewhere.

Democratic Teacher Unionism Rises Up

Finally, we focus this book on the Midwest because something special is taking place in Chicago in the teacher union movement. Over the years, as Jack Gerson relates, teacher union leadership at the highest levels of state and national organization have largely acted as a conservative break on more progressive forces within the teacher movement. This has especially been the case in Chicago where what historian's call "business unionism" and "bread and butter unionism" has characterized the Chicago Teachers Union (CTU) for most of its history over the last 40 years. This kind of unionism has been removed from and often times stood in opposition to the communities teachers serve while largely focusing on salaries, benefits and offering predictable electoral support for Democratic candidates locally and nationally.

In Chicago the Chicago Teachers Union has been revitalized through the leadership of President Karen Lewis and the organizing of the Caucus of Rank and File Educators (CORE) by uniting and inspiring militant teachers, support staff and community organizations to challenge the neoliberal reorganization, chartering and privatizing of the Chicago Public Schools under Commercial Club Curriculum. Renewing the democratic principles of the first teacher union formed by Margaret Haley over a century ago in Chicago, the new CTU rank and file has directly confronted the class and racial nature of corporate school reform in Chicago in ways that provide some key precepts for transformative teacher unionism across the nation. Most importantly, CORE has been willing to stand toe-to-toe against the efforts of corporate managerialism and attacks on teachers and collective bargaining while every step of the way uniting with parents and citizens who wish to regain dominion over their student's public education.

The rebirth of democratic, militant teacher unionism was clearly evident to Chicago and the world when almost 5,000 of the 30,000 member CTU, the week after the NATO Summit in May of 2012, marched en masse from their rally in the Auditorium Theatre and Grant Park, up Michigan Avenue, through the Financial District and to the Chicago Board of Education in one of the greatest displays of union strength in generations. As reported by a CTU coordinator, Jackson Potter, teachers have had enough:

You've got thousands of teachers who are fed up, and they've said you can't disrespect our schools, our students, the parents we serve, and the profession we've dedicated our lives to . . . [this is] an incredible force of humanity, we're saying we care about our schools deeply and we're not going to let you shut them down, allow for oversize classrooms, deprive them of art, music, world language, of facility expenditures that they need and deserve, to have air conditioning, library, recess facilities . . . and if you do that there's going to be a big fight on your hands.[2]

The ghosts of Chicago's great labor militants and advocates for racial justice past were evident in spirit at the CTU protest on this warm day in May. Chicago is returning from being a company town to a union shop, recalling the city where teacher unionism was born and where American workers had for half a century—between the great 8 hour movement of the 1880s to the bloody fights in the 1930s—fought to form unions and insure basic principles of democracy.

The unity of teachers in the streets and their 90 percent strike vote certainly has the attention of the corporate elite of the Commercial Club of Chicago. Plastered across the Chicago print, visual and sound media the next day was the inspiring spectacle of red shirted teachers as they weaved their route through the arteries of the Chicago financial center. But for the anti-union, bad teacher bias of corporate owned media, it was a development in Chicago, the now self-proclaimed global city and third largest urban center in the United States, which the whole country should have been seeing, but was not. This direct challenge to the corporate Chicago's designs on public education was not just an event that Commercial Club elites might choose to ignore; it was the latest demonstrative sign of an awakening process of popular and teacher resistance to the unworkable, failing plans of corporate Chicago to remove the public and any semblance of democracy from public school.

Regional histories have a vital role in the study of social, political and economic phenomena. They provide unique, place specific developments often unknown to not only those who live elsewhere, but even to those who inhabit that specific place. Such studies have the power to help us see ourselves and our local struggles more clearly, to see what is unique in our place and to offer parallel and contrast with others confronting similar phenomena elsewhere. We believe what follows in this volume extends this valuable function to the widening national and international struggle to preserve public education, democracy and union teacher rights.

Notes

1. *Counterpunch*, http://www.counterpunch.org/2012/06/15/supreme-insult/#_edn3
2. See http://www.peoplestribune.org/pdfs/pt.2012.07.pdf *People's Tribune Online*, July 2012.

Preface

The chapters of this book are organized into four parts, each representing what education feels like under the increasingly shrill call for market alignment or what we refer to especially in Part III as "neoliberalism." Neoliberalism has been theorized as a political economy where the political state (government) is intentionally weakened, provides a rationale for a market state (corporations, foundations and their proxies) to effectively takeover and manage the political system. The greatest concern regarding this process is the outsourcing of the long established function of modern government—the common good—to the highest bidders, often venture capitalists. Furthermore, neoliberalism includes an imperious attack on traditional labor rights.

A key feature of neoliberalism, specific to public education, emphasizes wresting local education decision-making away from the citizens, and handing it over to private interests. This process is accompanied with the calculated imposition of an *audit culture* on the social space of the school. An over-emphasis on competition ensues whereby students become subject to intense monitoring and control, their standardized test scores become more highly quantified and scrutinized, and, furthermore, their scores are re-purposed (surely violating content validity) in order to reward and punish teachers and principals, schools and school districts, and even teacher education and institutions of higher learning. The feature and these processes—the neoliberal education plan—have serious implications for American society at large (as well as other countries, such as Haiti, as we are to find), and should be cause for concern to everyone, not only policy analysts and academic scholars.

Each part of the book reveals what we as authors believe every educator ultimately knows to be true; education under "market alignment" creates tremendous strain on all the stakeholders. Currently being shaped by the Obama administration, the education design *Blueprint for Reform* provides a script for what has become the pressure cooker that is the modern day public school. But it is the phrase and the program "Race to the Top" that captures the spirit of this frantic period better than any other.

Subsequently, the following introduction, "Race to the Top, Running for the Money," begins by laying out the Obama administration's core initiatives from

Blueprint for Reform and Race to the Top for reshaping public education: linking students' standardized tests scores to teacher performance in order to determine who is eligible to be a *Highly Effective Teacher (HET)*; replacing teacher made curriculum with a national curriculum based on the *Common Core State Standards* (CCSS); and eliminating the caps on charter schools to expand the *Turnaround.*

Acknowledgements

This manuscript reflects a diversity of views, experiences, and expressions, and posed a challenge to weave through on a single common thread. Nonetheless it is grounded by a tension and passion that runs throughout, connecting all the stories: vigilance for better society with an educated public, and strong schools. To that end, we gratefully acknowledge the following persons for their support in moving this project forward to completion.

We are indebted to the insights and the edits of our peer reviewers, Bill Watkins, Erica Meiners, George Wood and Susan Ohanian. Much appreciated are our graduate assistants, including Damaris Allen who compiled the publication and copyright materials, Sarah Drury for her careful review as a wordsmith, and Bianca Greenwald for several transcriptions (some still on the cutting floor; another book perhaps).

Thank you Dawn Harris, for your administrative support at NLU in general.

Thanks to University Press of America: Brooke Bascietto, Laura Grzybowski and Lindsay Macdonald for stewarding this project from beginning to finish; Emily Natsios and Gwen E. Kirby for copy review; and Piper Owens especially, for overall coordination of the final copy submission, copy review and critically, for your patience with our request(s) to extend the publishing materials' deadline! Last and not least, thank you to Ginger Price, Pat Duffy, and Barbara Berne for your steadfast dedication as mothers and teachers.

Introduction
Racing to the Top, Running for the Money
Todd Alan Price, John Duffy and Tania Giordani

The Race to the Top program (RTT), a $4.35 billion fund created under the
American Recovery and Reinvestment Act of 2009 (ARRA), is the largest
competitive education grant program in U.S. history. The RTT Fund (referred
to in the ARRA as the State Incentive Grant Fund) is designed to provide
incentives to states to implement large-scale, system-changing reforms that
result in improved student achievement, narrowed achievement gaps, and
increased graduation and college enrollment rates.[1]

What is Race to the Top?

The story behind the education program Race to the Top begins with the critical
meeting between Jonathan Schnur, education reformer and co-creator of New
Leaders for New Schools, and the White House staff. In his book *Class
Warfare: Inside the Fight to Fix America's Schools* (2011), Stephen Brill
documents how—from the very beginning—the Obama transition team was
committed to using incentives to spur education reform. Brill describes Schnur
as the mastermind behind this approach:

> Schnur had written a three-page memo summarizing how the Obama
> administration would take the $800 billion economic stimulus package the
> president was about to propose and carve out $15 billion as a jackpot to be
> divided among ten to fifteen states that won a contest related to education
> reform.[2]

Schnur recounts the incident during a speech he gave before the Stanford
School of Business. At the historic transition team gathering, Schnur, President
Obama, and other domestic policy makers are assembled in the room vetting
education policy. Much debate goes back and forth, according to Schnur, but at
one point, as he recalls, Obama stopped the conversation saying:

Racing to the Top, Running for the Money!

> We have to prioritize, what are in the best interests of children; what are the
> ways that adults can support this; and in doing so, *let's not poke the unions in
> the eye.*[3]

Schnur then proposes his idea to let the states compete for federal education
money. Obama was keen on a competition; not all states should get the funds.
He believed grants should be awarded to sponsor long-term development, the
use of data to drive continuous test score improvement, and most importantly
the creation of highly effective teachers and leaders.

Following that meeting, a group of education policy insiders—including a
hedge fund-sponsored, wing of the Democratic National Committee, Democrats
for Education Reform (DFER)—codified into language this novel program. This
is the result, from language in the federal register:

> On February 17, 2009, President Obama signed into law the ARRA, historic
> legislation designed to stimulate the economy, support job creation, and invest
> in critical sectors, including education. The ARRA laid the foundation for
> education reform by supporting investments in innovative strategies that are
> most likely to lead to improved results for students, long-term gains in school
> and school system capacity, and increased productivity and effectiveness. In
> particular, the ARRA authorized and provided $4.35 billion for the RTT Fund,
> a competitive grant program designed to encourage and reward states creating
> the conditions for education innovation and reform by implementing ambitious
> plans in four core areas: enhancing standards and assessments, improving the
> collection and use of data, increasing teacher effectiveness and achieving
> equity in teacher distribution, and turning around struggling schools.[4]

After the development of detailed requirements and the establishment of grant
evaluation team(s), Secretary of Education Arne Duncan, with the President in
supporting role, released the application for RTT funds in a statement at the
Department of Education, Washington D.C. on July 24th, 2009:[5]

> For states, for district leaders, for unions, for businesses, and for non-profits,
> the race to the top is the equivalent of education's reform the moon shot, and
> the president is determined, I am determined, and our team is determined not to
> miss this opportunity.[6]

Over the next several months, Secretary Duncan pitched the law at every
stop, embarking on an "education reform tour" and relying on the odd couple of
Reverend Al Sharpton and former House Speaker Newt Gingrich in tow. Since
then RTT has become enshrined, part of the Senate's version of proposed
reauthorization of the Elementary Secondary Education Act (ESEA). It has
continued in its most recent iteration as a funding source for "innovation." More
importantly, however, "race to the top" works as a metaphor; it embodies the
administration's attempt to double down on accountability, ratchet up high
stakes testing, increase the adoption of new national curriculum standards and
assessments, and bind teacher evaluation to student test performance
nationwide. In other words, it has entirely altered the public education
landscape.

Rallying around the "Highly Effective Teacher"

One year after the Race to the Top dedication, a *Washington Post* article declared, "across the country, public education is in the midst of a quiet revolution." The article staked its claim on "the voluntary adherence to national standards and student performance-based teacher compensation" as evidence of a "major movement" in "our" education system.[7] For those tasked with preparing the next generation of teachers to respond to this mounting call-to-arms—including the authors of this book—it has been anything but quiet.

Indeed, for several years, traditional teacher education institutions have been subjected to loud, shrill, even irrational criticism from mainstream media. Foundations located outside of the profession[8] have joined in the chorus; but even more pointedly, criticism has increasingly rained on the profession from inside of the profession itself.[9] The ringing indictment sounds like this: teacher education colleges fail to produce the teachers "we" need, and even more compellingly, fail to place enough highly qualified teacher candidates into urban school systems where the highest need resides.[10] Furthermore, the argument goes, when they do, urban school districts fail to retain the effective ones.

Is teacher education to blame for the lack of highly qualified teachers? Is public education failing? Do we need education reform or education revolution? To consider these questions, and to understand the impact of long standing, withering teach criticism, it is important to examine how government and the teacher education profession itself have both informed and responded to the so-called "debate" over teachers.

First off, the federal government under the George W. Bush administration framed the argument and essentially controlled the terms of the debate. Labeling most schools as failing, their signature domestic program, NCLB (passed overwhelmingly across party lines by Congress) seemingly captured the high ground, reducing public education to civil rights for children. Indeed, the genius behind NCLB lay in linking the welfare of children to an excellent teacher at the head of the classroom and shifting focus away from chronic conditions of poverty. The nagging, inequitable school funding formula, which dooms most inner city school districts to substandard resources, old textbooks, and classrooms held in trailers, was thus eclipsed. The Bush team, given a pass from having to address the unequal distribution of resources—and subsequent reduction of opportunities for millions of students—conjured up a new standard bearer and focus for the entire reform effort(s): the "highly qualified teacher."

This brilliant move set off a ferocious debate within teacher education circles: what do we mean by "highly qualified teacher"? By what standards, whose definition? The Feds were elusive; they seemed to indicate a subject matter expert (SME). Many beleaguered school districts sought waivers from the vaguely defined "highly qualified teacher" formula; none were immediately forthcoming. Some veteran teachers were able to be "grandfathered" in, take professional development; still others tested out. New teachers in training were required to take more courses in methods. Professional education organizations such as the National Board for Professional Teaching Standards (NBPTS) had begun to recruit and crank out "National Board Certified" teachers after the initial *Nation at Risk* (1983) report, which faulted public education for a lapsed economy. After NCLB, they would increase their efforts, to be able to raise the bar of teachers who would teach across state lines and in accordance with the general parameters. School districts increasingly began to consider getting into the "business" of certifying highly qualified teachers, contracting out to a budding industry of education service providers, or exploring options to do the certification internally.

But it was the Aspen Institute that made the critical leap, changing entirely the rules of the game. A policy think tank charged by the federal government with surveying the country and preparing a report to be used for the pending reauthorization of NCLB, Aspen under former Governors Tommy Thompson of Wisconsin and Roy Barnes from Colorado proposed an additional 'e' for 'effective' to be included with the HQT, as in the "highly qualified *effective* teacher" (HQET):

> The Commission believes that it is time to raise the bar and allow all teachers to demonstrate their *effectiveness* in the classroom rather than just their *qualifications* for entering it. This is a significant change and must be implemented in a way that is fair to teachers. Teachers who are held to this higher standard also need and deserve more support. Those who are not initially successful in producing measurable learning gains in the classroom must be given access to effective professional development to help them succeed. Those who are unable to demonstrate effectiveness in the classroom after a reasonable period of time of receiving support should no longer teach those students most in need of help.[11]

With this proposal, Aspen got out in front of other policy makers, opening the door to what had up until this point been the exclusive domain of higher education, asserting that other entities outside of the traditional teacher education colleges knew better about what type of teachers were needed.

Following Aspen's press release and announcement, other professional education organizations followed suit, including the National Education Association (NEA), the Association for Supervision and Curriculum Development (ASCD), the National Council for the Accreditation of Teacher Education (NCATE), and the Higher Education Commission (HEC).

With the reauthorization stalling before Congress in September 2007 and as the Bush administration faded into obscurity, NCLB became an anachronism. Education policy appeared to be receding in importance, compared with the rest of the national agenda; nonetheless, the "effective" criterion caught on. With the inauguration of President Barack Hussein Obama in January of 2009, education became a signature strategy once again of a newly elected president. RTT replaced, at least in the political imagination, NCLB. The government in a time of economic crises aimed to "incentivize" school reform instead of "sanctioning" schools as was pro forma for the Bush administration. Coupled with major philanthropic donations, repeated, incessant calls for increasing teacher education oversight, and shifting state and national standards . . . the

Obama administration, borrowing from Aspen, literally created the "highly effective teacher" (HET).

Second, significant debates in teacher education correlated with the federal government's call to make more "rigorous" the "training" of teachers. Obama's department of education conspicuously dropped the 'Q' with the belief that qualifications of teachers make little difference in student achievement. Less conspicuous was their assertion, from the Secretary of Education Arne Duncan that Master's Degrees were of no consequence for student achievement. Teacher educators were caught up in this quandary; how to make better teachers with less education?

In this climate, teacher education as a profession was opened up, or perhaps opened itself up, to significant scrutiny, audits, and power struggles over turf. Who should teach the teachers? Whose teachers should teach the students? Subsequently and predictably, alternative teacher certification programs gained significant ground, filling the identified need for highly effective urban teachers.

One Country, Under Common Core

Another major change RTT calls for is the implementation of *Common Core States Standards* (CCSS). Follows on the heels of years of comparisons between state report cards and the National Assessment of Education Progress (NAEP), in order to receive the RTT "incentive" funds, states must now align their evaluation system(s) with the new, national standards.

The idea of a common core of knowledge is not new. It emerged in the 80s with E.D. Hirsch, author of *Cultural Literacy*.[12] Hirsch argued there were objective facts that every child must know, but he went further to assert that there was one overarching "American" experience on which all education needed to be based, a common culture. Following this budding idea, the movement picked up steam, emerging alongside the standards and outcomes-based education movement(s). The National Governor's Association (NGA),[13] (along with the Business Roundtable, their partner at national education summits) during the Bush-Clinton administration(s), became empowered and used that power to make a clarion call for "world class standards". NGA crafted a strategic game plan GOALS 2000, with the intention of corralling every school in every state under the same standards, same rubric, and same assessment. At the time, the end of the 20th century this was voluntary; there were no national standards with any consequence for the nation's schools, No Child Left Behind was not yet available as a tool ("leverage" as the Undersecretary of Education was famously known to have coined it) to sanction the schools for failing to embrace a system of evaluation and produce an evidentiary warrant that their school and students were achieving. Instead, there was an emerging consensus between government and big business that education was too important to be left to the educators and something needed to be done. Thus the nation's leaders elected to focus all their sights on world class standards. In doing so, NGA's heads of state sought to "win" the economic race with global competitors, believing that by raising the bar, they would invariably be increasing the graduation rate, a major concern of everyone, especially parents, America would emerge victorious. But to what end?

The 21st century interest in national standards can be attributed to the ascendency of two distinct and yet entirely aligned financial and political constituencies. The first major constituencies are big business interests—ranging from the previously mentioned Business Roundtable and the United States Chamber of Commerce. Playing an increasingly partisan and aggressive role is the American Legislative Exchange Council (ALEC), a body that has been found to write the language that is cut and pasted for state legislative deliberation and consideration. The second major constituency are the non-profit and/or not-for-profit foundations—perhaps the top three and most influential in education being the Bill and Melinda Gates Foundation, the Eli and Edythe Broad Foundation, and the Walton Family Foundation. There are also a number of "think tanks" that span from right of center to left liberal (see for example, the more notable of the policy wonks, the Fordham Institute. American Enterprise, Cato, Bradley Foundation on the so-called right wing and the Center for American Progress, People for the American Way, and The New America Foundation, considered by pundits to be part of the left spectrum). Certainly there are organizations/foundations such as the Carnegie Institute who play a major role in all areas of policy, decision-making, innovation and research.

The point is that while the roles of these business, philanthropy, and think tank organizations in education reform may differ, their agendas, with slight variations (and perhaps to the surprise of educators at large) are in harmony, quite indistinguishable: *they aim to remove the governance of public education from local control* and place the nation's system of schools entirely under the surveillance and control of both the federal government, a government that it should be noted is increasingly relying on ideas and direction from the private sector. In fact, for most persons, astute analysts paying attention, the modus operandi of the federal government and the private sector is difficult, often quite impossible to discern (note the bail outs of the banks, entirely by the taxpayers, or the subsidization of the healthcare insurance industry, again, taxpayers).

Common schools were places where people from different social and economic classes co-mingled, where they met to reach a common goal of education, through locally conceived community standards. Locally formed standards with a global focus are needed for citizens to participate effectively in a democratic plurality. The danger with "Common Core State Standards" is that it could eviscerate the inherent wisdom of the local, community standards, and with it democratic plurality. Gone would be the idea of a patchwork of locally defined common schools, contributing in novel ways toward the global goal of creating a knowledgeable citizenry. The drumbeat for Common Core State Standards seems much like a national corps marching to the same drum. One can imagine, without too much of a stretch, "common schools for the common good" being replaced with "common core curriculum."

Chartering Public Education

Mythologized in the *Waiting for Superman* movie, and despite research evidence that most charter schools are sub-par, charter schools are according to RTT the model for public education reform. To our way of thinking this is the third and most significant, major change of RTT: the states must "eliminate pre-existing caps on charter schools" in order to receive the funds. We believe the caps provided a necessary and intelligent safeguard, put in place by state legislatures in order to prevent poorly organized charter schools from being allowed to continue to draw from the public revenues, revenues which are, after all, taxpayer money. The sound rationale for the caps being in place in the first place was that when charter schools fail, and they often do, they close down and take the revenues with them. The students must then, by law, be allowed to return to the public schools minus the revenues lost during the failed charter school experiment. Nonetheless, even with this risk (and reality) of poorly performing charter schools under-serving students, the Obama administration brushes this concern off, and stands strongly behind the removal of the state caps. Like the Bush administration before them, they subsequently laud the expansion of charter schools as a prototype for school reform.

Conclusion: Students Shuffled Down the Road

RTT focuses on turn around schools and global competitiveness but ignores gentrification and the disruption of neighborhoods, as witnessed in Chicago. Schools have been closed down in neighborhoods where public housing projects once existed only to be replaced by expensive townhouses and high rises. Pauline Lipman has already documented this. But Tania Giordani adds that many neighborhood schools that were closed have reopened with a new curriculum and have selective enrollment criteria, such as the International Baccalaureate programs. Giordani notes that the problem that is not being discussed is access. Giordani states, "They [commercial developers] go into the neighborhoods, build these schools but the neighborhood students can't get in." So the idea is that the schools under public education reform agendas like RTT and its parent, Renaissance 2010, might in some instances be getting better, yet while schools are reformed, the students that are below radar level are not going to be served. Furthermore, struggling schools that are showing progress are forced to enroll students from failing schools. In turn, the receiving schools' progress not only ceases, but also in many instances, their scores drop leading to the yet another round of closures of their school. Giordani wonders, "How are you going to serve the students who were left behind and not able to get into the new schools?"

We are all collectively left with the NCLB law and RTT initiative. NCLB is evocative of a noble idea, leaving no child behind, but it had the result of making those very students identified for special attention, perceived as liabilities. Schools that had just been removed from probation have had to consider: if we accept these transfer students, we may be closed. Giordani sums it all up as follows, "What is lost is the focus on the students, parents and community as these students are being shuffled from one school to another."

Under such hazardous conditions with *Race to the Top,* we wonder, what road are we driving on? Where are we really driving the kids too?

Failing Teachers?

Race to the Top, as well as the No Child Left Behind act, fall apart if their fundamental assertion, that "teachers are failing," is a false premise. Yet when "we" as a nation "talk" about failing schools, rarely do teacher's voices take center stage. Rather "we" as a nation are led to conclude, via mainstream media pundits and tired worn out clichés, that it is ultimately the teachers who fail, not the bankers, politicians, journalists, or lawyers per se. Nor do "we", except for a few notable exceptions such as Jonathan Kozol in *The Shame of the Nation,*[14] fault ourselves as a society at large for failing public education. "We" are not to talk about misplaced priorities, aging school buildings with leaky roofs, overcrowded classes with near impossible teaching conditions, and diminished, cut-to-the-bone budgets.

Instead, "we" are directed to vilify the teachers, to gossip about, to insinuate, and to pontificate that teachers are to blame for all the social ills, not only the struggling students. As our teachers have often astutely observed, it is analogous to blaming doctors for cholera outbreaks or blaming reporters for bring bad news. Andrea Lee, one of the chapter authors, argues that

> . . . we don't hear enough about the fact that these are the same teachers who inspire hundreds of thousands of public students to do their best and as a result gain entry into the most competitive public and private universities and colleges in the country and world, and they [in turn] were taught by traditional public school teachers who dedicated their lives to this profession.

> Even in Chicago, its top and nationally recognized public schools [students] are taught by inspirational *unionized* educators.

> Instead, we are forced to believe that all teachers are to blame for a failing national public school system.

Even in passing conversations, the authors note, with colleagues, neighbors, and community members, the prevalent notion literally appears to be that anyone and everyone can become a teacher. Often enough, ambitious and thoughtful parents send their child to a charter school under the belief that charters are simply better than the traditional public school counterparts, and "that then becomes the reality to them", as author Tania Giordani asserts, the intended outcome. Still most charters fail. Rarely among parents (except among teachers as parents) is there any conversation, according to Giordani—a parent and a teacher from Chicago, one of the most charterized school districts in the country—about "whether the charter is indeed better, or what happens if the charter closes, let alone whether the teachers who teach in charter schools are actually more effective."

While teacher effectiveness is a great concern of the federal government under Race to the Top, for many higher education faculties it is not the only concern. We are equally concerned about the aims, means and ends of public education . . . and *sustaining* effective teachers. Political agendas like administrations come and go, but teachers remain, the bulwark of the human resource that holds up the education institution itself. Research indicates that teacher experience consistently correlates with student achievement. RTT's reliance on alternative certification organizations almost seems to run counter to this idea, of experience and sustainability. The *Teach for America* program, for example, is wedded to the idea that the teacher/resident be immediately placed into the classroom—yet with a commitment only to teach two years.

Staying in the long race remains a goal for the authors of this book.

Notes

1. Department of Education, *Race to the Top Fund*, 34 CFR Subtitle B, Chapter II [Docket ID ED-2009-OESE-0006] RIN 1810-AB07. (Federal Register/Vol. 74, No. 221/Wednesday, November 18, 2009/Rules and Regulations). Accessed December 8, 2011 at http://www.gpo.gov/fdsys/pkg/FR-2009-11-18/pdf/E9-27426.pdf
2. Steven Brill, *Class Warfare: Inside the Fight to Fix America's Schools.* (New York: Simon & Schuster. 2011).
3. see *Business of Education Conference: Jonathan Schnur*
http://youtu.be/gQN_3i7ejC8
4. Accessed December 8, 2011, see
http://www2.ed.gov/programs/racetothetop/interim-notice-proposed-requirements.pdf
5. U.S. Department of Education, *The Race to the Top Begins, Remarks by Secretary Arne Duncan*, (July 24, 2009). Accessed December 8, 2011 at
http://www.ed.gov/news/speeches/race-top-begins
6. see http://www.youtube.com/watch?v=xsPGVO_4pkw
7. Valerie Strauss, Duncan and education's "quiet revolution", (*Washington Post*, July 12, 2010) Posted at 6:00 AM ET, 07/27/2010.
8. Commission on No Child Left Behind (Aspen Institute). *Beyond NCLB: Fulfilling the Promise to Our Nation's Children.* (Washington, D.C.: Aspen Institute, 2007); Kate Walsh & Sandy Jacobs, *Alternative Certification isn't Alternative*. (Thomas B. Fordham Institute, 2007). See
http://www.nctq.org/p/publications/docs/Alternative_Certification_Isnt_Alternative.pdf; See also Chester E. Finn and Diane Ravitch, *Beyond the Basics: Achieving a Liberal Education for All Children.* (Washington, DC.: Thomas B. Fordham Institute, 2007).
9. See Marilyn Cochran-Smith and Ken Zeichner (Editors), *Studying Teacher Education: The Report of the AERA Panel on Research and Teacher Education.* (Mahweh, N.J.: Lawrence Erlbaum Publishers. 2005); L. S. Shulman, "Teacher education does not exist." (*Stanford Educator*, Fall, 2005): 7.
10. See Linda Darling-Hammond, and John Bransford, *Preparing Teachers for a Changing World: What Teachers Should Learn and Be Able to Do.* (San Francisco, CA: Jossey-Bass, 2005).
11. Aspen Institute, p. 47.

12. E. D. Hirsch, Joseph F. Kett, and James S. Trefil, *Cultural Literacy: What Every American Needs to Know,* (Boston: Houghton Mifflin, 1987); E. D. Hirsch, Joseph F. Kett, and James S. Trefil, *The Dictionary of Cultural literacy,* (Boston: Houghton Mifflin, 1988).

13. At the urging of then President George Herbert Walker Bush, NGA convened a major education summit—chaired by then Governor William Jefferson Clinton—outlining in broad strokes national education reform legislation: *America 2000*: see United States, *America 2000.* (Washington, D.C.: U.S. Dept. of Education, 1991). Congress, having failed under Bush to pass this legislation into law, succeeded during the Clinton administration, pushing similar language through and enacting into law *Goals 2000*: see H.R. 1804—103rd Congress: Goals 2000: Educate America Act, (*GovTrack.us (database of federal legislation)*, 1993) This law was largely voluntary, without sanctioning power, yet it was critical in increasing the role of not only the Governors in education policymaking, but that of the federal government (grants, research, and administrative oversight), non-profit organizations and foundations (grants and incentives), and business (models and leadership). These organizations would be given significant power over the public's schools once the *No Child Left Behind Act* was ratified in 2002. Retrieved December 8, 2011, from http://www.govtrack.us/congress/bill.xpd?bill=h103-180

14. Jonathan Kozol, *The Shame of the Nation: The Restoration of Apartheid Schooling in America.* (New York: Crown Publishers, 2005).

Part I
A Critical View of Chicago
Public School Reform

The first chapter is titled "Commercial Club Curriculum: Big Business Against the Common School." Co-authored by Todd Alan Price and John Duffy, this chapter reflects the story of the rapid growth of the city of Chicago where fortunes were made providing great promise of prosperity. But alongside the fortunes made by some was squalor. European immigrants came to work, to toil away in the underbelly of the modern factory, their children often beside them. But because of social reformers and child labor laws, children were soon ushered out of these sweatshops to be enrolled into the schools where they could learn to become Americans. Following the European immigrants, by the first decades of the 20th century, were African-Americans who migrated in growing numbers to the promised land of the North . . . only to be segregated to "Bronzeville". Yet school also offered their families the possibility of a better life than the one they left behind.

The early venture capitalists, seeing the influx of both the European immigrants and Southern Blacks making the great Northern migration, reimaged the organization of the modern day city to better serve their class interests. Endeavoring not only to transform neighborhoods, their aim was to socially engineer the schools by moving around the teachers and marshaling the students through a dual-track system. The Commercial Club Curriculum (CCC) that followed served some well, and many others minimally so; the outcomes either way were fairly well pre-determined. This chapter explains how the idea of a free common school system with universal education for all was compromised and corrupted by commercial interests . . . but was also the site of resistance by those who would dare to claim the dream of social and economic mobility.

In Chapter 2, "A Dream Deferred: The Commodification of Chicago Public Schools," Tania Giordani and Andrea Lee paint a stark picture of the problems students and families face transitioning out of and into different schools. The interviews they conduct of parents, who get the run around and are often treated as pawns in the education reform game, are powerful and demonstrate that the so-called "turnaround" process in Chicago is causing dislocation and fragmentation in communities where concentrated poverty remains unaddressed.

"Citizen Teachers and Curricular Activism," the third chapter by John Duffy describes the impact and response of teachers to corporate reform under Commercial Club sponsored programs in Chicago. Duffy first describes the inequitable impact of these reforms on his graduate teachers working hard to make a difference in the lives of their African American and Latino(a) students. Then he relates the organizing of resistance of teacher educators at his college as they attempted to reverse regressive policies constraining teacher education colleges in Illinois. He relates how he and a group of fellow teacher educators worked to ensure human rights in schools by speaking out as democratic citizens, and continuing to push forward, to sustain the legacy of the Civil Rights Movement in neoliberal times.

Terry Jo Smith's Chapter 4, "Standard Scores and Non-Standard Lives: A Recipe for Systemic Violence," paints a vivid picture of a phony race up close and personal in a particular school. It is the same kind of race being foisted upon students and schools across the country that pits students and schools against one another in a race to the bottom. It is a competition that on its face is unfair, but it is run every day and in the form of high-stakes testing and teacher/school accountability. Smith argues that callous words such as "no excuses" and "try harder" fail to change the conditions under which students compete. Instead, they merely continue the "systemic violence" being perpetuated on communities and the residents within who hobble under the burden of urban neglect and decay and concentrated poverty. When, as she notes, school budgets for inner city schools range from 1/4 of those in the burbs, one wonders, having read this tale of crying children failing to make the "mark," how in the world can we continue to uphold the "standard" of being on the same page with so many non-standard lives?

"Science Left Behind: Reflections from a Chicago Public School Student of Science," the fifth chapter of Part I, is the autobiography of Theresa Robinson who recounts the personal tale of a student of science who becomes a teacher of teachers of science. Her concern is whether the science test is all that remains of the science curriculum in inner city schools like the one she hailed from.

Chapter 1
Commercial Club Curriculum:
Big Business Against the Common School
Todd Alan Price and John Duffy

A study conducted by the Commercial Club of Chicago found that academic gains made by elementary students in the mayor-controlled Chicago Public Schools "appear to be due to changes in the tests made by the Illinois State Board of Education, rather than real improvements in student learning." The study described the performance of Chicago's high schools as "abysmal."[1]

Neighborhood Schools and Common Schools

It is important to step back and remember that public schools were once filled with the children of families who lived and worked in the surrounding neighborhood. Neighborhood schools as they would come to be known, played a unique role, serving as the bedrock of the community. Where those schools were poorly resourced, it was so only because the neighborhoods were poor.

The legendary Horace Mann in the middle 1800s sought to make neighborhood schools more effective; he standardized the schools, improved the textbooks, required chalkboards, instituted better desks and chairs, and saw to it that normal school-educated teachers and their students met in a scheduled common location. Together with other public education reformers, a "common school" movement took form (eloquently and visually depicted in a public television documentary *School, the story of American public education*).[2]

The realization of the common school was especially compelling to poor European families during the 1880s and 90s. Their neighborhood schools, especially in urban segregated communities like those in Chicago or Milwaukee, were composed of recent émigrés—students and teachers lived together in the same neighborhoods—from Ireland, Germany, Italy, Poland and other European countries. The young, female working-class teachers who taught in these schools were adamant about protecting their jobs and believed that teaching credentials were immaterial to that of gaining experience by teaching in their own neighborhoods. But because many of their urban area neighborhoods remained poor, the common schools they taught in were under resourced and of inferior quality, compared to schools in more established middle-class neighborhoods. The working-class teachers were frequently blamed for poor outcomes, resultant largely from conditions outside their immediate control.

Counter to the working-class teachers were the "progressives" largely a cadre of white middle-class Anglo men coming from the best teacher colleges in the country. Margaret Haley, one of the working-class teachers and a leading union leader in Chicago at the beginning of the twentieth century referred to this group as "sheepskins." These social engineers aimed to, so they claimed, to save the schools and bring about a new standard for educational management.

The idea of the neighborhood school was ironically the first target for these *administrative* progressives during the early 1900s. The rationale of their assault was this: neighborhood schools protected under educated teachers. The reformers' new standard for education was a "cult of efficiency."[3] With support from the mayor and high society (big business—manufacturing, commerce and trade), power needed to be wrested away from the local boroughs and ward bosses and centralized within mayoral appointed councils with credentialing relegated to teacher education institutions deemed worthy.

Marjorie Murphy, author of *Blackboard Unions* is particularly helpful in relaying this important historical shift. Murphy argues that administrative progressives at the top of the higher education chain were tasked with assigning the curriculum and administering that curriculum from the central office of the superintendent. Teachers deemed unqualified would be displaced from their neighborhood schools and directed to secure further education at Teachers College (at a cost the progressive administrators surely must have known was more than working-class women of diverse ethnic backgrounds could afford).[4] A new "scientific management" curriculum was settled upon and the barely high school educated, neighborhood teacher was replaced by a technically proficient, university educated professional: the credentialed teacher.[5]

During this process of "professionalization", gender, class and race played a critical role. First and foremost teaching in urban settings and elsewhere was gendered. Females largely comprised the work force; progressive males on the other hand constituted the teacher preparation faculty as well as the school management. Gender was also used to distinguish who did and did not possess the "official knowledge" concerning preferred and legitimated best practice(s) of the day. Class determined who would be able to afford the "best" schools; clearly elite institutions like Teachers College were largely out of reach for most working people. Chicago would subsequently become the site of the first teacher unions. Race also played a pivotal role in Chicago as non-Anglo students emigrating from the Southern and Eastern European countries, and blacks migrating North from the feudal system of the Southern states, found themselves tracked in at the vocational end of a dual track system[6] described in the next section.

Vocations and Occupations

In her sweeping, tour de force *School Reform, Corporate Style*, Dorothy Shipps reveals how early venture capitalists—while continuing to make fortunes off of speculation—drove educational reform from the 1880s up through the early twentieth century.[7] Titans of industry like the Pullman and Rockefeller families formed civic groups, managed by their appointed proxies. Given the composition of these groups, public policy discussions naturally led to the conclusion that the urban space needed to be transformed. The goal became to socially engineer the city and residents toward serving the needs of industry and financial capital.

Shipps attributes the successful transformation of the urban space along these lines to the emergence of the Commercial Club of Chicago. An exclusive coalition of financial and investment partners, this high status organization leveraged it power toward the creation of a "dual track system" of schools. An arm of the Commercial Club of Chicago, the Civic Committee on Education, would see to the details and become an influential lobbyist well into the 21st century.

What then was the dual track system in practice? Essentially it was a curriculum plan: one for the working-class sons and daughters of recent émigrés and another for their assumed managers: middle-class families' children. The aim of Commercial Club of Chicago captains of industry was to fit the working-class students into factory work . . . using vocational curriculum and tracked classes . . . confirming their own status as social policy engineers, and ushering in a new era of "managerialism."

Not coincidentally the factory work was conveniently housed in and owned by the same Commercial Club of Chicago members. To enroll the students into vocational classes and crank out workers in order to fill available job slots . . . it all seemed like the perfect plan.

In the early part of the 19th century, the Commercial Club of Chicago and allies sought to exercise their business prerogative further, turning to a veritable vocational school model. Yet the vocational school model, aligned with managerialism, vocationalism, and the dual track system it inspired, ran into some problems.

First organized labor groups like the AFL-CIO (under the leadership of union boss Samuel Gompers) wanted something different: a full education for workers, one infused with social and economic mobility, not merely a vocational school that would narrowly fit students into slots. Second, the vocational school model ran into further problems when it was of necessity partnered to the University of Chicago for further curriculum and instruction development, which involved deeper questions about what courses would be required, who would teach them, and where the teaching and learning would take place. Cutting against the managerialism grain, pedagogues like John Dewey refined the curricular aims away from the "fitting" of students into pre-determined *vocations*, and toward a focus on the habits of living and learning, what he described as *occupations*.

It is clear in Shipps' articulate rendering of this education policy history that by the early 1900s the Chicago Public Schools was immersed in a great experiment between progressive education and *Commercial Club Curriculum*. On one hand, *Commercial Club Curriculum* offered vocational schools to the growing immigrant classes. On the other hand, progressive education was making inroads amongst the middle-class private schools. To the sons and daughters of the upper-class, an expensive private school education in New York and the East coast was reserved.

In this tumultuous time the recently retired City School Superintendent Edwin G. Cooley seemed to have had the greatest impact on discussions and actions translating to educational politics and policy making. In 1915 he made a report to the Commercial Club of Chicago entitled *Vocational Education in Europe*. This report would be, in effect, "speaking for them" at other local government councils and committees. Cooley and his upper-class allies simply called for reshaping the schools, building their capacity for industry and socially engineering the city in the interests of efficiency. Shipps summarizes Cooley's proposal in the following passage:

> The main argument in Cooley's two-volume report supported Robinson's [another educator] belief that the vocational schools of Germany had accelerated its industrial development and solidified its nation building. For club members the examples of Germany and to a lesser extent Switzerland, Scotland, and Austria pointed to one answer for the economic and educational future of the United States of America: a wholly independent system of public vocational schools to ensure that the nation used its labor resources efficiently.[8]

The dual track envisioned a management track afforded to the upper middle-class, or those families who, having earned their pedigree through hard work and amassed great fortune, could assume to occupy their station at the head of the ship of industry. Alternately, a vocational track would be placed upon the workers, newly arriving immigrants, to whom the ship of industry depended to turn it engines.

Contesting this two-track system were *pedagogical* progressives education model and democratic ideas of labor unionists.[9] In this alternative to Commercial Club Curriculum all citizens were to have a curriculum oriented toward the productive capacity, individual developmental needs and potential of the whole child. In this more democratic and equitable alternative tracking to fit would be discarded for learning to live. Occupations[10] referred not to training, narrowing and closing in on a particular set of job skills, but instead to the teaching and learning, grounded in lived experiences and life skills. Curriculum would be distributed equally between the intellectual, artistic, civic and social domains, to the enrichment and fulfillment of all children.

Several other characteristics of administrative progressivism were established in this early period. These characteristics would resurface with a vengeance in the twenty-first century: mayoral control of school boards, merit pay, charter schools, and standardized testing. Wayne Urban, labor historian, explains in the early 1900s that: "the Chicago Teaching Federation (CTF) and the Loeb members of the board clashed over a reported deficit of six hundred thousand dollars in the school budget.[11] Loeb, a mayoral appointed education official, used the squabble to launch an investigation into the "economy and efficiency" of the schools. Notable was his solution to the crisis—to systematically cut salaries of the teachers.

Unionism: The First Sparks

Yet the working class teachers fought back. Margaret Haley, an Irish radical teacher unionist managed to find sources of hidden, uncollected tax money that corporations had refused to pay.[12] Haley and others demanded that city hall do its job to collect the funds:[13]

> In Chicago despite impressive mass meetings, the voteless teachers remained unsuccessful until 1899 when Catherine Goggin and Margaret Haley launched what they called the "the teachers tax crusade.[14]

In court, the union teachers had their say and in 1899 managed to rattle the corporate property cages. A total of $600,000, a large sum at the time, was wrested free to at last address the teachers' grievances.

Commercial Club Curriculum: A Privileged Process

Nearly one hundred years later, Shipps describes as a "privileged process," the means by which the Commercial Club of Chicago and other business association allies came together and crafted the key reform initiative for Chicago, the country and perhaps the world. That initiative was the *1995 School Reform* which centralized the management (after the previous decentralizing and recentralizing *1988 School Reform Law*) of the Chicago Public School district under mayoral control.[15] This mayoral control legislation was in fact informed by the Republican revolution driving the 1994 Congressional elections when Speaker of the House Newt Gingrich launched Contract with America. Illinois' legislature also had a revolution of its own. Through the efforts of Republican leaders working in tandem with Republican Governor James Edgar the pro-management *1995 School Reform Law* moved through the Illinois General Assembly and was signed into law.

Under the *1995 School Reform Law* Mayor Daley was given the charge to select a CEO of the schools and to constitute a Board of Trustees.[16] He appointed CEO Paul Vallas who stabilized the budget and instituted more intense high-stakes testing and other reforms. Among the Vallas changes was reducing the power of the local school councils (LSC) which under the *1988 School Reform Law* were given wide latitude to hire and dismiss principals and make other decisions at the neighborhood level, in effect, empowering many parents and community members to take part in their school. Shipps describes the critical juxtaposition of racialized politics, corporate calls for deregulation, and struggles that mixed into school reform:

Race played a critical role in the Chicago School Reform law of 1988.

Following Mayor Harold Washington's earnest Education Summit and then his tragic and untimely death, a split amongst the stakeholders, followed by a merging which occurred between the low income parents and families and the major corporate interests to get something done. This merging resulted in an unprecedented experiment in deregulation. The corporate groups wanted site based management, and free market competition, while the parent groups wanted greater voice and a decentralization of the school board and the teachers' union.[17]

It remains an open question how much the re-centralization under the 1995 law helped African-American youth who comprise much of CPS. The reliance on a single high-stakes standardized test did little to give confidence to underachieving students. Nonetheless, in 2004 the mayor decided to move further down the road of centralization with the backing of the Commercial Club of Chicago, setting up a dual system of schools called *Renaissance 2010*. This system would feature an alternative school system of "Contract" "Performance", and "Charter" type schools.

There has been extensive criticism by teachers and parents of the centralized, top down approach to Chicago school reform. It is especially telling to note that Civic Committee, to found fault with the reform efforts stretching back to the beginning of mayoral control. The Civic Committee's latest report *Still Left Behind,* released in the summer of 2009 argues, and presents data, that test scores have not gone up appreciably amongst inner city students. Nonetheless, this same report argues to double down, to move aggressively toward a charter schools and merit pay system, the answer they believe, to dealing with the overall low performance of Chicago students. These initiatives dovetail well with the Federal Department of Education reforms called for in Race to the Top. The Civic Committee's cry for more charter schools is dubious given an also summer-released report out of Stanford that found charter schools to be marginal at best toward improving public schools, and, comparatively speaking, doing rather poorly when placed next to traditional public schools.[18]

Shipps summarizes the conundrum of the CCC and like-minded allies who have shape, if not directly controlled Chicago school reform. As Shipps notes, the corporate elite in Chicago over the years continue to evaluate school changes, and then having found fault with the reform, they merely move on:

> Ironically, corporate leaders apparently do not recognize their own part in the reforms they now judge to be failures, justifying their next reform as if it were an uncommon investment of corporate energy in improving the schools.[19]

Furthermore, an article in the newspaper *Crain's Chicago Business* lauds the leaders of the Civic Committee of the Commercial Club who in another report urge investors to capitalize on purchasing, rehabbing and renting vacated public school buildings. Here, the unofficial behind the scenes voice for Chicago school reform glibly makes the argument that these modern day tragedies, the closing of Chicago's so called failing schools, offer a great opportunity for venture capitalists to invest and earn a sure profit while at the same time supporting the expansion of the charter school model.[20]

Conclusion

In researching, gathering our team of fellow writers and composing this volume we have found ourselves moving back and forth living and working as educational activists, teachers and writers. Our work in teacher education often places us in contradictory situations: what does it mean to try and create the highly qualified and effective teacher in an age of Commercial Club Curriculum? What is revealed about our own institution and practice in relation to the pressures and contradictions Commercial Club Curriculum imposes on both our universities and the schools and teachers we also work with daily? We understand we are at the same time products of a complex history that has preceded us and that we in turn have joined in making history. In doing so, we have invoked the insight of William Faulkner when he said "The past is never dead; it's not even past."[21] Thus, we have attempted to connect the current agenda of public school reform in Chicago with both the recent and century old history of how Commercial Club Curriculum has sought to rationalize and order public schools in a narrowly, undemocratic and economically functionalist manner and how that design in its present multiple manifestations is being taken to a national scale by the U.S. Department of Education with the support of President Barack Obama and through the leadership of Secretary Arne Duncan.

In the spirit of Paulo Freire (1970)[22] we have also with our co-writers set about the serious work of demythologizing the past and our living present. In our narratives and dialogues with teachers, citizens, and community activists, and in our roles as citizen teacher educators we have found ourselves in difficult conversations with the leaders of our own college that we find loaded with tensions and contradictions with our collectively expressed dedication to democracy, social justice and equity. We cannot avoid such tensions, and in fact believe a better future is only possible by courageously engaging them in our own families, neighborhoods, schools, and then taking those lessons to the larger political structures that govern our lives. Those who we admire in the past and today model this approach well.

At the end of the nineteenth and the turn of the twentieth century, the United States found itself in a similar situation as today. Corporate and governmental elites at the opening of the new era stressed the importance of global economic superiority as central to national survival, and thus launched global military expeditions to Latin America, the Pacific and Asia to insure that domination. All of this was taking place as racial and class divisions accelerated the polarization of the American people. Yet at the same time, new voices challenged injustices based on gender, race and economic disparity. 'Social Meliorists' were rising to meet these deep challenges, advancing the idea of a democratic, just and inclusive society.

As the century unfolded and advanced, leading American educators like Jane Addams, W.E.B. Dubois, Margaret Haley, John Dewey, Harold Rugg, George Counts and others would join those conversations with actions, in a common crusade toward a very different social order than that represented by the purveyors of Commercial Club Curriculum. New ideas about environmental protection, racial justice, gender equity and the democratic rights of workers, including strong voices questioning an increasing imperialist conception of U.S. global power, all contributed to a renewed vision.

It is our hope that the chapters which follow help continue, expand and deepen not only our conversations, but also our ability to act boldly as we make the connections between our struggle today and earlier fights for social, political and economic justice. In doing so we will, with our students, colleagues and the larger communities we serve, as the voices that follow in this volume so richly document, reclaim, preserve and widen the vital role of public education in building a just democratic society.

Notes

1. Civic Committee of the Commercial Club of Chicago, "Still Left Behind: Student Learning in Chicago's Public Schools." (The Commercial Club of Chicago, June 2009).

2. Sarah Mondale and Sarah B. Patton, *School, the story of American public education.* (Boston: Beacon Press, 2001).

3. Raymond E. Callahan, *Education and the Cult of Efficiency.* (The University of Chicago Press, 1962).

4. Marjorie Murphy, *Blackboard Unions: the AFT and the NEA, 1900-1980.* (Ithaca, N.Y.: Cornell University Press, 1990).

5. Ibid.

6. William Henry Watkins, *The White Architects of Black education: Ideology and Power in America: 1865-1954.* (New York: Teachers college press, 2001).

7. Dorothy Shipps, *School Reform, Corporate style: Chicago 1880-2000.* (University Press of Kansas, 2006).

8. Ibid.

9. See Murphy, 1990, where she describes how teacher councils fought against the Chicago Commercial Club sponsored dual-track system.

10. See "The Dewey School" in Herbert M. Kliebard, *The Struggle for the American Curriculum 1893-1958.* (New York, NY 10001: Routledge & Kegan Paul, Inc., 1986).

11. See Wayne J. Urban, *Why Teachers Organized.* (Wayne State University Press in Detroit, 1982) p. 83.

12. Ibid.

13. Urban, p. 33.

14. Urban, p. 39.

15. See *Business Influence in Chicago School Reform: 1988-1995*; see also Stefanie Chambers "Urban Education Reform and Minority Political Empowerment," *Political Science Quarterly* Vol. 117, No. 4 (Winter, 2002-2003), pp. 643-665. *The Academy of Political Science* Stable URL: http://www.jstor.org/stable/798138

16. The best, most authoritative sources concerning this event is the *Catalyst,* a Chicago periodical that studies all facets of Chicago education reform: see Michael Klonsky, "GOP clears field, Daley runs with the ball" in the *Catalyst.* (Linda Lenz, ed.: The Community Renewal Society, Volume VII, Number 1, September 1995).

17. See Shipps, 2006.

18. See Center for Research on Education Outcomes (CREDO), *Multiple Choice: Charter School Performance in 16 States.* (Stanford, CA: Stanford University, June 2009). Other reports contest the Civic Committee's conclusion that more charters are needed: see *Designs for Change, 2001.*
See http://www.designsforchange.org/pdfs/ITBS0401.pdf. The abandonment of the small

schools initiative/the transformative high schools project, in favor of charters, is clearly aligned with the Civic Committee report.

19. See Shipps, 2006.

20. Greg Hinz, "Venture capitalist Bruce Rauner floats plan to raise cash for public schools while supporting charters." (*This Week's Crain's,* July 26, 2010).

21. *Requiem for a Nun,* (1951) Act 1, sc. 3.

22. Paulo Freire, *Pedagogy of the Oppressed.* (New York: Continuum. 2000).

Chapter 2
A Dream Deferred: The Commodification of Chicago Public Schools

Tania Giordani and Andrea Lee

Chicago's Mayor Richard M. Daley unveiled Renaissance 2010, an education initiative to open 100 new schools as alternative school choice options for children and parents in the Chicago Public Schools (CPS) District. This chapter highlights the journey and stories of parents and children who attended these new schools in search of a high quality education. Some of these schools are no longer in operation leaving these families to seek alternative options. While many reports focus on the test scores of the schools that have been closed, consolidated, phased-out, or turned around, very few, if any, discuss the impact these processes have had on parents and their children.

The Mid-South is one of the many Chicago neighborhoods that have been greatly impacted by Renaissance 2010. The Mid-South represents only a microcosm of the current state of the entire Chicago Public School System (CPS) and its instability. This chapter addresses what happens to families when public schools are marketed and sold as private school options, only to have families learn that at the end of the day, the new schools are still public schools with similar challenges: high teacher turnover; continual student mobility; attendance, discipline, and academics problems; and insufficient parent involvement.

The True Victims of Renaissance 2010

In the spring of 2004, Chicago Mayor Richard M, alongside the Chicago Public Schools Chief Executive Officer Arne Duncan, announced a bold, new, innovative school reform effort, aiming to address the needs of a school district whose schools were failing, underutilized, and/or housed in dilapidated buildings. Renaissance 2010[1] (R2010) called for the creation of 100 new charter schools, contract schools, and performance schools by the year 2010.

Pauline Lipman (2002) in *Making the Global City, Making Inequality: The Political Economy and Cultural Politics of Chicago School Policy* argues that

R2010 was actually aimed making neighborhoods more attractive to white collar workers; a new professional class. Coupled with a bid to make Chicago a "Global City" in order to host the Olympics, R2010 spearheaded the drive toward gentrification of the city and served to dislocate many community members from their neighborhoods. At the same time R2010 spurred growth of "new" schools for "new" community members in otherwise pre-existing, but newly refurbished neighborhood schools.[2]

Citywide, there was dissent and skepticism about R2010 for several reasons. Citizens and parents feared that the creation of 100 new schools would mean that CPS would need to close 100 existing schools. R2010 had also been announced with a board resolution that provided no clear guidelines about the process of creating new schools and closing schools. In addition, there was little information provided about who would be eligible to open up these schools (CPS or independent contractors), what type of schools they would be (performance, contract, charter, or traditional neighborhood), where these schools would be located, and in what buildings they would be housed. Many also questioned whether the type of school in a proposed area would be determined by an expressed need of the community or would be created simply because an operator had a great idea for a new school.

An example illustrates the policy confusion citizens confronted in Chicago in the near Southwest side Latino(a) neighborhood of Pilsen. In this instance the Board of Education approved the closure of an academically successful school due to low enrollment, announced plans to demolish the school, and made plans to sell the land it was situated on.[3] When construction and repairs on the school took place during the months between the board's announcement and the end of the school year, CPS would offer no explanations to concerned parents and teachers upset with these developments. Following the school closure in June of 2004, CPS contracted in July of 2004 with a charter operator, United Neighborhood Organization (UNO). UNO would temporarily relocate in the same school that was up until this point slated to be razed.

Through the Pilsen school closure process and the closing of other neighborhood schools, more and more of the community believed that mayoral control of the CPS school system was unresponsive and that the CPS board refused to seek authentic and meaningful community support as it carried out R2010 and other school reform in Chicago. Compounding the growing community disaffection for school closures was strong evidence that schools being closed or considered for closing were located on the footprints of the City of Chicago's major Chicago Housing Authority's 10 Year Plan for Transformation. Most of the public housing being demolished was in close proximity, either to the Northwest, West or South of the nearby downtown retail, entertainment, business and financial center of Chicago. Citizens, parents and community activist soon began to understand that the demolition of public housing, which was to be replaced by mixed-income housing, was the reason for why the schools too had to come down, or be closed. These impacted communities and families came to suspect that gentrification, facilitated by moving out occupants of public housing, particularly in these new mixed-income developments, was the real impetus to prey on schools that historically had been more academically at-risk and that served many of the neediest students throughout the city. They soon found out that these suspicions were correct.

Community groups and families residing in neighborhoods affected by R2010 rallied together to oppose school closures, demanded real community involvement in developing school reform plans and denounced the lack of transparency on how CPS targeted schools for closure, and pointed to the absence of research on benefits for students that supposedly would come from the closing and re-opening of schools. In commenting on the CPS school closing process Julie Woestehoff, Executive Director of Parents United for Responsible Education (PURE) asserts that:

> the top-down nature of the R2010 process was necessary to CPS in order to carry out the changes that parents, teachers, students and the community so ardently opposed. CPS determined from the beginning that they were going to go ahead with the plan despite any opposition, so they needed to plan behind closed doors and ignore the loud protests when they finally shared their plans. The TACs and other supposed "representative" groups were just window dressing for this unfortunate exercise in bad government. It's not just that the whole process was secretive and top-down—the plans themselves have been harmful to children and communities, which is the major message the opponents of R2010 were communicating at every hearing and Board meeting. To do things to communities against their will and in spite of the dire predictions (many of which have come true) is simply irresponsible and unworthy of government.

> Now Arne Duncan is trying to do that same thing across the nation despite the same uproar of opposition.[4]

Moreover, the community groups learned that a major civic institution, the Civic Committee of the Commercial Club of Chicago (2003), came out with a report in July 2003 entitled *Left Behind*,[5] a detailed report on Chicago Public School performance. It highlighted dismal progress of our elementary and high schools after reviewing four years of test scores. However, while it applauded the then Chicago CEO and its appointed Board of Education, it put a great deal of burden on teachers and the unions for not being held accountable when it comes to student learning. It also lauded competition as a key to improving performance of public schools and called for greater reforms that included raising the Chicago school cap to 100 charter schools as the best way to help Chicago neighborhoods with failing schools.

In 1996, the State of Illinois General Assembly created legislation that enabled a limited number of charters across the State. At that time Chicago could have 18. In 2005 an amendment to the Illinois Charter legislation increased the cap to 30. This past 2009, legislation was passed (SB 612) to increase charters across the State to 120 total, where Chicago's cap rose from 30 to 75, where five of these schools are reserved for high school drop outs.[6] However, due to the cap on charters, it is believed that R2010 was created to open schools in a way that expanded the definition of charter school as well as creating other variations for school governance and accountability. Regardless, the cap on charters would ultimately be entirely eviscerated vis-à-vis Race to the Top.

In spite of communities across the city of various races and ethnicities coming together to decry this so-called school reform effort and ask for greater funding and accountability in place of Renaissance 2010, the Chicago Public Schools moved forward with its plan. The Mid-South community, known as Chicago's historical black belt, has been impacted the greatest when it comes to school closings and school openings driven by Renaissance 2010.

R2010 and the Chicago Mid-South Side Schools

The Mid-South side includes the U.S. Census-recognized community areas of Douglas, Grand Boulevard, Oakland, and Kenwood. African American residents of Chicago could only own a house in portions of this area referred to as Bronzeville, the historical Black Belt[7]. The Mid-South side also included the largest composition of Chicago Housing Authority (CHA) public housing complexes in Chicago, possibly the largest public housing area(s) in the country.

As of August 2010, 20 Mid-South schools had closed and 15 schools had opened under R2010 or "turnaround."[8] CPS "back-labeled" several schools such as Williams Multiplex and National Teachers Academy—designated these schools as R2010 schools—even though they opened 1-2 years prior to the official 2004 R2010 unveiling. As of February 2010, CPS proposed to close one more elementary school, and turnaround a local high school. This high school turnaround could also replace a high performing small school, Wells Prep, which shares the same building.

The Mid-South Side opposition to R2010 is the most compelling when people argue that the CPS commitment to R2010 is part of the larger Chicago Housing Authority's Plan for Transformation—taking down low income public housing and replacing with mixed income housing. As is the case when public housing is demolished, the enrollments at local schools are drastically impacted (going down precipitously, in some cases). However, in spite of all families not wanting to leave their community, CPS began closing schools as an integral strategy in 2001 while citing under-enrollment and low-performance. Even worse, CPS closed these schools and sent families to nearby, equally struggling schools. At times, CPS closed schools, identified nearby "receiving" schools the students could attend, and then years later closed those same receiving schools, all without accepting any accountability for the impact of their decisions.

Natalie Moore from WBEZ's Chicago Public Radio interviewed one parent, Ms. Tanya Dickens Whitehead (2009). Ms. Whitehead's son was from the closed Donoghue School.

> It got turned into a charter school. The district did give parents information about the new school. [But] We weren't given any information about how we could put our children into that charter school.[9]

He was then transferred to another neighborhood school, Doolittle. Ms. Whitehead and her son lived in Ida B. Wells Public Housing and were not selected to live in the new Oakwood Shores mixed income housing after they razed her public housing building. Thus, through a housing emergency relocation, she was moved from Ida B. Wells to Wentworth Gardens. Since a neighborhood school was nearby, she transferred her son to a third school, Abbott, where he was happy to learn in a small classroom environment. However, CPS chose in 2009 to close this school due to low-enrollment and proceeded to send the children to the nearby lower-performing school of Hendricks. Ms. Whitehead refused to send her son there.

In another instance, CPS insisted on opening up two schools in the same shared building; KIPP Global Youth Village serving 4-8th grade students and Big Picture Metro High Schools, serving high school students. Within six years of opening, CPS closed both schools at different points in time, blaming the decisions on the school's inadequate curriculum and funding problems. Such developments again call into question the process and accountability for opening up new schools. It also requires us to ask why any community facing school closings or openings should not be engaged from start to finish since active community involvement is indispensable for any school to succeed.

A Parent's Journey

While it may appear that CPS is closing underperforming schools and replacing them with new schools that will offer students an opportunity of attaining a better education, what realistic chances do students have when parents are not informed in a timely manner?

Mary, the mother of three elementary school aged children described her experience saying: "We were among the first people to get one of those brutal notices of [our school] closing." Mary reported that two to three weeks before the end of the school year, she was told that her children's school would not reopen for the next school year. Mary, who was also the chairperson of her Local School Council (the local governing board), was not only shocked by this devastating news, she was furious that the notice of the school closing came after the deadline had passed for applying for magnet schools and other high performing schools that may have given her children a better chance of attaining a quality education.

Another story involves Ann, mother of four boys (two in elementary school and two in high school). Ann states that as a result of the public schools successively closing in her neighborhood, Darius, her oldest son attended three different schools. Because of the instability (and uncertainty) in her neighborhood schools, with great trepidation, Ann decided to enroll her children in separate charter schools. Ann stated:

> Not having the choice to send [my children] to the school across the street, it's been pretty bad for the family. Of course you want your children close to you so if something happens, you can go right there. Instead the baby had to go to school outside the neighborhood.

Many other parents share this sentiment and experience. Shirley, a mother of three school-aged children (one in elementary, one in high school), told us that "The closings and openings caused me to transfer my children several times". Although her children once attended school in the Mid-South her children now attend schools 10 miles away in the North Lawndale neighborhood; one of her children attends a R2010 school while the other two attend a charter school.

Shirley says that while she is happy with the schools her children attend, she wishes these schools were in her neighborhood. Since Shirley does not have a car, her children have the added expense of paying for public transportation to get to and from school. Shirley states:

> I am out on faith and prayer and hoping that I find enough money to keep my children at [their schools]. CTA (Chicago Transit Authority) is a fairly expensive avenue for me because I send so many children to school out of the neighborhood.

She continues, "I know many families who stay in the neighborhood for school because transportation is not an option." Unfortunately many of the children of these families are caught (or stuck) in the continuous cycle of their child's school closing and having then to transfer to another school.

New Schools: Dreams, Hopes, Promises or Illusions

Another under-reported and little understood reality is that the opening and closing of schools along with the transferring of children in and out of schools, within and outside their neighborhood is a complex phenomenon. As mentioned earlier, one of the R2010 goals is to create new schools within CPS. These schools, as defined by CPS, would all be high quality schools. Since many parents in Mid-South neighborhoods are quite aware that their neighborhood schools are underperforming (as determined by their ISAT scores) and lack resources and access to technology, these parents are easily lured by the promise that new schools offer.

As schools closed in the Mid-South, 14 schools opened in the same closed buildings. Unfortunately, the majority of students in these new schools were not from the immediate neighborhood. It forces the question of why CPS CEO Arne Duncan (2001-2009) frequently talks of his tough decisions to close failing schools, yet he is not accountable for ensuring the students from closed schools are guaranteed enrollment at the new schools. Better yet, why not open new schools to serve the most at-risk students. Due to lottery enrollment a parent must cross their fingers and hope their child gets in, or be admitted to a school where there are no selective enrollment criteria. Too many children and families are being counseled out of applying before they even get near a highly desired school. Consequently most of our families do not benefit from these new R2010 schools where most of the students come from outside of the neighborhood. In communities that have historically been neglected and left behind due to extreme poverty, public housing and race, people on the street have come to see that school closings are being used to more quickly move existing families out of the community, and the new schools are intended to attract new, higher income families into the neighborhood.

The real question we need to ask is that if these new schools cannot educate the neediest of students, then are these schools better than their recently closed counterparts? This is the challenge most of our new schools have failed to take up.

Ann, who eagerly enrolled her fifth grade son into a R2010 schools said she did so because she was told that "it was going to be just outstanding and the facility would be great; it's a multi-million dollar building." Many parents like Ann soon discovered that although this new school was "state of the art" in terms of technology, science labs and other physical "attributes", the quality of his education was not any better than the school their child previously attended and according to some parents, the education and the school environment was actually worse.

Enrolling any child in a R2010 is always a risk since families are entering untested waters. The schools have no history; there are no parents to ask how the school works, and there is no data that tells anything how the school has performed. But many parents are willing to take this risk in hopes that their child will have access to a high performing school.

Unsatisfied with her son's new school, Ann transferred her son to Performing Arts Academy, another charter school in hopes of finding a school that would make good on its promises. This time around Ann and her son were very pleased. Ann then told her son "Ok this is going to be your last school and this is going to be the school you graduate from and he did". Ann was so pleased with the school that she tried to enroll one of her other sons. Unfortunately, he was not accepted. Soon after Ann's son graduated from Performing Arts Academy, the school closed, just as KIPP Global Village Academy and Big Picture Metro High School, two Mid-South R2010 schools, did within 6 years of opening.

If the story only ended here for Ann, but it doesn't. Ann's youngest son, a third grader attended their neighborhood school. In January of this year CPS announced that they were consolidating his school.

Because some of the new schools have entrance requirement, families with multiple children often find themselves having only one child who qualifies and is accepted. Then parents are left in an awful and complicated predicament where siblings may be attending different schools in different parts of the city. On top of that burden, many of these parents are single parents. And since CPS does not offer free bussing, transportation costs often contribute to students eventually dropping from schools outside their neighborhood.

Looking Back

Ironically, in June 2009, the Commercial Club of Chicago (CCC), a key business group that backed the creation of R2010 issued an updated report entitled *Still Left Behind.*[10] It claimed that many of CPS' localized efforts were still not making a significant dent, and it called for more aggressive expansion for charters and contract schools, as well as merit pay for teachers. The CCC and other elite civic and business groups continue to argue that CPS should focus on expanding school options, but they have yet to truly address how to educate the majority of its public school students. All agree this remains CPS' greatest challenge. Everyone continues to agree that we are in an education crisis, but not all agree on how to address it.

However, not all of the research in Chicago concluded that the answer to improving education was through R2010 efforts. A study out of the Consortium of Chicago Public School Research found the following after examining the impacts that closing underperforming school had on students at closed schools:

- Most students from closed schools due to their lower academic performance ended up in similarly weak schools.
- The year of the school-closing announcement negatively impacts reading and math scores.
- Repeated mobility occurred with students from closed schools to the receiving school, with many then moving to another new school. Attendance at Summer Bridge and summer school were also impacted negatively following school closings.
- Learning opportunity of students from displaced schools depended greatly on the quality of the receiving schools.[11]

A local publication, *Catalyst Magazine* for CPS found that even when parents have choice, 30% of African American parents opting out of neighborhood schools for "school choice" ended up in similarly struggling schools compared with 9% of Latino students and 1% of White students.[12] In high schools, nearly 25% of African American high school students who opt out of neighborhood schools end up in high schools scoring in the lowest 25 percentile on the ACT tests. This demonstrates that even with choice, African American communities are still not being provided higher quality opportunities. Still they are indoctrinated in the belief that school choice will be better. *Catalyst's* analysis also emphasizes the need to provide dialogues and venues for parents to better understand what a high quality school looks like, compared to being told new schools are by nature better for your children academically.

In the same *Catalyst* article cited, the Illinois Facilities Fund (IIF) found that in the most under-served communities, children are still waiting for high quality schools. In fact 227,900 students remain on a waiting list in the neediest communities, yet only 15,000 new seats have opened up, many in communities that don't have the education need.

Education as a Business, Students as Employees

In Washington, D.C., the Chancellor of schools Michelle Rhee aimed entirely at ramping up test preparation, and in this endeavor was firing teachers and principals and setting outcomes where schools were being forced to dramatically change their test scores in a short amount of time. Meanwhile the Gates Foundation's "small schools initiative" was dropped in Chicago; in its place funding was repurposed toward what were thought to be high-impact practices in effective classroom teaching. All of these approaches (test prep, small schools, leveraged practices) have been tried in Chicago . . . yielding mixed results.

However, in spite of what we have all learned in Chicago, the trend has been to treat our students as employees. They are punished and forced to relocate if they do not perform, and later admitted to new schools only if they are seen as desirable students. Schools are throwing out their entire staffs and educators, no matter which ones are teaching and inspiring our children. This comes in conflict with helping to retain new teachers, because they are often the first to go in spite of the fact that many of them have strong ideals and bring tremendous energy to their teaching. This mechanism of blaming all teachers when schools don't advance their test scores also sacrifices veteran teachers who have come to understand our children, their families, and the communities they are from.

These senior teachers are often our leaders who guide other educators. The mechanisms of reviewing our schools and student test scores as a bottom line budgetary issue used to determine the life or death of a school without considering learning and progress taking place undermines what public education should be about and contradicts what good teachers are trained to do.

Lessons Learned

It is important to listen to and document the experiences of parents, because it helps educators and policy makers look at school reform efforts more critically to determine if those most under-served are gaining from such policies. Or are these policies augmenting a two-tier public education system for those who are able to choose.

Through the stories of the parents interviewed and from our own community's experiences with closings and openings, these are some of the lessons we have gleaned:

- Communities need improved timely notification of school closings
- CPS has to make decisions fair and transparent
- There must be integrated community and school planning, particularly being sympathetic to housing mobility so that the school district may reduce school mobility when possible
- Parents should not have to choose a school outside of their neighborhood or even "a bus ride away"
- CPS must reduce repeated forced mobility and instead develop a comprehensive education master plan
- Choice is an option only if families have the means
- Public education is being subsidized through these new schools, but the real issue is that no matter who is paying, we have to come to terms with the true cost for a high quality public education for all children.
- Highly publicized new schools are making big promises, but falling short in having quality education.
- These new schools may be falling short because it's too early to tell if they will be successful, but then why replicate new schools so quickly?

- New schools, often run by non-educators, means we are testing theories out on our children, without evidence that they have the answers to educate all of our children, or lack the funding to continue it. The opening and then closing of KIPP and Big Picture is an example.
- There are no guarantees for sibling admittance
- Even if your school was on a previous year's list, families and schools never feel as though CPS will not return to close them.
- Most of these new schools, especially charters, do not accept a proportionate number of students who require more expensive specialized services, as well as English language learners. There is evidence that new schools are creaming the crop of higher performing students, leaving neighborhood schools with more challenged students
- Closings and openings are occurring in communities that are experiencing drastic gentrification with parallel social and economic changes.

On the Horizon

While new schools have provided options to some families, they should not be the central focus of education reform since the evidence is clear that new schools in Chicago disproportionately help children often already in advantaged positions for higher quality educational opportunities. Instead of R2010 as the school reform answer, CPS should begin addressing how to help the vast majority of students not served by new school openings. We must involve parents as team members and as important stakeholders in their child's education, and not see them as the problem or enemy. We must agree that all children may learn, but that our Chicago Public School business administrators must be willing to know what it will truly take to adequately and effectively educate our children so they have opportunities for success after high school.

The national trend is to run all school operations like a business. CPS' former CEO, Arne Duncan, was appointed the United States Secretary of Education under Chicago's own President Barack Obama. The result is rhetoric and now policies that are forcing states to close under-performing schools while offering incentives with huge dollars attached to expand charter schools. In addition, states that do not have charter schools need to create charter schools if they want federal money. In short, states are being pressured to follow a template resembling R2010 when there is no Chicago or national research suggesting that the new federal model is worthy.

Unfortunately, the outgoing Chicago's Mayor Richard M. Daley set in motion a plan to expand R2010 indefinitely, and now, in sync with the Obama administration, the new mayor, Rahm Emanuel, has called for expansion of the school turnaround, school closings, new schools and charter approaches discussed in this chapter. R2010 continues even though 2010 is long gone, but the unfulfilled promises and even greater problems created still persist for CPS, for parents, teachers, students and the community at large.

Notes

1. In establishing guidelines to reach this goal, the Chicago Public Schools (CPS) identified 2 options for new schools in addition to the charter option. The options are contract schools and performance schools. Contract schools have autonomy like a charter; they abide by CPS policies only if agreed upon in advance. In this process the CPS board comes to terms with the school operator through an agreed upon local "contract" to operate the school. This option is closest to a charter, but does not have the same level of autonomy a charter gets. A performance school has more limited autonomy and must follow CPS policies and board of education rules. However, unlike contract and charter schools, it hires Chicago Teachers Union (CTU) educators. A performance school operates most like a school governed fully by the Board but is granted certain exemptions from CPS rules and procedures.

2. Pauline Lipman, "Making the Global City, Making Inequality: The Political Economy and Cultural Politics of Chicago School Policy," *American Educational Research Journal*, 39 (2) (June 20, 2002): 379-419.

3. Chip Mitchell, "Neighborhood Fights to Keep Charter School Out," *City Room*, WBEZ Chicago Public Radio, August 27, 2009.
http://www.chicagopublicradio.org/Content.aspx?audioID=36408

4. Interview of PURE director, by the co-authors.

5. Civic Committee of the Commercial Club of Chicago, 2003, *Left Behind: A Report of the Education Committee*, Chicago: Commercial Club of Chicago.
http://www.commercialclubchicago.org/civiccommittee/initiatives/education/LEFT_BEH IND.pdf

6. See (105 ILCS 5/27A-4; Sec. 27A-4. General Provisions. Section(b))
http://www.ilga.gov/legislation/ilcs/ilcs4.asp?DocName=010500050HArt.+27A&ActID=1005&ChapAct=105 ILCS 5/&ChapterID=17&ChapterName=SCHOOLS&SectionID=17524&SeqStart=156200000&SeqEnd=157900000&ActName=School+Code

7. The Black Belt was the only sector of Chicago where blacks could legally live or own property until the 1940s, when the Supreme Court proclaimed that restrictive covenants based on race were unconstitutional. See Jennifer Farwell, "Bronzeville and Beyond: The Future Looks Bright for Chicago's Historic African American Places," *Preservation*, February 13, 2009.
http://www.preservationnation.org/magazine/story-of-the-week/2009/chicago-bronzeville.html

8. While the students remain at the existing school in the "turnaround" process, the entire staff—administrators and teachers—is replaced.

9. See Natalie Moore, "Fewer Neighborhood Schools Exist in CPS," *City Room*, WBEZ Chicago Public Radio, March 24, 2009.
http://www.chicagopublicradio.org/Content.aspx?audioID=32995

10. See Civic Committee of the Commercial Club of Chicago, *Still Left Behind: Student Learning in Chicago's Public Schools*, Civic Committee (Chicago), 2009.
http://www.chicagobusiness.com/downloads/CPS.pdf

11. See E. Allensworth, *Impacts on Closing Schools*, University of Chicago Consortium on Chicago School Research, October, 2009.

12. See John Myers, "The Challenge of Choice," *Catalyst Chicago*, November 2008.
http://www.catalyst-chicago.org/news/index.php?item=2486&cat=23

Chapter 3
Citizen Teachers and Curricular Activism
John Duffy

When I started my high school teaching career at a racially integrated but quickly re-segregating comprehensive high school (Proviso East) in 1972 near Chicago, within weeks my students confronted me with what they experienced as an inequitable, racially isolating and occupationally rationalized academic tracking system. Two articulate and highly politicized students, one black and the other white, challenged me to see that this system was forcing them and the 4,000 fellow students into separate and grossly unequal school experiences in what at that time was one of a few integrated high schools in the Chicago area. Other African American students passionately complained that their history books talked too much about slavery with little mention of modern liberation heroes like Fred Hampton who just a few years ago walked the halls of their school before he came to lead the Black Panther Party in Illinois, only to be assassinated in a Chicago and Cook County police conspiracy and collaboration with the FBI. This event would transform Chicago politics, lead to the election of Harold Washington as the city's first and only Black mayor, as well as open the flood gates of community based efforts to challenge the centralized, unresponsive board of education in the 1980s.

But in the 1970s at Proviso East High School my students, their parents and several community organizations were running face to face with what education scholars later would call "second generation segregation."[1]

The new structures and procedures for maintaining unequal educational opportunity, even as communities and schools integrated, were numerous and included: the massive and disproportionate suspension and expulsion of black students, an epidemic in the growth of black students assigned to special education, grossly unequal allocation of resources such as class size, a racially segregated gifted curriculum, the racial exclusiveness in assigning teachers to different schools and the racial isolation of students in egregiously unequal curriculum through academic tracking. I was fortunate to have students who challenged me to join with them and community groups to end these injustices and work for a school community curriculum council, similar in some ways to the local school councils (LSC) adopted by Chicago Public Schools (CPS) in the late 80s. For four years and through the negotiation of two teacher contracts the *Coalition for Outstanding Proviso Education* (C.O.P.E.) that we formed worked to create the council to plan the future of the school's curriculum in the face of an accelerated disinvestment in education resources and an attempt to down-track the school's curriculum by the white dominated school board. After a four year struggle, C.O.P.E., while unsuccessful in getting the council accepted by the school board, was able to force major compromises following a series of "curriculum hearings" conducted by university "experts" brought in from several noted universities.

As a social studies teacher and advocate of a new brand of "educational unionism" that worked in collaboration with the community, I continued to work for racially just curriculum and the elimination of the racial, gender and class based inequities that plagued "second generation segregation" in both my school and in the nearby community of Oak Park, Illinois where I lived. In response to ongoing concerns around the achievement gap between white and black students, in the late 1990s the Oak Park, high school district and elementary school district joined the Minority Student Achievement Network, a collaboration of school districts across the country where local governments were attempted to structure managed racial integration of housing and schools. Today, as is the case in most school districts, the learning gap, at least as reflected in standardized test scores, persists in Oak Park.

Over several years in the 1980s a multi-racial alliance of progressive, equity minded parents, teachers and citizens were able to bring significant changes in support of racial equity in the elementary schools while supporting the continued commitment to maintaining a racially diverse community of homes and apartments.

In Proviso Township, adjacent to Oak Park, a gradual re-segregation of the high school district took place during the 1970s and 1980s leading to schools that are today made up of over 90 percent African American and Latino(a) students with a 50 percent poverty rate. In January of 2011, all three high schools were declared turnaround schools under federal Race to the Top (RTT) requirements for repeated failure to meet the test scores mandated by NCLB. Proviso in many ways is following along a path of recent school history similar to the Chicago Public Schools (CPS). Parents and citizens have been repeatedly disappointed by the school's high dropout rate, the district's unresponsiveness to parent and citizen input, and ineffective efforts at substantial improvement by school leadership. Proviso's turnaround declaration follows on the heels five years ago of the creation of a Proviso magnet math and science school which siphoned off the most academically advanced students from the other two campuses. The establishment of charter schools seems to be around the corner if the prevailing pattern continues.

In 1991, I left Proviso East High School and spent the last 15 years of public school teaching at Hinsdale Central High School, which though more white and affluent, also was more ethnically diverse. During this time I continued to design curriculum and professional collaboration that countered the limitations of academic tracking while supporting mainstreaming and inclusion focused classrooms. Then in 2007, a year after retiring from highs school teaching, I began graduate teacher education working with Chicago Public School teachers in an interdisciplinary Masters of Education program that was centered around National Board Certification which had become one of the many mantras sponsored by agencies organized and funded behind the scenes by the corporate allies and members of the Commercial Club of Chicago. And so it seems to me that in many ways I have come full circle in my career in public education.

With my graduate teachers, just as with my students in the early 70s, I am confronting the undemocratic educational designs of what Watkins (2001) called the "white architects of black education."[1] For those unfamiliar with the history of Chicago, there was a direct line between New England business entrepreneurs and the foundations of corporate Chicago during the mid-nineteenth century.[2] While Northern corporate money fashioned and shaped a subservient racist education system in collaboration with many white aristocrats in the South in the late 1800s and early 1900s, the Commercial Club of Chicago (CCC) attempted in the twentieth century to shape a school system that served the class and racial interests of Chicago elites.[3] They would not go unchallenged. Democratically-minded teachers and citizens have throughout the generations have resisted the corporate shaped school order that fell so short of achieving the unrealized ideals of public education as they had evolved from Jefferson thinking of schooling as essential for a democratic republic the early 1800s, through Mann's annual reform efforts in the 1840s and 50s to John Dewey's progressive vision, Jane Addams' *Social Meliorism*, W.E.B. Du Bois' call for "the talented tenth" of college educated African American youth and Margaret Haley's' labor activism on behalf of democratic unions and schools in the first decades of the twentieth century. It is this legacy of vision and resistance that I joined when I entered the classroom in 1972 and that we as teacher educators and co-authors commit ourselves to, both in the scholarship of this book, in our intervention around public policy, and in our solidarity with the teachers we teach, and with the communities and colleagues we stand with in alliance.

Opportunity and Conundrum: Professional Teacher Training

A year after retiring from high school teaching, I began working with National Board Certification candidates in National College of Education's M.Ed. graduate program in the summer of 2007 in Chicago and continued through the early months of 2010. When I started this teaching, I was told by the liaison from Chicago Public Education Fund (the management organization for corporate money behind Chicago school innovations) that the fund believed, in a similar manner as then Chicago public schools CEO Arne Duncan, of how instructional reform would emerge. They argued, without empirical evidence, that if a struggling Chicago school, more than likely a high poverty school composed largely of African-American and Latino students, developed a critical mass of NBC teachers, that school would most likely experience a renewal and most importantly increase their scores on standardized tests, the critical measure that CPS and the Chicago corporate community used to define success.

Despite the many wonderful attributes of National Board for Professional Teaching Standards (NBPTS),[4] I had serious doubts about the "critical mass" scenario presented as well as the NBPTS lack of commitment to a critical perspective on issues of school equity and social justice. As easy as it was to notice in Chicago, it was easier still to notice, when I attended for four days the NBPTS national conference in Washington, D.C., that the burden of failing schools was completely placed on the shoulders of our nation's widely so-called unprepared, inadequate, and un-informed teaching profession. The mantra of every speaker I heard at large breakfast and luncheon symposiums, with one exception, was the repeated call to upgrade our teaching profession *less we continue our global economic downward spiral.* While I certainly did not see every session, I noticed a common discourse throughout the convention. At the dining room presentations I saw and heard only two classroom teachers present in front of the large audiences of teachers, teacher educators, and business and civic leaders attending these sessions. The only teacher on the panel reviewing NCLB called for a national curriculum and not a peep of dissent, save my controlled and restrained gasp, rose from the silent audience.

A second teacher prominently showcased before the whole convention was the nationally acclaimed teacher, author and educational entrepreneur Ron Clark who wowed, entertained and comically cracked up a large luncheon audience with a performance that combined the best of Pee Wee Herman and Jon Stewart. This he did without so much as one mention of a fellow teacher or the promise of teacher collaboration, the necessity for networks, collective intelligence, political organizing or the need for school resource equity in taking on the challenges we all face in poverty schools across the urban and rural American landscape. Despite his passionate commitment to the success of all students and invitation to build trusting relationships with parents in inner-city contexts, here was newest officially Oprah-sanctioned educational hero, screaming, laughing, jumping on tables, and running across the stage in ways that rivaled Bruce Springsteen, while dramatically reinforcing the underlying neoconservative and neoliberal corporate myths that the shortcomings of public education are primarily the consequence of the shortage of highly qualified individual teachers.

Over and over again for four days, major leaders in the NBPTS establishment, with only one exception, kept in step and aligned with the ideology of NCLB and what the public has habitually heard of public education ever since the release of *A Nation at Risk* in 1983. The focus of one presenter after another was an emphasis on high stakes outcomes—teacher testing and student testing. Sadly absent even amongst those addressing the racial divide surrounding National Board Certification was any discussion of the grossly unequal inputs surrounding teacher pre-service and in-service training, school resources, and advanced teacher certification. If anyone was concerned about the accelerating misdistribution of American wealth and its detrimental consequences for our nation's children, the near last ranking of U.S. schools among industrial democracies for equity in public school resources, the disturbing reality that one fourth of our children still live in poverty, the persistent and deep racial divide around teacher achievement of National Board Certification, the expanding privatization of public education, and the persistent drumbeat for wider school choice, even as the Organization for Economic Cooperation and Development (OECD) warns of how broadening school choice *actually undermines equity* (2009)[5], these discussions were virtually absent at this convention in our nation's capital. Instead, as has been the case in Chicago, the shortcomings of our schools, in the entrepreneurial spirit surrounding the board certification process, was almost wholly placed on teachers, who just as they are primarily responsible for our schools shortcomings, can also be responsible for their redemption

CPS Teachers, Commercial Club Curriculum

My teachers, like most who enter the NBPTS certification process, did so for a combination of reasons--for personal monetary aggrandizement, for the status such certification brings, and to serve the students and communities better. Unfortunately, many of the teachers I work with do this in face of the contradictory, corporate designed and increasingly undemocratic nature of Chicago school operations. So with a mix of practical and idealistic motives for National Board Certification these teachers have come to understand more deeply the obstacles to realizing better schools. Now they face an even more centralized system, constructed by an even more charter-focused school oligarchy, the Civic Committee of the Commercial Club, with intimate ties to the Obama administration.

Some of my Chicago teachers taught in so-called turnaround schools, others in struggling neighborhood schools, and still others in lauded charter schools in the neighborhoods of the West Side and South Side which rim the gentrifying areas just West and South of the Chicago loop. As these teachers moved through the preparation of their National Board portfolios, geared up for their assessment center exams and completed related courses in curriculum, instruction, educational foundations, multiculturalism and child development, they soon began to notice a major disconnect between what they were learning and doing around national professional standards and the manner that Chicago schools were being run. The Commercial Club Curriculum regimen that was being imposed on these teachers came into direct contradiction with what they believed were the needs of their students, their own professional integrity and long established teacher union rights that had been gutted by school reorganization under the new mayoral appointed school board beginning in 1995.

Teachers Mark and Kimberly

Mark, one of the high school social studies teachers in our cohort, grew up in the North Lawndale neighborhood of the West Side, maneuvered through the dangerous streets during his youth and then went to college in Minnesota before returning to the West Side to commit himself to helping children have the same opportunities he experienced.

Mark teaches at a Chicago high school that faces some of the greatest challenges in urban education—gang activity, high poverty, and widespread unemployment with the concomitant problems of schools that are not measuring up to the standards demanded by the intense regime of high stakes testing students and teachers face in Chicago. And then one evening Superintendent Arne Duncan appeared on the six o'clock news in the Winter of 2008 and announced the closing of 18 more Chicago public schools and then he called out Mark's school as a failing school where the entire faculty would be replaced with teachers and leaders being trained in the Academy of Urban School Leadership (AUSL), a Chicago corporate and Gates Foundation funded alternative certification program for training teachers for Chicago public schools. The leaders from the fast track certification program would bring in all new teachers, administrators and curriculum to turn the school around. Sadly, this was the third time such a move had taken place in five years at Mark's school. Mark and a second colleague of his in our program and I were shocked and outraged that their indefatigable efforts in their classrooms and in their National Board preparation were summarily being dismissed as another chapter in Chicago school failure. From that cold late February day through the end of the year over half of Mark's students discouraged by more public ridicule and undemocratically imposed school board restructuring stopped coming to class.

Ironically, just a month before CPS announced the closing of Mark's high school and other schools, National College of Education held a community forum and symposium for graduate students and faculty to explore and discuss the problematic impact of race and class on children's chances for equal educational opportunity. A large group of participants attended, but no specific resolutions or follow up took place when I inquired as to what we would do with the testimonies gathered in the breakout dialogues. I could not help but ask if other faculty and administrators saw some tension and contradiction between our college vision statement which passionately calls for democracy, equity and social justice in America's schools and our faculty and administration's collective silence as all these Chicago schools were being closed without the democratic input of the parents, community organizations and teachers being impacted.

The most disturbing part of these closings, as I soon learned, was that the teachers and leaders being brought in were coming out of our alternative certification program to replace dismissed teachers in our National Board preparation graduate program. After spending a cold morning on a downtown picket line protesting with community groups, union teachers and students, I called on all members of the college to wonder how two wonderful, dedicated teachers in one of our graduate programs, labeled as incompetent by CPS CEO Duncan, were being replaced by graduate students from another one of our programs. While I praised the dedicated work many colleagues had done in supporting teacher growth and equity in large numbers of Chicago schools over the years, I also suggested that our university seemed to be on the wrong side of the widening community divide on school renewal in Chicago. Soon after these comments I received an email from the director of the alternative certification program asking me for details and further affirmation of my graduate teachers' talents and quality. He then urged me not to take up with him the argument over the school closings.

Sensing that my two teachers were about to step out of the problematic Chicago syndrome newspaper journalist Mike Royko referred to as being "no one, who nobody sent," I wrote supportive letters on their behalf. My two graduate students soon were invited to interview for their jobs, told of the wonderful new curriculum they would get to teach, and eventually along with 20 percent of their colleagues were invited back to their born again school, now a large city high school and no longer the small high school alternative that had lost favor with corporate sponsors of school change. All of these developments are representative of how quickly corporate sponsored urban school solutions lose favor among their very sponsors who want immediate high yield returns on their venture capital. The Gates Foundation threw hundreds of millions of dollars into the creation of small high school around the nation. By the summer of 2009, it was all over as the foundation now placed their future money toward urban high school reform on the rapid expansion of charter schools as the latest sure-fire answer for struggling high poverty urban high schools.

Then, not even two years into Mark's school's reorganization, only a few months after Arne Duncan rode the "triumphs" of Chicago school reform to become Secretary of Education[6], the Civic Committee Report of the Commercial Club of Chicago (2009) declared school reform a failure and in sync with Gates Foundation called for a massive expansion of charter schools in Chicago. This transpired too while a Stanford University (2009) study on the impact of Chicago charters found but limited success in improving math for lower grade students of poverty backgrounds.[7] In the area of reading Chicago charters, according to this report, were significantly underperforming regular public schools in Chicago. Finally, CPS, on the heels of these two reports, announced the failure of their latest high school restructuring effort based on only the first benchmark evaluation of the Kaplan developed high school curriculum that teachers, in schools like Mark's, have been mandated to teach.

Mark's fellow graduate student Kimberly had the good fortune to teach in one of the most lauded of all elementary level Chicago charter schools. Her school was located just a short distance from where Mark grew up and now lives. As you will see and hear from Kimberly, her charter school, despite highly touted test scores, was far from the ideal teachers sought under corporate controlled school renewal in Chicago.

Kimberly, an African American mother of six grown children and grandmother of many, has had a remarkable and admirable educational journey. She overcame years of occupational tracking in CPS to eventually realize that she possessed great talents and a calling to teach which were not being fulfilled in her job as a hairdresser. After growing up in the Cabrini Green public housing community in Chicago, she wanted more for her children than the CPS neighborhood schools were offering so she enrolled her youngest children in one of Chicago's first charters on the West Side where she also started doing volunteer support work. She eventually began to teach at the school when she obtained her bachelor's degree.

As one of my graduate students working to get her National Board Certification and Master's degree Kimberly focused her individual research on what she had come to view as the disturbing contradictions and problems of teaching in what CPS officials would hail as one of Chicago's model charter schools. Kimberly continued to believe in the idealistic goals of the charter school movement, but the longer she taught, the more she came to resent what she came to see as serious injustices she noticed as the school's only art teacher. Her doubts about her school situation developed even in a charter school that had benefits that far outstripped the local public schools that surround it on the West Side. It has the highest published test scores of West Side schools, sits in a new, beautifully designed and decorated building and is blessed with significant additional funds from Chicago corporate sponsors. In many ways it had become an educational oasis in one of the most economically distressed neighborhoods of the city. Nonetheless, for Kimberly and other teachers these benefits have started to be outweighed by the relentless demands and pressures charter school teaching, like all teaching, demands of its teachers.

As the pressure on charters to boost students test grades has increased, and as her school has expanded through replication, Kimberly has come to resent her yearly talk with her ever changing principal, four in the last 7 years. She fights for more time to teach art and obtain a salary that is commensurate with her ongoing dedication to advancing her knowledge of art through continuous professional development at various Chicago art foundations and through her National Board preparation. Each year she becomes more angry that charter teachers are denied collective bargaining, work almost two weeks longer than regular CPS teachers, but like regular CPS schools in the North Lawndale neighborhood where Dr. King took up temporary residence as the Civil Rights Movement shifted mass direct action to Chicago housing, jobs and school issues in 1966, she has witnessed a persistent narrowing of the school's curriculum in an effort to ramp up students test scores. And the collegiality Kimberly loves and thrives on is more and more difficult with the exhausting schedule, which she believes is partly responsible for teacher attrition rates this past year of 50 percent.

Other teachers in our program Kimberly studied with have come to resent the ever-expanding creation of more charter schools and the loss of some of their better students to these schools. They sadly lament the even greater pressure to teach in ways that conflict with what they are learning in their NBPTS study. Some have told how their principals tell them to not worry about teaching science or social studies since these subjects will not, in their eyes, be reflected in citywide test scores. Some teachers are professionally insulted by newly prescribed and scripted curriculum. My high school teachers see major contradictions between National Board standards and see the Kaplan created curriculum funded by the Gates Foundation to be incongruent with their commitment to differentiate their teaching, materials and assessments in culturally responsive ways and in the spirit and letter of the national teaching standards that Commercial Club Curriculum praises.

Recently, I caught up with my student Mark after his first month back to school. He continues to teach in his second year at his CPS turnaround school, which is now prominently profiled in National College press releases as a glowing example of how leaders and teachers trained in its corporately subsidized AUSL alternative certification program can provide the teachers and leaders who can re-energize, rededicate and save underperforming Chicago high schools. A massive, recently announced 2009 Department of Education grant of almost $20 million over five years that will insure the National College/AUSL/CPS turnaround model for replication across the city. This grant ironically comes, as noted earlier, just after the Gates Foundation withdrew its multi-million dollar support for restructuring and curriculum renewal in collaboration with CPS administration in a network of high schools called Transformation Schools. The Turnaround model will now compete with Charter school alternatives while both approaches will soon be adopting a strongly business endorsed performance pay structure for teachers.

In the meantime, Mark struggles to maintain his spirit as he wrestles with a litany of contradictions he experiences with the new curriculum he is mandated to teach in his school's turnaround experiment. According to Mark, the curriculum screws are being turned even tighter as his social studies lessons are coming to be an almost verbatim instructional formula. He is outraged that the his belief in strong disciplinary content balanced with individualized differentiation, especially in materials and assessment, a principle we studied and explored and that is deeply in harmony with NBC core principles, are absent in what he calls a technocratic approach to teaching, emphasizing methods, skills and scripted classroom contexts that are woefully short on critical content or a culturally responsive outlook. Instead, leaders espouse the principle that the context kids bring to school does not matter. As Mark questions practices like these that disregard any commitment to individualization, he is counseled by his principal to not speak up so much in meetings.

Mark tells of how he has come to understand who is calling the shots and wonders if he will have the stamina to carry on in his school undergoing its third principal in five years, as it has gone from a large traditional neighborhood high school to a small school and now under turnaround status back to a large high school. Perhaps what most discourages Mark is the certainty turnaround school leaders have about what they are doing. As he points out, the most important element in serving students in schools like his is building a sense of community with students' needs first. But under the new organization of his turnaround, he gains or loses half of his division students with each semester change. When I asked about teacher input and evaluative participation in the new system of curriculum and instruction being lauded as the solution to student learning needs, he told me that when leaders seek feedback, they only want ratings on the technocratic innovations they sponsor, and never wish to speak about teacher concerns about the culture of the school and the underlying premises for curriculum and testing. When I wonder if he is tempted to just walk away and try another school, Mark expresses his heartfelt hope that he is not asked to leave (principals can release any teachers from the school without due process, and free them to find another possible CPS school that may want them) and then he sadly and painfully laments that "they don't want you to think anymore." Mark then pauses, there is a moment of silence, and in frustration, but also with his usual tenacious resolve he cries, "I am working with the kids I went to school to serve, that's why I came back to the West Side." As we conclude our conversation, I can't help but wonder how without a full, democratic civic and professional voice any teacher could continue to teach in this latest version and organization of Commercial Club Curriculum.

Curricular Advocacy

Both I and my fellow editor Todd Price are teacher educators but define ourselves more fully as citizen teachers. As citizen teachers, in addition to our focus on helping our students and ourselves develop the essential knowledge, pedagogical skills, critical frameworks and political perspectives to build classrooms and schools focused on democratic living and social justice, we believe critical citizen teachers need to fully participate in the democratic deliberative life of our departments, college, university, and the communities where we live. We believe it our democratic civic duty to respond to, influence and shape the public policy of educational organizations especially as that policy expands or limits the possibilities for democracy, equity, and equality in public schools and society. As we have argued, Commercial Club Curriculum has attempted to constrain the civic voices and labor organizing rights of teachers in turn around schools like Mark's and charter schools like Kimberly's. Now, in unison with Obama education policy, it has called for a rapid expansion of charter schools to replace regular public schools with the assertion that pubic school reform in Chicago has failed. In a complimentary, parallel manner, the National Council for the Accreditation of Teacher Education (NCATE), the American Association for Colleges of Teacher Education (AACTE) and NBPTS are defining professional standards in ways that further attempt to remove from the dispositions of "highly qualified" teachers the principles, moral and ethical commitments and participation in the civic culture all schools require of teachers, but which are especially vital in schools and communities facing the worse consequences of social, economic, environmental and political injustice in urban, suburban and rural America.

IACTE and "Troubling" Dispositions

As critical "citizen teachers," we are concerned with the removal of required educational foundations courses as essential to teacher preparation by NCATE, the elimination of social justice from the list of dispositions that highly qualified teachers demonstrate, and the removal of sexual orientation from NCATE description of the human diversity teachers should be trained and committed to addressing in their classroom lives. Let us briefly explicate our critique of how NBPTS presents a narrow functionalist conception for teachers' standards of professional behavior when acting as professional change agents; then, we will turn to the deliberation around social justice and sexual orientation involving our college's participation in the Illinois Association of Colleges for Teacher Education (IACTE).

There is widespread support for the NBPTS instructional and content standards as a template for advancing the professional skills and knowledge of experienced teachers. Despite mixed evidence on how much NBC teachers influence student achievement and a significant attack on NBPTS from right wing opponents, the corporate advocates of teacher education reform, including the Commercial Club of Chicago and its surrogate the Chicago Public Education Fund, vigorously endorse the NBC belief that the strength of teacher involvement and collaboration with parents and community agencies are important to improving teacher effectiveness. Yet, evidence of high professional standards regarding out of school professional engagement, a major requirement of NBPTS for all certification areas, in a manner similar to NCATE standards, fosters a narrow, instrumentalist, functional definition of professionalism. In the NBC professional portfolio entry evidence of professional work outside the classroom can only be used as a demonstration of professional accomplishment *if the teacher can tie this work directly to some improvement in student achievement.* Thus, the most publicly recognized, federal and state subsidized definition of "highly qualified teachers," in a manner similar to NCATE, marginalizes social justice and political advocacy activist teachers often take up in a career long dedication to changing the range of societal constraints that have influenced school inequities for generations. Teachers we have worked with believe their understanding and mastery of NBC core principles will help their children achieve, but they consistently found little direct connection between national board principles, standards and altering the serious impositions like dire poverty, violence, environmental hazards, nutrition, mental health needs and limited employment opportunities that place such severe limits on the families and communities of their students.

In another example of how professional standards are being defined in ways that further attempt to remove from the dispositions of "highly qualified" teachers the principles, moral and ethical commitments and participation in the civic culture, is the American Association for Colleges of Teacher Education (AACTE). AACTE, with its 750 member colleges that prepare 90 percent of American teachers, and its state affiliates like the Illinois Association for Colleges of Teacher Education (IACTE) are the leading organizations for advancing and coordinating the interests of teacher education across the nation. For the past two years we have been engaged in wrestling with how we live up to our university's diversity and inclusion policy regarding sexual orientation and our personal commitment to calling for the IACTE to not hold meetings at member colleges who are not in compliance with the 2006 Illinois Human Rights Act which prohibits discrimination based on sexual orientation. We joined in alliance with teacher educators at Northeastern University, DePaul University and the School of the Art Institute of Chicago, all fellow Chicago members of IACTE. We rallied in support of Therese Quinn and Erica Meiners' (2008) principled direct action[8] where they asked teacher educators in face-to-face conversations at the IACTE meeting being held at Wheaton College to sign a pledge titled "Embrace Love, Not Condemnation." Subsequently both Quinn and Meiners' colleges received letters asking school administrators to discipline them for their actions. Quinn and Meiners then planned to place a motion before the IACTE administrative board to ensure that the organization's meetings no longer be held at schools like Wheaton which were not in compliance with the Illinois Human Rights Act.

In support of Quinn and Meiners' courageous and principled action and their proposal to have IACTE ban meetings held at schools that discriminated against LGBQT students, we called for the deans and faculty of our college, the National College of Education (NCE) in Chicago to support the resolution. A discussion of the motion at the November 2008 NCE meeting showed a divided faculty and the proposal to support the meetings resolution was tabled for further study and investigation as various current and former administrators of the college told of how there were good people at Wheaton College and that they contributed valuable resources over the years that kept the operation of IACTE viable. They related how they had friendly, respectful and productive relations at Wheaton and other schools that discriminated against LGBQT students and failed to prepare either their pre-service or graduate teachers to address the LGBQT diversity they would find in their school classrooms. Other opponents of the resolution claimed we had no business telling Wheaton College how to run their community, even though supporters of the resolution did not challenge Wheaton's internal decision, but instead directed our concern for the contradiction between our own university's diversity statement and what we came to see as a regressive 1973 approved and never revised, diversity and multicultural policy published on the IACTE Homepage.[9]

Out of this effort to confront what we saw as a disturbing contradiction in what our college professed and what it was willing to do regarding its commitment to social justice, a group of straight, gay, lesbian and bi-sexual faculty formed a LGBTQ Interest Group to carry our concerns to the higher levels of university administration, present the case to the Diversity and Inclusion Council and launch a series of curriculum development and support efforts, including a professional development grant to build more openness, understanding, support, acceptance and safety for LGBTQ faculty and students. We continue to press these difficult conversations, have organized a series of informational and artistic events around National Coming-Out Week, Human Rights Week, and a winter workshop on LGBTQ awareness and teaching. In the meantime, we wrestle with the difficult conversation about when and if we as a group will make a full case before the University Provost and President to support the meetings' resolution.

Postscript

In Oak Park near Chicago, I recently moderated a Town Hall Meeting called by citizens who were concerned that the testing regime imposed by NCLB and local school reforms for the last generation had shown little if any progress in raising test scores for African American students at Oak Park and River Forest High School. Furthermore, as several speakers pointed out, the African American achievement gap has persisted in a school that has been reluctant to confront long documented inequities in the curriculum and instruction that different groups of student's experience.

Several participants at this town hall meeting also expressed once again long stated concerns that curriculum tracking at the school was a major factor that contributed substantially to inequitable as well often highly segregated learning. This traditional school structure and the racial segregation tracking encourages continues in a community where civic leaders and citizens commonly sing the praises of 'managed integration'. In my opening remarks as the moderator of the meeting, I suggested that the challenges for teachers to address the persistent skewed inequities in the school's academic curriculum outcomes would soon be compounded as Illinois teachers and principals, like most states around the country receiving NCLB waivers under RTT, will soon have their evaluations and even pay tied substantially to improvements in student test performance.

Some citizens at this town hall meeting doubted these new Common Core State Standards would actually have a positive impact on teaching and learning, but instead, would likely amp up the pressure to narrow the curriculum, especially for the African American population who overwhelmingly are not making cut scores which are used for defining success. The segments of the community that have benefited under the existing curriculum structure of the Oak Park and River Forest High School have resisted until recently to even question, even acknowledge that the school may play an important role in contributing to these disparities. And even when it tries, the school has found it difficult to replicate features that appear to enhance minority achievement in other communities. A few people at the meeting proffered a more radical analysis, proposing that the tracking system, testing system, and their grossly uneven outcomes were part of a design that worked well with the needs of the American social and economic system and the corporate interests driving the new accountability models. Other individuals went so far as to claim the school system was doing what the larger society not only expected, but desired.

Despite this evening of dire, often sad and disturbing testimonies from parents and some students, most participants left the gathering committed to carrying on in search of the idealistic promises of racially integrated schools. Yet in the hall, after all but a few of the crowd had departed for home, for the first time I heard one parent speak of considering the need for a charter option in Oak Park. Ironically, a charter advocacy group formed in the neighboring Proviso Township High School district had recently introduced and then withdrew from state consideration a proposal for a charter high school. I can't help but think that the extension of the Chicago chartering phenomena to both middle class and working class racially segregated and integrated school districts on the West and South Side of Chicago seems to be just around the corner.

Notes

1. William Watkins, *The White Architects of Black Education: Ideology and Power in the South, 1865-1954*. (New York: Teachers College Press, 2001).

2. See Donald Miller, *City of the Century: The Epic of Chicago and the Making of America*, New York: Simon & Schuster, 1997; and Kevin Phillips, *The Cousins' Wars: Religion, Politics, Civil Warfare, and the Triumph of Anglo-America*, (New York: Basic Books, 1998).

3. See Pauline Lipman, *Race, Class, and Power in School Restructuring*, Albany, NY: State University of New York Press, 1998; and Dorothy Shipps, *School Reform, Corporate Style. Chicago 1880-2000*, (University Press of Kansas, 2006). p. 3.

4. See National Board for Professional Teaching Standards Core Propositions for K-12 Teachers, http://www.nbpts.org/thestandards/thefivecorepropo

5. See Simon S. Field, M. Kuczera and B. Pont, *No More Failures: Ten Steps to Equity in Education*, Summary and Policy Recommendations for the Organization for Economic Cooperation and Development, 2010, http://www.oecd.org/home/0,2987,en_2649_201185_1_1_1_1_1,00.html

6. For a critique and challenge to Duncan's claims of major success in Chicago, See J. Brown, E. Gutstein, and P. Lipman, "Arne Duncan and the Chicago Success Story: Myth or Reality?" http://www.rethinkingschools.org/restrict.asp?path=archive/23_03/arne233.shtml

7. See *Multiple Choice: Charter School Performance in Sixteen States*, Center for Research on Education Outcomes (CREDO) (Stanford University, Stanford, CA., June 2009) at http://credo.stanford.edu, and *Still Left Behind: Student Learning in Chicago*, Report of the Civic Committee of the Commercial Club of Chicago, 2009, at http://www.civiccommittee.org/Still%20Left%20Behind%20v2.pdf

9. Details of which informed their book; see T. Quinn & E. Meiners, *Flaunt it! Queers organizing for public education and justice*, (New York: Peter Lang, 2009).

10. That, in a thinly veiled reference to sexual orientation diversity, AACTE would continue "the support of explorations in alternative and emerging lifestyles." See *No One Model American*, (AACTE, 1973).

Chapter 4
Standard Scores and Non-Standard Lives:
A Recipe for Systemic Violence
Terry Jo Smith

A couple of hundred years ago, Kant told us that the one thing we're not permitted to do, morally speaking, is to treat people as means to an end, as tools or instruments to achieve other objectives. It's been a while since I've read him, but I don't recall that he made an exception for really short people who don't eat their vegetables. Thus, it will not do to sacrifice children on the altar of accountability, to use them in a giant high-stakes experiment and ignore the very real harm it does. Alfie Kohn in Ohanian, 2002, p. x

In the late 1990s I spent a day a week at City School (names have been changed), a K-8 school on the west side of Chicago, that was in its second year of "probation." I witnessed a systemic violence there,[1] an institutional brutality that was hurled upon students, families, teachers, and administrators. The violence was perpetrated from beyond the school itself and was going under the guise of urban reform. I was at the school the days the high stakes test scores were received by the principal and then the students and teachers. This was a week in which the violence was visible and palpable. Because I write to process emotions, think things through and to research[2] I wrote a narrative back then, a thick description of the week, to carefully construct my own understandings. That narrative is the centerpiece of this chapter.

I return to this narrative because it haunts me. The systemic violence I witnessed has spread across the nation. Back then, such practices as the threat of a failing school being "reconstituted," a student failed based on a single test score, and teachers being relegated to use scripted curricula, were relatively new phenomena. The panic and discouragement it wrought was raw and so, not yet embedded enough within school experience to be invisible or "normal." Thus emotions were strong and reactions were pointed. Today, this systemic violence is a given, is widespread, is more prevalent in schools. It has been codified in the No Child Left Behind Act (NCLB) and given a whip and farther reach through the Race to the Top (RTT) initiative.

> Systemic violence is not intentional harm visited on the unlucky by vicious in-
> dividuals. Rather, it is the unintentional consequences of procedures imple-
> mented by well-meaning authorities in a belief that the practices are in the best
> interests of students. Systemic violence is insidious because those involved,
> both perpetrators and victims, are often unaware of its existence.[3]

I began my work in City School after having taught in the inner city in Mi-
ami for several years. I left the classroom just before the high states testing
frenzy began to get underway. My work at City School, as a consultant, was my
first exposure to the social and emotional impact these punishing, top-down
policies had on students, teachers and administrators. The account included in
this chapter is a slice of life, a contextual rendering of a few days in the life of a
school and my interpretation of what I experienced on "judgment day," when
the results of the standardized test entered into the school, casting blame and
shame. This is a social account that attempts to tease out the intersections of
policy, theory, and practice within the institutional arrangements of schooling.
The lived impact of educational policy can't be read on school report cards, it
can't be aggregated, and it shouldn't be ignored.

Long ago Paulo Freire (2003) made a compelling case about the importance
and centrality of the relational dynamics in education, particularly when related
to teaching disenfranchised and marginalized people. He argued that the nature
of relationship between teachers and students and the institutional norms that
provide support for those relationships, are critical components in regard to education holding the potential to be liberatory. He is unequivocal when he states,

> The Solution is not (nor can it be) found in the banking concept. On the con-
> trary, banking education maintains and even stimulates the contradiction
> through . . . attitudes and practices, which mirror oppressive society as a
> whole.[4]

Like many educators around the world, his insights still impact my seeing.
When, I look at urban reform, I always have an eye to the nature of sanctioned
relationships, to what comprises curricula, to how power is enacted and by
whom.

The following narrative was constructed in the late 1990s when I was
spending a day a week at City School. My engagement there provided insights
into the impacts of urban reform that was a forerunner for NCLB and RTT. Having recently left the classroom and eager to stay actively involved in urban
schools, I offered the principal to help in any way I could. Given my experience
and interest was in working with students considered behaviorally disordered, he
asked me to work with the two teachers who were experiencing the most severe
behavior problems in their classrooms and with the students who were posing
those problems. I split my time between observing and helping out in these two
classrooms and talking with students in a small office I was given in the base-
ment. I also visited other classrooms in the school, had conversations with
teachers in the lunchroom, and had weekly conversations with the principal.

Tensions

Amidst some laughing and learning and loving, what I've found in my time at City School were many struggles: struggles between students, teachers and administrators; struggles with time and demands; struggles with feelings of frustration and hopelessness; and struggles to keep the war that raged in the neighborhood beyond the doors out of the school. One of the most prominent struggles was lived out by the teachers as they tried to respond to their students' needs and the dictates of district policies that were based on the assumption that the problems facing this school district were due to teachers who weren't working hard enough, holding high enough expectations, nor caring enough about students' progress. Behind these damning attributions, were the subtle accusations that the teachers weren't teaching the right way and perhaps were not smart enough or prepared well enough to do so. To overcome the weaknesses of bad teaching, a prescribed "teacher proof" curriculum was adopted. In fact, I was told that the teachers were expected to be on a certain page on any given day. High stakes tests were instituted to hold teachers and students accountable.

Ms. Lewis was the teacher in one of the two classes I worked with regularly. She taught in a self-contained, general education, eighth-grade room with 28 students. Over half the students had failed the previous year based on one standardized test (the IOWA). This year, the students were angry and being fed the same lifeless, standardized curriculum they had "failed" in the year before. It was curriculum that didn't touch their hearts, and thus, never made too lasting an impression on their minds. The students were angry and disengaged and the teacher, a rookie, was at a loss. When I talked to her about using a more engaging curriculum with the students she said she wasn't free to do so, there was certain material she was supposed to teach each day and assess each week. There were scripts she was supposed to read. Her classroom was a free-for-all on many days. She sincerely wanted to teach the kids, sincerely cared about them, but she had never been prepared to deal with their anger and resistance, nor the pain and sadness that fueled it. She was learning, they were teaching, and as is too often the case in the inner city, the lessons were sometimes brutal.

However, this rookie teacher wasn't the only one struggling with student resistance and apathy. As I sat with a group of teachers in the cafeteria and listened to them talk, they voiced their perplexity at students who were defiant and unmotivated. One veteran teacher commented that things were getting worse; the students more disrespectful, the neighborhood more dangerous, and the district demands more ridiculous. Another teacher said with a mixture of frustration and much sadness, "They can't give us kids who don't care and expect us to teach. They have to give us kids who care."

Yet when I talked with many of the students one on one and in small groups, they were brimming over with things they cared about. They were just not the same things the teachers wanted them to care about. When I gave students a chance to talk, stories poured forth from them like water from a clogged pipe once the obstruction has been cleared. The students told me stories about parents and siblings being on drugs, of being left with relatives, of fathers in jail for life, of being born into a gang family, of a revolving door of fathers in the house, of siblings in and out of jail, of using drugs and selling drugs, getting in fights, of racist teachers and neighborhood violence. They were growing up into a world they didn't create but could not escape.

The students also told me stories about cultural pride, bonds of love and loyalty, families and friends who loved them fiercely, defying the many systems that attempted to control and regulate their lives, teachers who cared about them, and about solidarity among students. They told me stories of boyfriends, best friends, and secret hopes for making a good life. These students cared deeply about many things. There was passion pulsing through the veins of this school that ran cold when it came up against lifeless curriculum, fill in the blank tests, and topics unrelated to the complexities and passions of their lives.

The kids are living in fast times and in dangerous places. Much of their life is dominated by powers beyond their control. They are after all, children. They have many sides to them. They are innocent children in some ways, and in other ways they know way too much about harsh realities children shouldn't have to know. They are a tight knit group. There is a familiarity and a bond among the students, and a united front against the teachers when the need arises. By the middle school age, the students' stand off against the teachers is perfected. Although there are hugs and conversations and some learning going on, the underlying dynamic that is ever present and seems to increase with the age of the student, is resistance to just about everything the teachers deem important. Teachers, with rare exceptions, are seen as outsiders to the students' worlds, members of one of the many systems that paint the students and their families as problems. More than one child commented that the only air conditioners in the entire school were in the principals' office. They are aware of dominant social hierarchies and their place near the bottom. Given these dynamics, "help" isn't always a welcome commodity.

I once watched Ms. Lewis' class shut down for over a week and refuse to work after she lectured them about her desire for them to get off of welfare and have choices in their lives. She tried to explain the engrained middle class notion that people on public aid drained those of us who worked hard for a living. She made the distinction between those people who really needed welfare because they were physically unable to work and those who milked the system for all they could get. She talked about doing well in school as the ticket to a respectable life. After her heartfelt speech that was sincerely meant to let her students know how much she cared about them and wanted for them, most of the students called her a racist (among other things) and resisted her best efforts to teach them. Ms. Lewis was surprised she had offended them and hurt them with her words.

Many of the students are torn between a street culture that is pervasive, immediate, alluring and dangerous and a school culture that tries very hard to suppress and repress that street culture. Many of the parents are torn between wanting their children to have the promise of a better life and their deep distrust of any "system" to deliver that promise. They are in agony over not always being in a position to protect their children from serious threats. Two of the girls in

Ms. Lewis' class have scars from gunshot wounds. One boy in her class was shot this year. I met his father when he came to school to get homework for his son while he recuperated. Ms. Lewis hugged the man and told him things would be OK. Mr. Kamp (the principal) showed me a police report detailing the crime activity for the previous month in the surrounding neighborhood. The students tell me stories of police violence and raids. One morning when I arrived the whole school was on lock-down. Students had been ushered inside before school, leaving book bags and other personal items outside. There was a raid on a house across the street and gun shots were fired. Not much formal learning occurred that day. The neighborhood is saturated; loss is a part of everyday life.

Judgment Day

One Tuesday, I just happened to be in Mr. Kamp's office right after he got results of the IOWA (standardized test) scores for the school. This was the test that determined if individual students would be retained, if the school would get off probation, if ultimately the faculty would keep their jobs. He was not his usual self and when I mentioned that he looked distracted he told me he had just received word that the reading scores had gone down from the previous year. I realized he was more than distracted when I saw tears well up in his eyes. He said he felt like going home. He was having a hard time being in the school. He needed to deal with his feelings and come back tomorrow. I had never seen this strong leader look so down. He had started his teaching career in this school and then come back to it as an administrator. He gave his heart and soul to this work. It was clear his heart was breaking.

"How could the reading scores go down?" he asked as he shook his head from side to side. "How could that happen with all we have done, all these programs? Teachers are working their fingers to the bone. We have extra reading classes and tutoring before and after school. Everyone is pitching in."

I saw Mr. Kamp later in the day when he stopped by Ms. Clark's class to tell the students he had heard good things about them from me. He didn't go home, and he didn't miss a chance to tell some kids he was proud of them. Once again, I was warmed by this man's enormous heart. I remembered when I first met him and told him I wanted to spend time in his school and help in whatever ways I could. I told him I missed being in schools and that City School was the kind of school I felt most comfortable in. He grinned at me and said, "You better watch out, there is something about this place that makes you fall in love with it." I could see in his face that he had been struck by cupid's arrow.

But Mr. Kamp, in spite of his big heart and deep insights into school and community, was in danger of losing his job as principal. City school was on "academic probation" because their standardized scores were lower than average. The school had three years to remedy this situation, bring test scores up, or the school would go under reorganization. This meant bringing in new faculty and administrators. They were at the end of year two.

I was at City School two days later when the teachers and students got the results of the IOWA. The teachers were gathered in the hallway before the morning bell rang, talking nervously about the day to come. As I walked up, Ms. Lewis came running over to me and hugged me. She was so nervous about the scores. "Oh good, you're here. Please stay in my class today. It's going to be a crazy day," she said. "Today we get the test results. I hope my kids did good."

Once the students came in they were as nervous as the teachers. For the students in eighth grade a low score meant being retained, many of them for the second time. It meant humiliation. Over half of the eighth grade class had been retained the previous year. The school, and especially the 8th grade wing, was piping with energy. Kids were bouncing off the walls. At lunchtime, the 8th grade teachers sat together in the lunchroom. This was the first time I had seen this happen. They were coming together for support, for comfort. They talked about which kids they had heard through the grapevine had passed and which had failed. They openly expressed their grief and disappointment when they heard students who had worked hard had not passed. They talked about how impossible it was to teach many of the kids who were living such difficult lives.

The individual scores were not given out until the end of the day. It was a day of raw nerves and blaming, a day of fear and prayers. Everyone's worth was on the line. It was judgment day and nearly everyone was telling stories to explain why things might not "measure up." I heard the teachers blame the kids, administration, parents, neighborhood, crime, and race. I heard the kids blame the teachers. But overall, I heard a lot of people who were just generally perplexed, because they were all working very hard. I heard a lot of frustration, a lot of sadness, and a lot of deep questioning of a system that put so much emphasis on a test.

There was talk of handing the scores to the kids at the door when the students left and that way if they went crazy it would be outside. A number of teachers moved their cars down the block because the students would be let out into the parking lot. They said last year the students really got out of control when they got the results. There were fights and vandalism, some windows were smashed and the police had been called. The air was very tense. After lunch, in Ms. Lewis' class the students chatted nervously and moved about. They were full of anxiety and asked a hundred times if the school had the results yet. They kept asking Ms. Lewis to go check. They told her she could pull some strings and find out the scores if she really wanted to.

At one point a group of about ten students pulled their chairs in a circle and held hands and began to pray. Rasheda led the prayer and said among other things, "please God, we ask you in Jesus' name to get good scores." She also thanked Jesus for bringing them together as a family in that room. I had talked to several of the students in the circle at an earlier time about their seeming lack of interest in academics or getting ready for the test. I asked them if they cared if they passed or not. They said they cared but they didn't seem to see the connection between studying, doing schoolwork and getting good scores. They complained that the work was boring. Now they were asking Jesus to pull off a miracle in the eleventh hour.

The administrators and counselors set out from the main office ten minutes before the dismissal bell. They took sealed envelopes with students' names and scores to each class and handed them to the teachers. They directed the students not to open the envelopes until they got outside. The students tore the envelopes open as soon as they had them in their hands. I stood watching the students' faces. I watched kids celebrate and jump up and say yes! YES! YES! YES!! And I watched kids burst into tears. Rasheda, who had worked very hard and had often gotten angry that the room was so chaotic, cried hysterically. She just broke down. Her counselor came in and took her outside. She went out in the hall and wept. Other kids who didn't make the mark sat there and shook their heads, wiped away tears, and hid their faces, as some of their classmates danced in circles and cheered around them. Alberto, a boy who rarely did his work and kept the room in an uproar, scored very high. It was about a 50/50 mix of celebration and devastation.

The students were ushered out of the building a minute after they got their test results. Some of the teachers gathered together again and talked about their scores and sheets. Ms. Lewis started to cry. At that point, Jeanette a student in her class who had been absent walked in and wanted to know her score. Ms. Lewis told her she didn't pass and Jeanette broke into tears.

"What am I gonna do?" She asked. "I studied and I tried. I knew that damn test was too hard. I knew I did good though. No way, how could I not have passed? Oh, my God," she sobbed,

> I won't be able to get a summer job, I won't be able to do nothing. What if I don't pass it in August? Oh no, What am I gonna do? I wish I didn't come to this damn school! I would have passed at my other school. The teachers help you on it there. They read something to you, answer your questions. HELP YOU! Oh no, what am I gonna do?

She sobbed as she collapsed in a chair and hid her face in her hands. Ms. Lewis hugged her and held her and tried hard to comfort her. She told her a test is like a snap shot and this could have been a bad picture/test day for her. She said maybe she could take it over, get a waiver because her scores had dropped. Or if she had to take it in August she could start studying right away to make sure she passed. Jeanette just cried.

Ms. Lewis took her to see Ms. Garcia, the assistant principal. Crying children were being comforted, talked with and held around the office. Angry parents were asking questions, holding children by the arms. Emotion was everywhere; blame, anger, self-doubt. The test scores had entered the building like a conquering army, defeating hope, wounding children, and contaminating the arena of learning, turning it into a place of fear.

Erasing Social Difference

One of the rarely spoken beliefs behind the practice of standardized testing is that students have standardized opportunities. Inequalities in students' opportunities are rationalized away by invoking the statistical ideal of the representative norm group. When the norming group of a standardized test is compiled it is constructed to make sure all kinds of lives are represented in the sample in ways that echo their percentages in society at large. Children who struggle with tougher life conditions, less resources, and poorly supported schools, are ranked in standardized scores up against a group sample that was comprised of children who for the most part had more and in some cases much more privilege and opportunity. Children who have a lot of opportunity, resources, stability, high educational opportunities are compared to a sample comprised mostly of students with less opportunity. It is no great mystery that poor and marginalized children tend to do poorly on standardized tests, and affluent students tend do very well, and all the others tend to fall in line as one might expect given their opportunities and challenges. The logic goes, that as long as some disadvantaged kids were in the norming group (even if they scored lower) that the comparison between kids with many advantages and those facing many obstacles is somehow "valid." Yet, anyone who lives the differences and suffers from the comparison knows this formula doesn't erase the inequalities. It simply moves the blame onto teachers and students as it obscures differences in opportunity and quality of education, life.

It's like having two children in a race. One child is given the best running shoes, a proper diet, great training facilities, a personal trainer, the best training equipment and a safe environment to support her development. From the time that child is young she knows she will be a runner; after all she is surrounded by runners. She is encouraged every step along the way. The second child is given old shoes, poor food, inadequate shelter, and is forced to grow up in a dangerous environment. Training for the race is seen as frivolous or at least secondary to more immediate concerns and demands of survival. This second child knows the odds are stacked against her, that the people who set up the race are related to the other child. The rules of the race are written in the other child's language. The racecourse is similar to the one the other child practices on. All of this is ignored while the race officials take great care to make sure that the running lanes on the course are exactly the same length, that the timer used to measure the runner's time is exactly the same, and that each runner starts at exactly the same place and time. In this simplistic way they believe they have created a fair race while all the conditions and moments of each child's life before the race are obscured. The results of the race are offered as proof of one child's superior ability and the others lack thereof.

Around the same time that I was working with City School, I was supervising student teachers in the affluent North Shore suburbs of Chicago that are known for excellent academic and enrichment programs, and especially for the high number of graduates who go on to Ivy League Universities. As shocked as I was at the poverty of the inner-city schools I had worked in, including City School, I was equally or more shocked at the resources these schools were afforded. Unlike the poverty and crime surrounding City School, these schools were located in neighborhoods where the average four-bedroom house cost $775,000 at that time. One school I learned a good deal about had an average working budget of $44,000,000. Four times more money was allocated per student at North Shore than at City School. Teachers' salaries were about double on the North Shore. My graduate students who taught in these affluent schools reported that their students felt extreme pressure to achieve, to compete, and excel. The push came from parents, from faculty and from within their selves. Many of the students had private tutors, took extra classes, and lived in the shadows of expectations from parents that they would not only succeed, but excel and become the movers and shakers of the world. They were, in essence, receiving educational training equivalent to the physical training for Olympic bound athletes. Their whole life and world was geared to compete and to win. Yet, they too had come to believe that what they achieved was not connected to these advantages, but a result of superior intelligence and a good work ethic.

Reification

Standardization is a process of reification. Reification is a practice of social forgetting. It refers to ways in which we author aspects of the social world and then forget our participation in that construction. Berger and Luckman (1995) describe reification as "the apprehension of the products of human activity *as if* they were something else other than human products—such as facts of human nature, results of cosmic laws, or manifestations of divine will."[5] Thus differences in language, opportunity, familiarity, education, and safety are somehow forgotten as we look at standardized scores as an objective measure of achievement or intelligence or both. Touted as an objective measure, standardized test scores are used as an implement of systemic violence. In essence, they justify the punishment of those against whom the race is rigged.

High stakes testing enacts cultural imperialism, what Young (1990) has described as involving "the universalization of a dominant group's experience and culture, and its establishment as a norm."[6] It would appear very unfair to have language and situations that are common to poor, inner city families on standardized tests because it would disadvantage those children who don't live in that world. Yet, their absence disadvantages the children who do. Instead, the dominant group asserts their norms as universals and "Often without noticing they do so" the dominant group "reinforces its position by bringing the other groups under the measure of its dominant norms".[7]

Systemic violence in education

> includes any practice or procedure that prevents students from learning, thus harming them. This may take the form of conventional practices that foster a climate of violence, or policies which appear to be neutral but which result in discriminatory effects

and

> includes any institutional practice or procedure that adversely impacts on individuals or groups by burdening them psychologically, mentally, culturally, spiritually, economically or physically.[8]

When I look at what I experienced and observed at city school, the impacts of the systemic violence seemed blatant. It shocked the students, their families, teachers and administrators. I witnessed this shocking and the tears. I saw the shaming and blaming. I witnessed kids giving up on their futures.

Back to the Present:
No Child Left Behind to Race to the Top

I've spent much of the last decade supporting the dissertation research of educational leaders. With only one exception out of the 200 plus administrators I've worked with in the past eight years, I've found they believe that the imposition of the harsh sanctions that drive NCLB compliance is a punishing force within their schools and districts, tying their hands and distracting them from focusing on the whole child and the school as a community. Just a few samplings from their research provides descriptions of the same forms of violence I saw at City School, though as you will see, while the violence struck the most vulnerable students and schools first, it has become pervasive in education leaving few schools unpunished. The pressures of being labeled as failing and the possibility of being reconstituted loom large. McCleverty-Sala-Dabaj (2010) describes the public shaming;

> Here's what we got for "failing": our official failing status was publicized on the interactive report card on line, the mandate of a letter to the community stating this status, the stigma attached to one who gets a public bad grade, and the opportunity to get some money.[9]

These school leaders are often put in the "head slave" position, in which their own survival as administrators is based on enforcing mandates that they don't believe serve the best interests of the school community. They become the punishers and enforcers of mandates they don't agree with. I've learned that the anguish I witnessed in Mr. Kamp the day the test scores came in, the inside understandings of his school community and the outside judgments based on criteria he did not find legitimate, were not an isolated thing. McCleverty-Sala-Dabaj (2010) describes her anguish after getting the results that her school has failed to make Adequate Yearly Progress (AYP) for the third year in a row:

> I, as the principal, feel the punitive pressure first. It comes in the form of time-taking paperwork and anxiety about getting the right message to my teachers. Contriving messages that inspire and encourage while chastising and being critical is so stressful that I begin to get physically sick. I try to unite them against the cause and onslaught of unfair benchmarks but feel deceitful. The truth is that I am certain that Willow Oak will never again make the AYP cut-offs required by No Child Left Behind.[10]

McCleverty-Sala-Dabaj is a school level administrator in an underfunded, overwhelmed district with a diverse, low-income population. Her building is in ill repair, her computer lab is 20 years old; her teachers are dedicated, talented veterans, with 30 students in their classrooms. Kapff (2007) on the other hand, is the district level director of assessment in affluent, highly acclaimed district. Yet she feels the same sting, the overwhelming sense of injustice when she gets the word that one of her schools does not make AYP. She reflects in her research journal:

> Isn't this a wonderful place to work and to send your children to school? We all thought so until the day when the State decided to send that "crazy" memo that must have been wrong. Surely they were wrong—how could WE be a failing school. Tears welled up in my eyes—this just isn't fair.[11]

After another school in her district is deemed failing the following year, Kapff (2007) focuses her research on listening to the stories of the school building principals as they begin to grapple with the impacts of NCLB. She watches strong, committed leaders lose their confidence, become depressed, and feel like they are selling out their most dear values in order to comply with an accountability system that does not take the lives of students into account. Kapff (2007) laments that the increasingly impossible improvement on test scores set up in NCLB and the punishments that enforce compliance are a "set up to be conflicted" and the core of the "conflict developed because of their struggle between wanting to do the right thing for kids, and needing to do what the district required to improve student achievement".[12]

Cerauli and Okler (2010) research the impacts of NCLB on the children in their district. They tell us that, "Happy children seem to lose their energy and enthusiasm as soon as they walk through our doors" (2010, p.4). They see a connection between the pressures of accountability and students losing voice as they lament that "it seems what independence and opinions our students come to school with, are slowly pushed down in favor of attitudes of compliance and a fearful desire to know the 'right' answer".[13]

These two district level administrators went in search of joy in their middle class, high achieving district . . . and it was in short supply. Their research revealed that those few teachers who did find ways to bring joy into the classroom, reported that they did so as a subversive activity, often swearing their students to secrecy so they would not be discovered. When asked to participate in their research on joy in the classroom, several teachers wondered if it was a trick to expose them. To Cerauli and Okler's dismay, they found that even the teachers who were identified as being joyful, separated the "fun" from teaching and instruction. Fun was the reward for hard work, not embedded in learning itself.

These few examples typify the overwhelming sentiments of the administrators I've worked with. While many are beginning to find promise in some of the data practices that have come along with reform, the fact that standardized testing is the ultimate measure of their students' progress and that punishment, sanctions, threats, and humiliation stand at the ready to enforce that one sadly flawed measure, have them disheartened and angry. They feel deeply conflicted about their own forced compliance in a system that they know is not in the best the interest of their students, teachers and communities.

Punishment and Freedom: Buying into the Race

My second major professional focus in the past decade has involved working with the students in a number of alternative certification programs that partner with my university. These are high achieving students, many with bachelor degrees from prestigious universities who are allowed to begin their teaching careers almost immediately and learn as they go. They are placed in hard to staff urban schools, including some "turnaround" schools, where the entire school has been reconstituted and its management handed over to a turnaround group. Each of these programs has one thing in common: they buy into the notion that improvement on standardized test scores is the key indicator of a schools success. "Closing the achievement gap" is their mantra. They are in alignment with the underlying precepts of NCLB and RTT and heavily supported by federal dollars. In my experience, once they are embedded within the realities of under resourced urban communities and schools, our new young alternative certification teachers are quick to critique and question the assumptions of "winning the race."

This new teaching force, which was originally touted as a way to fill critical shortages in urban education, can no longer be justified in that way. My sense is that they are seen as the new "breed" who more readily buy into a technological, data driven, race focused education. Experienced teachers are being laid off around the country. We have a severe shortage of money in education, not teachers. Yet, one of the provisions necessary to compete for the Race to the Top money being dangled in front of states with dwindling resources and mounting accountability pressures, is the need to utilize alternative routes to certification. This often seems rather counter-intuitive if one finds any merit at all in teachers' experience, yet we have seen a trend of experienced teachers being the casualties in Reductions in Force (RIFs), school closings and reconstitutions, while young, new teachers are hired who have not yet learned how to teach.

Since teachers unions have rightfully protested, they too, along with colleges of education, have been associated with failure and might well be in the process of being rendered obsolete. The uncertainty of the financial downturn, the overall desperation in relationship to resources, have acted as powerful motivators to have educators work against their own and their students best interests just to survive. It may well be that we have all become head slaves in the service of NCLB and RTT.

Freire and Dewey must be weeping in their graves, as this United States of America, regulates the very life out of education and deregulates markets. A seemingly heartless federal government has schools compete for meager educational dollars to fund an educational system that enacts the slave/master dynamic at every level. In a context of fear, shaming and deprivation, compliance with this systemic violence is coerced through of all things, a race. A metaphor that is so apt and so unselfconsciously offered, that it feels like a slap in the face—a system of winners and losers.

In a system that is so heavily run by the whip, you can't have freedom. Not at any level. And thus, the last decade has been one in which extreme forms of institutional control permeate the contexts of schooling. The many, many administrators I know feel their hands are tied with the mandates of reform. They are visible and vulnerable and at best try to shield their teachers and students from the most painful punishments of the state. As for students, the more affluent ones are often robbed of joy in learning and the children who live in poverty are subjected to harsh militaristic forms of discipline that would be best suited for prisons. If you think I exaggerate, note that one of the new gurus of many of the alternative certification programs is Doug Lemov (2010) who unapologetically provides strategies of control in the service of higher test scores. He writes:

> As you circulate, your goal should be to remain facing as much of the class as possible...Turning your back, by contrast, invites opportunistic behavior. The most powerful position to be in with another person is where you can see him, he knows you can see him, and he can't see you.[14]

Other Lemov strategies involve narrating every move students are required to make, controlling their every moment, while teachers are told to move around the room so they "make it clear to students that you own the room—that it is normal for you to go anywhere you want in the classroom at any time."[15] Having recently visited a school in which Lemov's strategies are implemented across the board I wept when I got back out to my car. I went home to write in my journal to process and make sense of a scene that broke my heart. I wrote:

> *I just got back from observing at Plantation Elementary (alias). I was stunned by the eerie quietness of the school, the absolute "discipline" of the uniformed children. Adults controlled everything. The older students looked up and quickly back down, as my group of white people walked in, walked around, were never introduced, gawked at them and left. They had no joy in their eyes, as they turned them down to their books. Their silence and obedience were what was on stage and they knew it. Next room, younger students sat slightly wiggling in chairs as teachers counted, cajoled, danced, praised, instructed. Children watched, listened, sat, responded, and waited silently for the next command. In the hallway, three classroom groups sat completely silently, startling me when I realized they were there. These silent obedient brown children are the accomplishment of the white men who tell me with a good amount of anger that they are proud of their silence. I think how many times this same scene has played out in American history and I feel sickened and saddened.*

Frank Smith (1998) points out that there are two kinds of learning. One he calls the official theory and it is based on a vision of learning that requires hard work and discipline. He notes this kind of learning is often quickly forgotten. The other he calls the classical theory and it involves learning through relationships and experience, it goes on whether we want it to or not and it is rarely forgotten. He uses a story of a young boy who is handed back a test on which he has scored poorly and is scolded by the teacher who asserts that he has learned almost nothing. Smith points out that to the contrary, he has learned some things that he will never forget:

> The student has registered the condemnatory look on the instructor's face, experienced the sickening feeling in the stomach, and concluded once more what a fruitless and punishing experience the entire learning situation can be. The student has lost a bit of confidence—and is unlikely to forget any of it.[16]

As I watch the schools that serve some of our most marginalized children come to resemble prisons, I wonder what students are learning about who they are in the world. Our narrow focus on closing the gap often obscures the social dynamics of urban reform. Often domestic violence against children is justified as being in their own best interest (Miller, 1990). The harsh whipping is for their own good, to teach them lessons that will prepare them for their future. Urban reform, even when it is brutal is couched in the same rhetoric.

Collateral Damage

What is the impact of the systemic violence that has taken a grip on American Education through the punishment embedded in NCLB and RTT? How do we measure it? In teardrops? In sullen silence? In anger? In the twisting feeling inside of one's gut? Franz Fanon (1963) described schools as playing the same role of holding the dividing line between groups in capitalist society that police stations and barracks play in the colonial world. He asserts that the subjugation of marginal groups, the "have nots" is accomplished through the structures, postures and social behaviors involved in schooling; "all these aesthetic expressions and respect for the established order serve to create around the exploited person an atmosphere of submission and inhibitions which lightens the task of policing considerably. In the capitalist countries, a multitude of teachers, counselors and "bewilderers" separate the exploited from those in power".[17]

Coercion, whether it comes in the form of the carrot or the stick, has detrimental impacts on those who are subject to it. Kohn (1990) points out that when institutional relationships are structured through coercion that several negative consequences occur; relationships are ruptured, creativity and chance taking are reduced, reasons for behaviors are ignored, and interest in learning shifts to interests in rewards and punishment. DeVries, Haney, & Zan's (1991) research suggests that children who are managed through authoritarian, top down behavioral orientation in school learn to engage with one another in a similar fashion. Likewise, children who are taught in classrooms where they are given an opportunity to collaborate, make decisions and have choices are better able to solve problems through negotiation rather than attempts to overpower one another when left to their own devices. DeVries, Haney & Zan (1991) summarize the impact of coercion on children's development:

> That is, coercion has three possible effects: Mindless conformity, rebellion, or calculation. By "calculation" I refer to following adult rules only when under surveillance and not following them when away from adult observation.[18]

School cultures that are based on coercion hinder moral development because they do not allow students the necessary conditions to reflect on their behaviors and do not provide role models of appropriate behavior (Kohlberg, 1984; DeVries, 1997; Piaget, 1969).[19] Behavior that is based on either avoiding punishment or getting a reward is what Kohlberg (1984) referred to as "premoral" behavior. There is no moral reasoning involved in forced compliance or behaviors geared towards incentives. Yet, schooling is how we mass socialize our children. Their moral development, according to Kohlberg, is shaped by the level of moral development embedded in the institutions in which they engage. DeVries concludes that teachers most likely don't know the impact of their top down behavioral methods on their students' social development.

Epp (2004) points out that "what makes systemic violence 'systemic' is the fact that there is no-one to blame. People applying the violence are only a part of a larger process. Administrators and teachers do what is expected of them. They follow protocol, they maintain standards."[20] Through NCLB and RTT, educators have been co-opted into a system that does violence to the very children they are committed to helping. Yet, they are powerless to impact change because the source is beyond their influence. They are in the powerless position that Lemov suggests that they use with children. That is, they are in a position where they are keenly aware that they are being watched, but they cannot see the person who is watching them. This of course is the essence of a "big brother" mentality and can be easily envisioned by the guard tower.

What is at "stake" in high "stakes" testing and punishment-based policies and practices? What is the impact on children of being harshly disciplined in order to compete? What is the effect of the winners and the losers? What happens when we conceptualize education as a race rather than the engaged preparation for participation in democracy? What happens to the hearts of children when learning and violence become one another? What can be said of a nation that creates school systems based on coercion and then turns a blind eye to the suffering of its children and their teachers? Is academic achievement conceptualized as simply the means by which we dominate others? Should learning be a race? Is what is at stake the very moral fiber of our nation?

The Problem with "Trying Harder"

Caught between a rock and a hard place, school leaders like Mr. Kamp and Andrea McCleverty-Sala-Dubaj have worked tirelessly to get their students to the "mark." While not believing in the morality of the policies and practices they have none-the-less been unwilling and unable to take their students out of the race. Even while understanding intimately why the race is not fair, they work tirelessly preparing students for the race and simultaneously doing all they can to alleviate the collateral damage. If they are not willing to prepare students for the race, they will lose their jobs and someone, perhaps less committed to their students and less aware of the systemic violence, will take their place. Because local control of education has been completely eroded by NCLB and RTT, the battle for our children's' hearts, souls and minds cannot be won from within the school system, even by the most valiant effort of individual educators. Though their efforts do matter to the children in their care, and are more important than ever given the violence of schooling.

It is hard to believe that the terrorism I witnessed in City School 15 years ago has gripped our nation's schools and become almost normalized. My alternative certification students have a hard time imagining education that is not conceived of as a race, as eliminating the gap, as a technological system of control. Yet, they know that they and their students are miserable in schools, that schools are punishing places. But the seasoned leaders and teachers I teach in the doctoral program know that things can be different. They watched this violence descend. They have been co-opted as head slaves and their guts wrench. I have been working with a group of doctoral students in Wisconsin for the past year and many of them have been involved in the protests against the union busting legislation that was passed there and continue to work in explicitly politicized ways for its repeal. Scott Swanson, a doctoral student and a high school English teacher, wrote how at the end of each school day he would don his protest gear and head to Capitol Square in Madison, Wisconsin.

> I found myself stuck in a maelstrom that I was forced to act upon; my reality, my lens, was no longer in focus. It was as if my internal calculator, when given the input of 2 plus 2, equaled 5. It didn't work. No longer was I thinking like a teacher, safe in my little English bubble, worrying about what will happen to Romeo, or whether or not Sir Gawain would indeed finish his quest; now I was moved to action, and as cliché as it sounds, all we could do was descend on the capitol and chant, along with a growing, boisterous, angry (but never unruly) crowd. Steadily the numbers rose and the public began to understand our plight.[21]

Because the violence is systemic and the source is outside of the education system itself, the battle must be fought in the national political arena. Teachers, administrators and researchers can no longer be satisfied with working very hard within the dictates of the current system. We can no longer conceive of ourselves or our work as apolitical. While schooling has always been deeply connected to power, and therefore political, the heavy-handed government regulation of schooling we've seen in the past decade is unprecedented in history. We must heed Dante's warning that "The hottest places in hell are reserved for those who in times of great moral crises maintain their neutrality." We need to march. We need to vote. We need to research the social, relational, cultural and lived experiences of schooling. We need to construct the counter narratives that expose the violence of the current moment. We need to make the systemic violence that has gripped education visible to the public, to our students, and to their families. We need to move from being paralyzed and blind-sided by the systemic violence that paints us and our students as lazy and inferior and become politicized. We need to stand up.

Notes

1. Juanita R. Epp and Ailsa M. Watkinson, eds. *Systemic Violence in Education: Promise Broken.* (New York: NY: State University of New York Press, 1997).

2. Laurel Richardson. "Writing: a method of inquiry," edited by N. K. Denzin and Y. S. Lincohn. 2nd ed., (Thousand Oaks, CA: Sage, 2000) p. 923-948.

3. Epp & Watkinson, 1996, p. 1.

4. Paulo Freire, *Pedagogy of the Oppressed.* 30th Anniversary Edition ed. (New York: NY: Continuum, 2003) p. 73.

5. Peter L. Berger and Thomas Luckman, "The dehumanized world." In *The truth about the truth,* edited by Walter Truett Anderson, p. 36-39. (New York: NY: Tarcher/Putnam, 1995) p. 36.

6. Iris Marion Young, *Justice and The Politics of Difference.* (Princeton, NJ: Princeton University Press, 1990), p. 59.

7. Young, 1990, p. 59.

8. Epp & Watkinson, 1996, p. x.

9. Andrea McCleverty-Sala-Dubaj, "Mosaic and Tessera: an educational love story in an era of accountability." Ed.D., (National Louis University, 2010), p. 62.

10. Ibid, p. 33.

11. Darlene Kapff, "Assessment practice as data: the stories of NCLB." Ed.D., (National Louis University, 2007), p. 149.

12. Kapff, p. 281.

13. Lisa Cerauli and Karen Okler, "Joyful classrooms, successful kids: a study in the connection between joy and learning." Ed.D., (National Louis University, 2010), p. 4-5.

14. Doug Lemov, *Teach Like a Champion, 49 Techniques That Put Students on the Path to College.* (San Francisco, CA: Jossey-Bass, 2010), p. 87.

15. Lemov, p. 89.

16. Frank Smith, *The Book of Learning and Forgetting.* (New York: NY: Teacher's College Press, 1998), p. 1.

17. Franz Fanon, *The Wretched of the Earth.* (New York: NY: Grove Press, 1963), p. 39.

18. Rheta DeVries, John P. Haney, and Betty Zan. "Socio-moral atmosphere in direct-instruction, eclectic, and constructivist kindergartens: a study of teachers' enacted interpersonal understanding." *Early Childhood Research Quarterly.* 6, no. 4 (1991): 473-517, p. 41.

19. Lawrence Kohlberg, *The Psychology of Moral Development.* (San Francisco, CA: Harper and Row, 1994); Rheta DeVries, "Piaget's social theory." *Educational Researcher* 26, no. 2 (1997): 4-17; Jean Piaget, *The Psychology of the Child.* (New York: NY: Basic Books, 1969).

20. Epp, p. 2.

21. Personal communication, March 4, 2011.

Chapter 5
Science Left Behind: Reflections from a Chicago Public School Student of Science
Theresa Robinson

The important thing in science is not so much to obtain new facts as to discover new ways of thinking about them.—Sir William Bragg

Our nation struggles to prepare our citizenry to be able to solve our many environmental and science-related societal problems. Our schools are in turn being called upon to lead this effort, and to produce a scientifically literate populace. This is the story of one school's attempt to improve science achievement as measured by standardized test scores in response to local and national mandates for school reform. In this chapter I will explore how school climate and culture are impacted by local initiatives such as Renaissance 2010 (R2010), the Chicago High School Redesign Initiative (CHSRI), national mandates such as No Child Left Behind (NCLB) and programs like Race to the Top (RTT). As a professional development coordinator for secondary teachers I was tasked to help build and support highly effective teachers in science curriculum and instruction. As a participant and observer, I encountered the unintended outcomes and barriers that school reform has placed on school culture, climate and science education. This essay describes how the issue of low science achievement was addressed and the methods employed in the school where I worked. I hope my analysis and description of this process, especially an understanding of the mistakes encountered, will inform others who attempt to improve science achievement, especially in urban school settings.

My Alma Mater

What do pilot Amelia Earhart, musician Herbie Hancock, Chicago politician Edward Vrdolyak, seventies soul singer Minnie Riperton, Blackstone Nation founder Jeff Fort (a prominent Chicago street gang) and myself, an assistant professor of science education, all have in common? We all attended and/or graduated from Hyde Park High School.

Hyde Park High School is a Chicago Public School (CPS) founded in 1874. It is located in the Woodlawn community, a neighborhood adjacent to the University of Chicago and the University's liberal, integrated Hyde Park Kenwood community. The Hyde Park Kenwood community is home to the 44th President of the United States, Barack Obama. The school is also exceedingly revealing because it provides a powerful window into local educational policy and proposed school change in relation to national policy, and because of its unique geographical position in relation to the ethnic, economical, and historically socially segregated communities of Chicago neighborhoods.

Hyde Park High School is relevant as a subject of study in school integration during both the pre and post *Brown v. Board of Education.* This relevance was due in part to the culture and ethnicity of the student body, but more importantly, because of social class and later urban renewal pressures the school underwent. Hyde Park High School was an example of a school caught between a national law for integration and local resistance to change. The school lived with a certain amount of success with increased integration for nearly twenty years between 1947 and 1967. However, due to increased government pressure to adhere to integration, the changing racial makeup of the surrounding Woodlawn community, and the construction of Kenwood High School in the Hyde Park neighborhood, White families moved their students out of Hyde Park High School. The liberal Whites were not as accepting of Blacks from a lower socioeconomic status in their school and the associated violence that came during the late 60s and 70s era. From 1967 forward Hyde Park High School became a predominantly African American high school. Although the racial and ethnic makeup of the school changed, what remained were the high standards for learning and achievement. Furthermore, although the student population had changed, many of the teachers remained. By the 1990s and the new millennium once again the school became the epicenter of change with local reforms and national mandates driving increased assessment of student progress. The school was caught between the national legislation of NCLB and local board of education decisions to close underperforming schools. I am concerned here with the impact such reforms have had on science teaching and their implications for student learning. I will begin with a look at the role Renaissance 2010 (R2010) has had in impacting science education at Hyde Park High School.

Renaissance 2010 was a local educational reform program launched in 2004. One of the hallmarks of the program was the turnaround of struggling schools. The program was supposed to help create new innovative schools using high performance measures, namely standardized tests. These "new" schools would be charter, contract, and performance schools.

The goal was for these "new" schools to have more freedom than traditional schools in return for higher productivity: test scores, attendance, and graduation rates. Hyde Park High School was on the receiving end of the school closures of then CPS CEO Arne Duncan and Mayor Richard Daley's R2010 program. R2010 takes students from low performing schools outside of their community and places them in other Chicago public schools. In fact Hyde Park was hit by a double whammy, being forced to accept more than 300 students more than any other receiving high school in the past two years because the other schools were closed to freshman *(Chicago Sun Times*, March, 12, 2006). In commenting on Renaissance 2010, Arne Duncan said "a school like Hyde Park received too many new kids," "overburdening" them. The article goes on to note that teachers and students are forced to live with a new culture of violence and its impact on education. This violence was in part due to overcrowding and different students who were brought together without concern for what might happen from rival neighborhoods in Chicago.

Race to the Top, the 4.35 billion dollar incentive program authorized under the American Recovery & Reinvestment Act of 2009 has also significantly impacted Hyde Park High School. RTT's competitive grant program encourages and rewards states that are implementing reforms by enhancing standards and assessments, improving collection and use of data, measuring and holding accountable teachers for their effectiveness in raising test scores, and turning around struggling schools. The RTT administrator is U.S. Secretary of Education Arne Duncan, former CEO of Chicago Public Schools. Much of the challenge for science education that accompanied R2010 has only become aggravated with new pressures brought about by RTT, the President's educational reform strategy.

Science Major, College Graduate

Hyde Park High School, a prestigious Chicago Public School, founded in 1874, was renamed the Hyde Park Career Academy (HPCA) in the early 1990s. It continued as a neighborhood school for students residing within the Woodlawn community of Chicago. With the creation of a magnet program, I, as well as students like me, because of our academic were able to attend the historically successful school even though we lived outside the school's boundary. As magnet program students, we took a sequence of courses designed to prepare us for college. Because other students were in career preparation tracks designed to prepare them for a vocation instead of college, the school's name changed from the original "Hyde Park High School" to "Hyde Park Career Academy."

During the years of my attendance, the school was still regarded as one of the academically stronger public schools in the city. The school remained renowned for its many areas of concentration that students could choose to study, including radio and television production, architecture, drafting, and medical preparation. The science department, in particular, was acknowledged and highly regarded for its academic rigor and demanding, talented teachers. The science curriculum offered courses in biology, advanced placement biology, chemistry, physics, anatomy and physiology.

As a student at HPCA, I was expected to fulfill department requirement for student participation in the science fair. I approached one of my teachers and explained to him that I wanted to do a project on the environment. Because of his involvement in a summer research program for teachers at the University of

Chicago's Department of Ecology and Evolution, I was able to conduct my research using their laboratories. My project advanced through school, district, and city levels of competition. Along with three other students from Chicago public schools, including the prestigious Whitney Young Magnet School and Von Steuben High School, the four of us represented the City of Chicago at the *International Science and Engineers Fair.*

The event was a great success and we immensely expanded our understanding of authentic scientific study. My project culminated with titled "Intraspecific and Interspecific Sperm Competition in Tribolium Castaneum and Tribolium Freeman Flour Beetles" which was published in the science journal *Heredity.* To a great degree, my accomplishment was a consequence of the way science teachers organized instruction at my school.

At Hyde Park High School, teachers in the science department emphasized project based learning, lab work and technique, and science in the community. In one environmental science class we visited the *Chicago Water Reclamation District* to learn about the process of treating water for human consumption. On another field trip we visited a landfill where I learned first-hand the impact humans can have on the environment. One long-standing project of the science department involved independently going to the zoo and conducting an animal study. Those experiences with science in high school furthered my interest in science and education. As a graduate of Hyde Park I knew I would study science in college. I decided to major in biology with the hopes of becoming a medical doctor, but after reading Jonathan Kozol's *Savage Inequalities,* [1] my interest shifted from medicine to education. I reflected on my experiences in high school science and decided to add secondary education to my biology major.

After completing a doctoral program in Curriculum and Instruction, with a concentration in science and environmental education, I returned to Chicago with one goal in mind: to carry on the tradition of high quality science programs in the Chicago Public Schools that I had experienced at Hyde Park. I accepted a position at the historic DuSable High School, but soon found it was not the same high school from my memories. The new DuSable High School had been divided into three small schools as part of the City of Chicago High School Redesign Initiative (CHSRI). [2] I was hired to teach at one of the three, a CPS Charter small school. As the school year began and I planned my lessons, I soon realized that although the names of some of the schools had changed the problems had not. Violence and students with special needs were central themes. I worked harder than I ever had to help the students succeed. I knew in my heart they could make the grade despite their many personal issues. Yet out of frustration with the administrations lack of support, daily violence, apathetic parents, and students with severe social and emotional problems, I did not return the following year. This was my brief and unhappy introduction to school reform in the City of Chicago.

Returning to Hyde Park Career Academy

Today, as an assistant professor in the Department of Secondary Education at National Louis University, I serve as the Science Program Coordinator. I teach courses in urban education and biology methods for secondary teachers. At one point in time, one of my other assignments was to serve as a professional development coordinator responsible for delivering professional development and providing instructional coaching for Chicago high school teachers. When the PD coordinator at Hyde Park High School found her job too challenging and the CPS administration sought a new coordinator, I accepted the position.

One of the first challenges working with the school was simply 'getting in'; convincing the teachers and administrators I was there to help and not simply take from them and their students. It was late spring, well into the school year when I started. As I walked into the building where I was once schooled, I immediately noticed a big difference from when I was a student. There was only one door open for the main entrance and there was a very long line that extended outside the building. Once I was able to cross the threshold there were huge metal detectors and scanning machines. During my time as a student, there were no metal detectors and we could enter the building through three or four different doors. This drastic change was a response to how many schools were undergoing drastic culturally changes resulting from high school restructuring.. According to a March 2006 Chicago Sun-Times report titled *School Closings Lead to Surges in Violence: Fear on Receiving End*, Hyde Park High School saw a 226% increase in reported violence from years past. This spike in violence was associated with and recognized by the teachers to be a consequence of , the closure of failing schools, and the absorption of those students from the failed schools into Hyde Park. Teachers saw the devastating effects, and some opted to bail out. As noted in the article, thirty-year veteran Betti Ziemba put it this way: "I left out of fear, I've had it, I quit, there's no way I'm going back there." Teacher Marie Chavez said she would not return to the school the following year because of a lack of support in addressing rising violence and discipline problems.[3]

Thus, to put it mildly, I was anxious the first time I returned to Hyde Park.

As I entered the main office, however, I was somewhat comforted because I recognized a familiar face. One of the three assistant principals was my former history teacher who was highly respected by students and colleagues alike. She had been responsible for many projects in the school, including a three-year interdisciplinary project with the art department to create murals depicting African Kings and Queens in the school stairways.

I approached her and explained my purpose and mission, but to my surprise, was rebuffed. She was either uninterested or too busy to pay attention to the opportunities I had enthusiastically proposed for the school community.

I left the building.

I returned to the school the next day. This time I sat in the main office for approximately three hours waiting to speak to the principal or an assistant principal about the federally funded science education grant. I left once again without making any headway. I was discouraged, yet determined to return and succeed,

This cycle of waiting to talk with someone occurred for the next two visits. On the fifth visit, as I walked through the metal detectors and had my bags scanned, I noticed another familiar face, one of the physical education teachers who sponsored the Booster Club to which I remembered being a member. She was working in the attendance office. She recognized me right away. As she invited me into her small office, managed by a parent volunteer and two staffers, we began to talk.

I started by explaining my charge as a professional development coordinator, what I was doing, and most importantly how no one at the school seemed to be interested in what services I had to offer. She explained that the theme of that school year's work was improving freshman attendance. A research report by the Consortium on Chicago School Research (CCSR) concluded that freshman year attendance and first quarter grades were the critical indicators of whether a given student would be on track to graduate. Therefore the school's leadership, in response to CPS board policy, made the recommendations of the CCCR report a priority and developed a plan to address freshman attendance. I was invited to participate.

The plan devised relied on me to become an integral part of the school environment. This included my running errands for the attendance coordinator, hanging bulletin boards, typing lists, printing attendance awards and other trivial tasks. When I reported back to my director in CPS and the professional development office, some said, "that's not why you are there." I did understand my colleagues' concerns, but I felt they didn't understand was that it was those menial tasks that allowed me to go upstairs and come in contact with teachers at Hyde Park.

The other benefit was that I learned who the people were who kept the school running. I became very familiar, for example, with the non-teaching staff including the janitors, attendance clerks, secretaries and administrative assistants. The attendance coordinator and I developed an attendance initiative. I also created eight by eleven posters with the motto "Good attendance + good grades = graduation."

I went around to each teacher's classroom and asked if I could hang the small poster their classroom. As I visited the classrooms, I met more of my former teachers. With curiosity they asked, 'what are you doing here?' Just the question I wanted them to ask and as I explained, I gathered more support.

As a professor in teacher preparation, I also had the pleasure to meet up with two of my former students, both now science teachers!

Once that phase was over and I had established a presence, I began to move more freely throughout the building. I had become part of the school community. I wasn't stopped anymore and I was allowed to enter the building without going through the long lines and metal detectors. Now I was able to talk with the science teachers about all that I had to offer and explain the teacher quality grant.

Highly Qualified Teachers of Science

The theme of the grant I was implementing was improving literacy in the content areas. If teachers wrote a unit plan that integrated literacy, the grant would purchase a set of classroom books. The first event, organized with permission from one of the assistant principals, was an offsite professional development day for the science department. The grant office supplied lunches and we had a half-day together. During the meeting we presented literacy strategies, vocabulary-building strategies and more.

During this first engagement with Hyde Park science teachers around pedagogy, to my surprise I soon learned that the science department had lost its program level cohesiveness. Nonetheless, based on the evaluations of this professional development day, the teachers felt it was worthwhile; they enjoyed the opportunity to be out of the building and have a professional conversation around teaching and learning. After this meeting I had firmly established myself as a colleague and professional development leader for the science department. We established departmental goals which included having regular department meetings and the development of curriculum maps for biology, chemistry, and environmental science.

I eventually moved from working solely with the science department to working with the school curriculum coordinator to plan the school wide professional development calendar for the year. I then presented to the school staff the opening session for the first professional development day. According to feedback from teachers, staff and administration it was highly successful. I leaned that one of the hidden issues staff was grappling over was the changing of the school mascot. Due to Illinois High School Association regulations the school's mascot could no longer be an Indian; and, they were now the Thunderbirds. This change was and still is contentious for much of the alumni, but especially fort the athletic department. More importantly, the issue divided teachers and staff who were there when they were Indians and those who were not. Statements were made like "we were a family", "we had pride in our school." I rationalized that the mascot issue was actually more of a symbolic issue, a sort of benchmark for the school culture rather than about the actual mascot and the derogatory connotations it stirred up for Native Americans. It represented a period in time for some when things were different at the school. I used these symbols in an opening slide to pull these emotions out. I asked the crowd if they knew what a thunderbird was. Appropriately someone from the social science department pointed out it is a Native American bird. We eventually reached the conclusion that although the mascot was no longer the Hyde Park Indians, students and alumni were now the Hyde Park Thunderbirds and had the ability to create a new culture and climate of family.

Caught in the Middle: Teaching Science or the Science Test?

At this point things began to become more complicated. he administrative team had interests other than best teaching practices and provided me with lots of direction for the next session they were eager for me to conduct. The problem was that the administrations interests were not aligned with the Department of Secondary Education and the Teacher Center. The Teachers Center, housed at Northeastern Illinois University, was there to provide support and professional development opportunities to effect improvement in student achievement. Yet, in several conversations with the assistant principal, he made it clear that improving test scores via more frequent and common assessments was the priority course.

I was committed, on the one hand, to the belief that there needed to be more curriculum mapping and assessment development. But on the other hand, the school to which I had devoted so much time and energy, and that had meant so much to me, was increasingly placing an emphasis on aligning the curriculum with the standardized science test, rather than to the student needs and the professional science standards. In the end I could not continue with the school administrations' plan.

In the meantime, the CPS School Board of Education assigned an area instructional coach to work with the various departments. The science department was assigned one of these coaches. The new coach was an employee of the central office and the teachers were held accountable for meeting and planning with her. This soon became problematic because the teachers did not have enough time to work with two coaches, so I was squeezed out. The board agenda of improving test scores via common assessments took precedence over my creating—with the teachers active involvement—unit plans that integrated reading, writing and communication.

My concern with the narrowed focus on high stakes testing would find its corollary in the local press. In August 2009, the Chicago Sun-Times newspaper did a special investigation, called "Grading Games." The investigation was fueled by teacher's complaints of unauthorized grade changes. Former Hyde Park teacher John Kugler revealed that pressure to goose up grades is 'part of the culture' at Hyde Park, a school, the newspaper noted, that was on academic probation where an increase in the number of freshman and senior F's could tip the scales and trigger federal sanctions, or even closure (March 10, 2010).[4] In other words, grade inflation was encouraged. According to a March 2010 report, Principal Trotter wrote a special memo to the grading coordinator that indicated that since the school was given too few teachers to start with, and had been expected to add five new teachers sometime between October 19 and November 9, all students should receive A's for their troubles. "In fairness to the students and the newly hired instructors," the letter said that all students should be getting first quarter A's, and instructions on what they needed to do to maintain those A's second quarter.[5]

A letter to the *Sun Times* editor, following the 2010 article about the special memo, said the real question, beyond the principal's awkward attempt to do what he thought was fair, concerned how and why students at HPCA could have no regular teachers for the first quarter of the school year. This essential question had an answer, given Chicago's problematic school reform efforts.

Teachers are allotted to CPS schools based on student population estimates from the previous year. Hyde Park Career Academy attendance was considerably lower the prior year; therefore nine teachers were laid off, including the one and only physics teacher. In the current year, enrollment mushroomed because other closed schools sending many of their students to HPCA, and thus the teacher shortage. While five new teachers were eventually hired, losing the only physics teacher severely impacted the science department.

The Chemistry Team

The chemistry team was dedicated to helping improve student-learning experiences through meeting student needs. The chemistry classes absorbed the students of the physics teacher laid off the year before. Subsequently, some chemistry teachers had classrooms of thirty to thirty five sophomores and juniors. Among the students who were displaced were those who had already taken chemistry. Several classrooms did not provide enough seats and students sat wherever possible. However challenging the situation, the chemistry teachers were dedicated to planning and preparing for teaching and learning. Most notable of the team was the department chair and lead chemistry teacher.

I worked closely with them and together we wrote a unit titled *Introducing Chemistry through An Inconvenient Truth*. We wanted students to understand that chemistry is a part of everyday life and to be able to answer the questions: Why is global warming important to study? Is there valid evidence for global warming and to what extent is human activity responsible for increased CO_2 production? The goal of the unit was to use literacy strategies and the book *An Inconvenient Truth* to introduce 10th and 11th grade students to chemistry. We wanted students to be able to use reading and writing to understand a science text, to develop the ability to interpret and evaluate scientific information (numerical, graphic, and written) and to use the scientific method to investigate a problem/issue.

The department chair and chemistry teacher organized a presentation from the *Alliance on Climate Education*. She reported back that the students were so engaged and impacted by the presentation that she was called to the office by one of the assistant principals about a student issue. Apparently, one student was so noticeably disturbed by the presentation and the plight of planet Earth that she was moved to tears. The teacher reflected that if she decided to use the presentation again, she would make sure to include an action steps stage so students would not leave feeling hopeless.

Although I continued to work with the chemistry team, my interaction with the other course teams became few and far between. The science teachers were simply overwhelmed by school initiatives, student issues, and teaching responsibilities that our project became just one more task to complete. All these things interfered with teachers planning time and ability to create and use innovative strategies to teach science. Teachers were burdened with department meetings, course team meetings, literacy team meetings, and school meetings. These meetings occurred mostly during their preparation and lunch periods, leaving little time during the day for collaboration and lesson planning. All of the meetings were justified by the need to improve test scores. Ironically, it did not work. As I came to understand the complexity of the school culture and pressure on teachers, I believe now that a vital responsibility of the Professional Development Coordinator should be to understand these conditions and develop strategies to work with teachers to support them so they can see the value of the proposed work to themselves and their students. The pressure to raise test scores at Hyde Park under NCLB and the disruptive pressure of ongoing school restructuring in Chicago have contributed to an ongoing decline in testing results.

To explain, the *Illinois Interactive Report Card* website created by Northern Illinois University (NIU) with support from the Illinois State Board of Education (ISBE) compiles data on Illinois schools and student performance on tests, including the Prairie State Achievement Exam (PSAE). The PSAE measures the performance of high school students in grade 11 in reading, mathematics, writing and science. Science test questions are derived from the ACT *Assessment of Science* and two *Work Keys* assessments: *Reading for Information* and *Applied Mathematics*.

According to Hyde Park Career Academy student data, retrieved from the PSAE 2001-2010, there was a steady decline in the past decade in science test scores. During academic year 2005, 20% of students tested met or exceeded the science standards. In 2006 and again in 2007, 15% met or exceeded the standards. By 2008, scores dipped again to 10%, and in 2009, they bottomed out at 7%. In 2010, scores showed a slight increase; 8% of students were found to be meeting or exceeding the standards.

Overall from 2001-2010 over half of all students tested in science did not meet the standards and fell below the standards. Clearly many students, still under NCLB, are being left behind.[6]

A Student of Science

As a participant and observer, I know the focus in science was taken away from designing curriculum and instruction that met the needs of the students. The shift has been toward a curriculum and instruction model aligned with the high stakes standardized tests. This bodes poorly for the students in Hyde Park and beyond.

Simply put, teachers need time and space to collaborate, create and be innovative. Teachers need a voice in the decisions being made with regards to their classrooms.

As a student in a science program at Hyde Park that developed in me the capacity to do authentic scientific study, I was honored by the Student Science Fair as one of the many CPS students who have participated and benefited from the Science Fair. As I stated in my essay on my award winning project,

> participating in the science fairs provided me the opportunity to explore my interests and that was made possible by my science teachers. It was through

participation in the various levels of the science fair that my passion for science was uncovered.

How best can we honor the students of science in the future? By preparing great teachers, and giving them the tools, skills and knowledge to teach science so their own students can pursue their passion the way I did through actively participating in science. Otherwise, we will continue to leave science and students behind.

Notes

1. Jonathan Kozol, *Savage Inequalities: Children in America's Schools.* (New York: Crown Pub. 1991).

2. This initiative aimed to provide populations of low-performing students in underserved areas of the city with high-quality, small high schools. These schools were formed (1) by converting large high schools into a number of small ones, which were called redesigned schools, or (2) by creating new-start schools. The Bill and Melinda Gates Foundation supported this initiative, with additional funding provided by local foundations. CHSRI ceased to exist as a separate entity in August 2008, leaving 17 small high schools still in full operation in their original locations. http://ccsr.uchicago.edu/publications/CCSR_CHSRI_Report-Final%5B1%5D.pdf

3. Rosalind Rossi, Mark Konkol and Art Golab, "School Closings Lead to Surges in Violence, Fear on Receiving End," (*Chicago Sun Times*, March 12, 2006).

4. Rosalind Rossi and Art Golab, "2,000 Grades Raised—Hyde Park Academy," (*Chicago Sun Times*, March 10, 2010).

5. Arlene Gloria Hirsch, Editorial, "CPS Bureaucrats Cheating Students," (*Chicago Sun Times,* March 12, 2010).

5. *Illinois Interactive Report Card, 2010.* Northern Illinois University; http://iirc.niu.edu/

Part II
Vouchers, Charters, and Mayoral Takeovers: Tools of the Great School Selloff

In Chapter 1, we describe "Commercial Club" interests as being at the heart of "education reform." Nowhere does this phenomena more starkly emerge than in Chapter 6, "Voucher Vultures: A Blueprint for Restructuring Milwaukee Public Schools" by Robert Miranda. Miranda describes in detail how Milwaukee education reform has been a fraud on the taxpayer. Pushed by "external forces," the plan from the get go has been privatization of the public school system using vouchers to siphon dollars from public resources. Miranda argues this process was choreographed in the Paul Hill book *Reinventing Education* and then carried out by politicians and school officials.

In Chapter 7, "Milwaukee League Comes to the Defense of Public Schools," Todd Alan Price details the thwarted attempt by the then Democratic Governor Jim Doyle and his would be successor, Milwaukee Mayor Tom Barrett, tried to dismantle the Milwaukee school board. This drama which was documented via newspaper and television media outlets was largely ignored by Madison liberals, much to their peril, as the outcome of the battle resulted in a split Democratic Party and a clear path for the election of Republican Governor Scott Walker, or what we refer to as the devastation of public education wrought by the "Backwards Walkerman."

In Chapter 8, "The Privatization Pandemic: Barbarians at the Schoolhouse Door," Geoff Berne provides a blistering condemnation of the misplaced priorities of the nation, faulting the "privatization pandemic" for the withering and decay of the public's schools.

In Chapter 9, "Clash Over Charter Schools in Ohio: Ted Strickland's Challenge to the Obama-Duncan Wrecking Ball," Geoff Berne describes Ohio as literally the crucible of public education, where the public schools face up to their very survival. In the state that produced the most American presidents, President Obama's support for charter schools runs into the reality that all too many charters are poorly administered by for-profit organizations. Privatization seems to displace real reform efforts of public education advocates such as former Governor Ted Strickland. Yet, in spite of an attack on public education in the latest form by Governor John Kasich, citizens have risen up to push back against the stripping of collective bargaining rights. But will the charter movement remain? And to what end?

Chapter 6
Voucher Vultures: Blueprint for Restructuring Milwaukee Public Schools
Robert Miranda

Trading Colors

As a teenager growing up in the 1970s on the Southside of Chicago, little did I care about education or what was happening inside or outside of my neighborhood; I was too busy trying to survive the streets.

Chicago was a big mean city then. No one was looking for books; we were looking for drugs. The social justice/civil rights movements in my community had slowly turned into "silver rights" battles. Many of the 1960s neighborhood revolutionaries began peddling marijuana and cocaine to youth throughout the community. The money we got from drug sales was needed. Not for school, clothing, or to pay bills, but to buy guns, to buy clothing that represented the gang's colors, to buy more drugs.

The Latin Souls were the majority of the Puerto Rican street gangs operating out of Chicago's Englewood district in the city's south side. At the height of the gang's activity, we had control of the 55th and Halsted area. To our south, our rivals were Black gangs, such as the "Black Peace Stone Rangers" and "Black Gangster Disciples"; to our north, Latino gangs, such as "Saints" and "Latin Kings" to our north; and to our west, White gangs, such as the "Insane Popes" and "Gaylords".

Being political by the time I became a senior member of the gang, my interest began to fade away from the streets, especially when the "Young Lords" no longer were around passing out their little red Mao books to the youth and preaching Puerto Rican independence. After witnessing several of my closest friends sent off to prison and/or shot, I knew that this was not what I wanted my life to be. I was lucky to be able to come to this conclusion early in my life. It was a lifestyle I knew I had to leave. I came to this resolve because of my father and mother. They may not know it, but if it were not for their continued meddling in my affairs, and insistence on having me attend one of the best high schools in the city, I too would have ended up dead or in prison at an early age.

So, I traded in my street colors whose meanings embodied death and destruction, for school colors of blue and gold, which at the time to me meant goals and dreams to be fulfilled.

De La Salle Institute was all-boys Catholic high school recognized for producing four of Chicago's mayors. It was a school that gave me hope, and greater understanding of my Catholic heritage, but fell short of giving me the fundamental knowledge of democracy. In my senior year, I took an interest in politics, especially after the fall of the Shah in Iran and the taking of American hostages at the American embassy. I began to take an interest in the ideas of American freedom and I wanted to learn more about this system of democracy. My family did not have money for college and my grades did not qualify for assistance, so I joined the United States Marines.

Once again, I traded in the maroon and black colors of the Latin Souls, stored away the blue and gold of De La Salle, and went for the red and gold of the Marine Corps. At the time I thought, like many others watching Ronald Reagan come into power, if there are colors to protect, why not the Red, White and Blue?

Red, White and Blue

After eight years of the Marines, I again found myself pondering the life I was living. I began to question my involvement in our nation's military campaigns such as Beirut, Lebanon and Nicaragua. I recall thinking to myself, how is it that these people are a threat to our country?

In 1988, I was in South Korea taking part in an annual military training mission with Korean Marines. One evening, I was having a conversation with a well-respected captain from my unit. I was a sergeant at the time; we began to talk about politics. It was during this conversation that I felt my life about to change again.

As we spoke, we got onto the topic of war. I could tell the captain hated war. As the conversation went on, he provided me with the name of a book authored by one of the Marine Corps legendary icons, Major General Smedley Darlington Butler, one of the few men in the history of the armed forces of the United States to receive two Medals of Honor. My captain said to me "Sergeant, if you really want to know what you are fighting for, read General Butler's book, *War is a Racket*." He said he admired my resolve to fight and die for democracy, but that our nation's military campaigns now and in the foreseeable future will have nothing to do with defending democracy or fighting for freedom. There will always be wars "to keep Wall Street fat and continue America's path to internal destruction similar to Rome."[1] Reading the book *War is a Racket*, I found that General Butler's views back in the early 1900s were still relevant today.

When my second enlistment ended, I took an honorable discharge and decided to go to school, get a college degree. It dawned on me that I needed to know more about this fragile democracy and why my education did not give me skills to learn what I learned outside of the classroom.

Education Reform is a Racket

In 1992, I enrolled at the University of Wisconsin-Milwaukee. For most of my undergraduate years I was an active student. I organized demonstrations, became president of the student government and led national campaigns for the Green Party. I then became interested in education reform in 1994. At the time, the superintendent of Milwaukee Public Schools was Dr. Howard Fuller. Dr. Fuller was seen as a progressive leader seeking to improve the education of urban children.

In 1995 Dr. Fuller came out publically supporting "choice" or more accurately "voucher" schools (which meant taxpayer money funneled to private schools). When that happened I knew I had to get involved. Around this time, I met Leon Todd, a member of the Milwaukee School Board who often stood against Dr. Fuller and his reform policies. I had a chance to meet with Leonard Minsky of the National Coalition for Universities in the Public Interest, referred to me by Ralph Nader whom I met at a university lecture in Milwaukee—he was blasting the North American Free Trade Agreement (NAFTA).

A few days after Nader and I spoke about Milwaukee education politics, Minsky arrived in Milwaukee. He and I then went over to meet with Leon Todd who provided us with materials the Milwaukee Schools Board of Directors were given by the Fuller administration. The information contained detailed plans on reforming Milwaukee Public Schools, including a manuscript authored by Paul T. Hill.

Exposing the Blueprint to Impose Vouchers in Milwaukee

Paul Hill's *Reinventing Public Education*, published early in 1995 by the RAND Corporation, contained a blueprint for restructuring and privatizing K-12 education that envisioned the complete replacement of the present system based on centralized public schools with a decentralized school "system" based on privatization.[2] In other words, Dr. Fuller was advocating for each school to become a privately owned corporation that would contract separately with school boards for the delivery of educational services. An essential part of the plan required the elimination of teachers unions nationwide.

Realizing what we had come across, we arranged a meeting with several executive directors and presidents representing teacher unions in Wisconsin.

Among those attending were Sam Carmen of the Milwaukee Teachers Education Association (MTEA) and Charles Lentz of the Wisconsin Educators Association Council (WEAC). The meeting was held clandestinely at a restaurant overlooking a lake in Delafield, Wisconsin. After explaining the purpose of the meeting, identifying the information and how it was obtained, a breakdown of the reform efforts being pursued by Dr. Fuller was then detailed to the union leadership.

The plan Dr. Fuller proposed for reforming MPS was corporate welfare to the highest degree. The book called for privatizing schools to replace the dismantled public school system. It was a plan we all agreed would in fact be more, rather than less, costly to the taxpayer, and would distribute educational services unequally. It was a plan that would, as Leonard Minsky said at the meeting, continue to allow "inner-city schools" to "fail" requiring the state to pump in more funding to achieve better results—precisely the situation that exists in the now "failing" public schools, except that there would be profits made to school entrepreneurs.

As we continued, we explained that basic costs as they now exist in the public school system would go up because the State and the taxpayer would be required to pay for the buildings and equipment up front and bear the costs of curriculum development and training for staff in a privatized system. If new state-of-the-art equipment were needed for contractors to meet their teaching obligations, the State would be required to provide it in order to protect the profits to be made.

As I sat watching the faces of the union leaders sitting at the table, listening to the presentation, I could not help but think to myself how surprised they looked. They seemed even more shocked when I laid out how the book outlines a detailed step-by-step plan, whereby state and local politicians, acting in concert with local businessmen, would quietly enact legislation that would make it possible to eliminate resistance from teacher unions, senior teachers, central administrators and other supporters of the public school system. Minsky added that the plan now in place in Milwaukee may have played a significant role in the successful attack on the Michigan Educational Association in 1994, and it seemed to be guiding the actions of politicians and business leaders there as well. It became clear to many of us then that Howard Fuller played a central role in bringing RAND (the sponsor of the *Reinventing Public Education* report, turned into book) to Milwaukee to discuss the plan, and that Fuller was continuing to act behind the scenes to achieve the plan's objectives.

Paul Hill's book openly advocates manipulation of community opinion by business leaders and politicians. Parents, in particular, are targeted as community support for privatization, and paid parents will provide the bellwether leadership for the greater number of parents who are too busy or too little educated to understand the true impact of privatization. It was explained that while the plan refers frequently to the "community" as though it envisions significant public participation in decision-making, the community referred to is ultimately "senior" business leaders acting in concert with "senior" politicians (e.g., the governor) behind the backs of the people and with ultimate contempt for the largest part of the electorate.

We told the union leadership that in our opinion the plan was conspiratorial, and that it laid out a formula for organizing the efforts of politicians and businessmen in support of conservative strategies and tactics worked out by right-wing foundations fed with corporate dollars. Changes in laws and other necessary "alignments" in the system to permit privatization would all take place behind the scenes, through cooperating "external forces."

What were these "external forces"? Well, Professor Hill tells us frankly they were key elements to helping change the political equation. They were the vital features needed to create new ideas different from those advanced by the interest groups normally concerned with public education. For example, superintendents can become change agents, but they normally need the support of external forces like the business community or the governor's office.

For Superintendent Fuller to pull off voucher education reform, a fundamental governance change had to occur. Such a change would only happen if community forces of great power were organized to demand and sustain it. Mayors and top business leaders, who define civic priorities and undertake projects as vast as downtown redevelopment and economic restructuring, would need to provide leadership for education governance changes. Grassroots campaigns to excite parents and community members—especially in minority communities could provide important support for governance changes. Once local leaders were won over, committed to reform, the best way to move a local school system toward private contracting would be to use governance change as a way of improving education in neighborhoods where the existing public schools had failed. "External forces" or privatization think-tank groups like RAND, the Bradley Foundation and the Heritage Foundation, to name a few, would need to "create new ideas that are different from those advanced by the interest groups, etc."[3] Paul Hill speaks about the teacher unions, students, and grassroots community leaders. In his book, Hill points out that the place to start privatizing education is with inner city schools that have "failed."

The reason Professor Hill suggests starting with inner city schools is because expectations are low and these schools will not have to face the quick criticism of middle class taxpayers should they perform badly. In any case, Hill's plan requires that performance standards and expectations be lowered or fixed at current levels, because if privatizing education is going to work, local education authorities must be capable of frank discussion with school contractors in order to deal with real issues.

However, what is realistic to expect in a school that serves a shifting population of new immigrants? If a contractor provides a school in a neighborhood where many resident students have, for years, failed to learn to read and dropped out in 9th grade, what is a reasonable performance expectation? It may be good politics to say that all schools are expected to get steadily better and that every student is expected to meet statewide standards, but a contracting system that did not take into account the student body and neighborhood needs would fail.[4]

What Hill is really saying is that if the school has failed there is no need for private contractors to do better. Further, taking account of neighborhood "needs" is a cryptic way of saying that these students do not "need" the same kind of education given to middle class students. In short, under privatization according to Paul Hill, schools in the inner city would continue to "fail" in fact, but the changed rhetoric of realism would mean that private schools could not be expected to do better than public schools had done with the same population in the past. This would not be failure but realism. Professor Hill declares that,

Today's public education system evades such frank discussions with rhetoric suggesting that it is unfair to expect less of some students than others. Many schools are evaluated on standards they cannot meet and then ritualistically condemned for failure—in the long run, all students can indeed learn to high standards. But in the short run it is better to have well-thought-through plans and demanding but realistic expectations, than to hope for magical solutions.[5]

However, in order to realize these privatizing ambitions, unions must first be abolished or at least eviscerated so that the power they maintain is to protect teacher salaries and benefits only. "Local union leaders will run service agencies, not industrial unions with great bargaining power."[6] A recent example of this is Wisconsin Governor Walker's recent removal of state workers' collective bargaining.[7]

Why Destroy Labor Unions?

Breaking the unions is critical, because a privatized system expects its initial profits to come from destroying teacher, support and maintenance staff salaries, as well as from lowering outlays on equipment and other school supplies. Hill says that if public schools were run under contract, the terms of employment for many teachers would change dramatically. Schools, or the contractors that run them, would employ teachers. Because they would be responsible for their own budgets and staffing patterns, schools could employ different mixes of junior and senior teachers and uncertified subject matter specialists, determine their own student/teacher ratios, and set their own pay scale.

The outcome? No school could afford to have a large staff composed entirely of highly paid senior teachers (as is now the case in many city schools) and few schools could survive if they relied entirely on low-cost inexperienced teachers.[8] As Hill puts it, lower salaries for everyone, fewer jobs for "senior" teachers and (in my opinion) an inferior education for all as there will surely be many more "low—cost inexperienced teachers" added to the mix to improve the profit picture in a privatized education system.

Teacher unions are the most important targets for rightwing privatization efforts, because in many states they are the largest source of organized power for the labor movement, and in Wisconsin they are the only statewide union capable of mobilizing resistance to the corporate education agenda. Education unions have this additional advantage in a fight back campaign—they consist largely of middle class, articulate members who can appeal to many others in the middle class whose children are largely in their care. From the corporate perspective, teacher unions are potential catalysts for rallying support for a labor agenda, and must be disbanded.

RAND's plan calls for the transformation of teacher unions into employment agencies, "matching" teachers and schools in a "free market," while unmatchable teachers would simply be discarded as unemployable in the district. In such a system, teachers who supported the union would clearly fall into the unmatchable category, and would not be rehired. Professor Hill speaks with brutal clarity of union leaders, administrators and senior teachers when he declares, "People whose jobs depended on the old system should not be given critical positions in the new structure".[9]

In addition, the plan outlined in his book calls for the schools to be deregulated and relieved of the necessity of conforming to state or federally mandated programs. Schools would not have to meet mandated standards or serve particular groups of students that require services tailored to their needs, such as minority and special needs students. The purpose here is to reduce the costs of education by not providing for students with special needs, making federal funds more freely available to contractors to take as profits.

Voucher Vultures Will Destroy Labor Unions

While Professor Hill and the RAND Corporation are open and frank about what they intend to do to unions, teachers, central (MPS) administrators, they are less than forthright about what it will cost the public both in the short and long run. What RAND and Professor Hill intend is that the public bear the entire cost and most of the risk for this truly questionable experiment. What RAND in fact envisions is a privatized school system based on private contracting in which all or most of the risks and costs of the new system are paid for by the taxpayer. Buildings and equipment will be provided at taxpayer expense.

Contracting lowers the risks of starting a school by guaranteeing contractors a building, a fixed minimum income, and full reimbursement for all costs for students enrolled above the minimum expected number. It lowers entrepreneurs' front-end costs and guarantees their cash flow.[10]

In conclusion, everything Hill plans is designed to create educational corporations that would bear none of the risks of capital costs and investment in the newly privatized schools, while attempting to ensure profits by facilitating the breakup of unions in order to dissolve present salary scales for all persons currently employed by the public school system. The likely outcome, in fact, is a school system distributing services according to the inner logic of the market in which people get what they pay for—the rich will continue to get superior educational services, and the poor or minorities will get only as much as they are getting now or less—if the teacher "mix" in fact results in fewer experienced teachers in the inner city schools. Students with special needs will get mainstreamed, and opportunities for escape from the inequities in inner city schools will all but disappear.

Continuing down this destructive path clearly places our national union in a perilous situation. The privatization of our system of education means the end to free thinking in order to make room for the free market. In a system of privatization, no longer will minds be rewarded for prolific ideas that elevate humanity and advance society. Such thoughts will be considered socialist and a threat to corporate culture. In a privatized system, minds that produce competitive ideas designed to undermine foreign economies and eliminate notions of collective social justice will be rewarded and honored as the standard all Americans should strive for.

Therefore, the time to defend the real meaning of our Red, White and Blue is here.

Notes

1. Smedley D. Butler, *War is a Racket.* (New York: Round table press, inc. 1935).
2. Paul T. Hill, *Reinventing public education.* (Santa Monica, CA: RAND. 1995).
3. Hill, p. 67.
4. Hill, p. 67.
5. Hill, p. 67.
6. Hill, p. 100.
7. For further information, see chapter 13 in this book.
8. Hill, p. 53.
9. Hill, p. 102.
10. Hill, p. 70.

Chapter 7
Milwaukee League Comes to the Defense of Public Schools
Todd Alan Price

Foreword

President Barack Hussein Obama proclaimed that his administration would award a total of $4.35 billion to states demonstrating a serious commitment to education reform. President Obama lectured that "in the 21st century, countries that out-educate us today will out-compete us tomorrow." Forgotten in this narrative was the debacle of the North American Free Trade Agreement (NAFTA) some fifteen years past, which outsourced family supporting, manufacturing, service, and the information economy jobs to other countries. Ignoring this, yet another U.S. President was sending forth the message that schools, not better trade agreements, must fix the economy, and that it was the schools' charge to take orders, educate, and outcompete the rest of the world, or else perish.

This warning is now emblazoned on the flag being first unfurled under President Ronald Reagan's administration and the infamous *Nation at Risk*, and since 2009 carried with relish by the Obama administration as it wages a zero tolerance war on America's public schools. Calling for austerity and "shared" sacrifice, while lavishly rewarding banking and the private health insurance industry as well as the military industrial complex, Obama repeating the sins of his presidential forerunners was placing public education on notice that it will either get in line with business, or be given the business, and foreclosed. In the name of Mammon and competition, reforming education by way of the Department of Education has unwittingly (or wittingly?) opened up the schoolhouse gates to corporate entrepreneurs whose main credential in education is tax avoidance and shortchanging kids. What was new with the Obama administration, different from his predecessors, is he is putting the process of converting public schools to private ownership into overdrive, pursuing this goal with a strong arm and a heavy hand not previously witnessed. The encouragement of chartering and privatization has now thanks to him and his administration's Race to the Top become a prime facie condition for receiving funding for federally required reforms.

Race to the Top requirements are rigidly prescriptive. The limited funding for education places states across the country in competition to be the lucky winners of a race to the top. Prizes are awarded according to which states clamp down hardest on low-achieving schools while reducing education reform to the level of an ESPN sports competition. To even be eligible, as President Obama emphasized during his November 4th, 2009 Madison, Wisconsin visit to the James Coleman Wright Middle School—a charter school—states were required to get rid of any "firewall" laws that inhibit school reform. Besides eliminating the caps on charter schools, another one of those firewalls was codified in the Race to the Top application as follows:

Eligibility Requirement (b)
At the time the State submits its application, there are no legal, statutory, or regulatory barriers at the State level to linking data on student achievement (as defined in this notice) or student growth (as defined in this notice) to teachers and principals for the purpose of teacher and principal evaluation.[1]

How would this new competitive game play out across the land? To provide a clue, we need only look at a large, urban school district serving a majority poor and minority student population where Education Secretary Arne Duncan attempted to impose a radical change.

Feds Pitch RTT . . . in Exchange for Mayoral Takeover!

Here is the story of an unprecedented federal intrusion into public education and the successful battle to push it back, brought about as a consequence of Race to the Top. It took place in Milwaukee, the largest city in Wisconsin.

In 2009, Wisconsin held a statewide superintendent race where I ran as a long shot candidate. My campaign platform was simple: to put the "public" back into public education and that the heart of the struggle for public education beat in Milwaukee. Although I failed to win, little did I know how prophetic and accurate those words would be; Milwaukee proved to be one of the major sites of the struggle, illustrating how the Federal Department of Education's aim is to take public education out of the hands of the people and turn it over to entrepreneurial powers.

The year 2009 would build and culminate with growing efforts by the city's perennial detractor of public education and business voice of Milwaukee, the powerful Metropolitan Milwaukee Association of Commerce (MMAC), and their corporate media megaphone, the *Milwaukee Journal/Sentinel* (MJS), to single out the Milwaukee Public Schools for the lion's share of criticism for overspending. At a time of budgeting crisis at all levels of government, a McKinsey & Co. report early in 2009 signaled that the Milwaukee Public Schools (MPS) needed to implement cost cutting:

Implementing a pre-pack model would allow MPS to reduce food service personnel by 358 FTEs (84 managers and 274 assistants). While such decisions are always difficult, they may be especially difficult amid current economic conditions.[2]

Yet even before this proposal, an invigorated, proactive MPS School Board had already created and implemented effective plans for monitoring spending, and outright cost cutting.[3] Nonetheless, the governor, mayor, and MPS officials had hastily come to the conclusion that a mayoral-appointed advisory board was better than a citizen-elected one, and they further believed that mayoral takeover of the critical operations of MPS was necessary to solve longstanding financial and academic problems.

Why mayoral takeover? The idea took root in June 4, 2009 when a handful of select officials from Milwaukee and the state of Wisconsin met privately with U.S. Secretary of Education Arne Duncan. Duncan's nationwide mission at the time was to motivate states to strive to compete for federal Race to the Top funds that would be awarded only to the states showing the greatest avidity for "unprecedented reform." In the absence of minutes of the meeting, it was automatically assumed that the mayoral takeover effort that started almost immediately following started here.

In the aftermath of the June 4th meeting there were, at first, according to MTEA and WEAC (the teacher unions) documents, reassurances that there would be no major governance overhaul.[4] Yet reported to the public by the Milwaukee School Board president himself were the contents of a letter saying that he, President Bonds, was resigning from Mayor Tom Barrett's advisory board because the mayor had indicated to him that the advisory board would indeed be moving in that direction.

And, as further noted by the *Milwaukee Shepherd Express,* the new board would convene meetings concerning the public's business in private.[5] This amounted to a "mayoral takeover," the precise radical change in governance that had been widely predicted by astute observers. Thus in an effort to bring all this behind the scenes planning (amidst public speculation) into the open, Milwaukee School Board President Michael Bonds had courageously (and effectively) blew the whistle. Since the lid had been blown the whistle. And now, since the lid had been blown off the cover, the mayor and the governor had to scramble. The political machinations in and around the revelation of a hostile mayoral takeover bid quickly triggered a nonstop succession of bombshell developments.

First following Bonds' intentional leak in Milwaukee there was another newsworthy leak in Madison that was attributed to a staffer from the administration of Democratic Governor James Doyle indicating that the sitting Governor would not seek re-election. Governor James Doyle had started his statewide service as Attorney General James Doyle. In that capacity he had been a staunch advocate for public education, having among other things spent a major part of his career fending off expansion of the controversial Milwaukee Parental Choice Program, the same voucher scheme which was documented in Robert Miranda's previous chapter. In recent years as Governor, however, Doyle was increasingly pulling funds away from the public institutions and the public sector workers. He most likely had considered the political calculus and realized that he was not going to win a second run for governor. As the end of his term approached, a mad scramble ensued where names were hastily assembled, added, and then dropped in a matter of a few short months from a list of prospective gubernatorial candidates.

Soon to follow was another bombshell coming out of the mayoral takeover-planning conclave: Governor Doyle further confounding the press with two more initiatives. First, he stated that it had always been his intention not to run for a third term. Campaign donations were still flowing into his campaign (even while the Governor's approval ratings were dropping) when this news of a secret plan to cop out on his candidacy and its supporters hit them in the face. This bombshell became doubly confusing because at the very same time that he was announcing his political withdrawal, Doyle chose that moment to fix the school system—the Milwaukee Public School System—with a mayoral takeover. But why, the question spread rapidly, had Doyle waited so long to try to "fix" the school system, and why choose the mayoral takeover as the remedy?

The Governor's actions were confusing to say the least: being rushed through in these past few months was a budget that would soon cripple school districts across the state by cutting perhaps $500 million. How did a hasty resignation and a rushed, austere budget factor into the Governor's green light for mayoral takeover? No one could figure this one out. Nonetheless, with Governor Doyle's avid support the process went into overdrive!

On August 31, 2009, governor and mayor made it official by announcing that the mayoral takeover bid was being pursued. In response, a full-blown grass roots movement emerged overnight. Parent groups, religious leaders, the NAACP, the Milwaukee Teachers Education Association (MTEA), city council members, state legislators, congressional representatives, most of the MPS school board itself and concerned citizens, including myself, came together in opposition. Perhaps the bottom line sentiment of all these groups can be found in the following statement of the MTEA:

> Mayoral takeover will not change the fundamental reform issue: the state's method of funding public schools.

But what would happen with mayoral takeover? We all assumed that the popularly elected school board would lose control of budget and oversight and cronyism would come rushing back in.

We already had two precedents. Case number one was New York City Mayor Michael Bloomberg who fired his appointed board members who refused to go along with his charge to flunk kids on the basis of one standardized test score. He had also hired a corporate lawyer to run the district. Case number two was Mayor Richard M. Daley of Chicago where, for the Midwest, the entire mayoral takeover debacle had started. Daley, like Bloomberg, fired his advisory board president when he refused to back the mayor's decision to hire as school CEO an accountant with no experience whatsoever in education, Ron Huberman, to replace the departing CEO, Arne Duncan. It would be no stretch to predict that Mayor Tom Barrett would do the same. Odds certainly favored Barrett appointing an outsider. The most likely candidate for Milwaukee superintendent would be someone from the Commercial Club world, perhaps from the Eli Broad Institute where charter schools with little public oversight are the primary school organization model. Parents would quickly find that they would have no say, zero input in their local schools.

Mayoral Takeover Sneaks into Milwaukee

The upheaval that resulted from the attempt to import mayoral takeover of schools to Milwaukee started with the mayoral election of 2004 in which the winner was a former Congressman with gubernatorial ambitions, Tom Barrett, who had been defeated by Jim Doyle in a 2002 primary contest for the Democratic gubernatorial nomination. Barrett had clearly harbored longstanding aspirations to bring in mayoral control with its incidental potential for building support around the state for another gubernatorial candidacy among voters historically unsympathetic to urban Milwaukee. He had come right out and put mayoral control in his '04 mayoral election platform, but its manifest unpopularity forced him to withdraw the idea soon after winning the election.

Still, the idea of mayoral takeover, and the gubernatorial ambitions that were coterminous with it, appears to have never left Mayor Barrett's agenda, and when opportunity knocked, he opened the door.

Hoping to inspire interest in the vaunted Race to the Top reform, Education Secretary Duncan made a ceremonial (and to my eyes as a spectator, somewhat lackluster) appearance at a May 2009 rally for public education in Ohio being hosted by a true education advocate in the form of Ohio Governor Ted Strickland. That was in May, and here in early June of 2009 he arrived in Madison, Wisconsin, offering federal funds in exchange for state school policy realignment. So, Duncan's Wisconsin appearance had come straight on the heels of his flatfooted visit to Columbus, Ohio, where he was frankly and shockingly for him, upstaged by Ohio Governor Ted Strickland (as will be described in chapter 9, by Geoff Berne, who attended the Ohio rally with me).

With a select group in attendance, Duncan lectured, counseled and urged, some would say coerced, top officials, including the governor and the mayor into competing for the Race to the Top funds. As reported by Alan J. Borsuk in "U.S. Education Secretary Pushes to Improve MPS," *Milwaukee Journal Sentinel* on June 4, 2009, Duncan had impressed upon the group the importance of this "unprecedented opportunity" and admonished the group saying: "don't blow it." Duncan, according to the article, "While not calling for a mayoral takeover of MPS," argued, "leadership needs to start at the top and that means the mayor."[6]

Following this high level visit, Mayor Barrett aimed to make good on the green light given by the Secretary. He set up an advisory board staffed with stakeholders in the education reform game.

The mayor then tried to get the School Board President Michael Bonds on board with the mayoral takeover scheme. Bonds, however, publicly sounded the alarm. In a letter to the rest of the school board he stated that he would not participate on an advisory board. According to Lisa Kaiser on August 13, 2009 in "Exclusive: MPS President Bonds Resigns from Mayor Barrett's Advisory Council," *Shepherd Express,* "Daily Dose," Bonds declared:

> I do not feel I can continue to serve on your public committee, while you and the Governor and other key actors are having private conversations about taking over the Milwaukee Public Schools (MPS) or changing its governance structure of which I am the president.[7]

The ripples from this declaration moved quickly. The unexpected revelation by Bonds in the form of an open letter pressured the mayor and governor to present the policy as if it had been carefully and fully researched.[8] This led Governor Jim Doyle and Mayor Tom Barrett to, on August 31, 2009, and for the first time, announce that achieving any significant reform in the Milwaukee Public School System would require the mayor literally leading the school system, including personally selecting the next City Superintendent.[9] At this time, however, no specific policy plan proposing mayoral control existed. The only opinion on organizational change was the report from the private consulting firm (the McKinsey Commission) that Governor Doyle signed. This advisory report called for cutbacks on employee benefits, giving kids pre-packaged lunches, and some other vague, cost-cutting measures.[10]

Why did the governor and mayor wait so long to propose such a drastic reform, one that would effectively dissolve direct, participatory, and democratic control over the MPS by handing over all school authority to the mayor, especially a mayor who was seeking to leave the position for higher office? Could it have been the money chase started by Obama and Duncan?

As if this wasn't enough, in yet another bizarre turn of events, Mayor Barrett was severely injured when he bravely intervened in a dispute at a Milwaukee county fair, and the assailant suddenly and viciously attacked him. The drama in the city of Milwaukee and the state of Wisconsin took a backseat as Barrett gained national celebrity status as a hero and victim, appearing on talk shows everywhere. As the mayor struggled to regain use of his hand, he soon resumed the offensive, debating the merits of the mayoral takeover at various school forums throughout the city. All the time he continued to play coy, while leaving little doubt that he would run for governor.

Meanwhile, the opposition grew rapidly. Before advancing forward with his election bid, Mayor Barrett had to deal with his constituency, up in arms over his proposed takeover of the Milwaukee Public School District. Finally, a day after the visit by President Obama and Secretary Duncan to Wisconsin, November 7, 2009, Mayor Tom Barrett officially announced his intention to run for Governor.

Confusion and Defiance to the Mayoral Takeover Threat

The scene was orchestrated but dramatic: well over thirty elected officials filled a narrow hall outside of the office of Milwaukee Democratic Congresswoman Gwendolyn Moore. With cameras from television networks capturing her every comment and in front of a throng of citywide supporters, school board members, and state representatives, Moore opened the press conference on Tuesday, September 8, 2009:

> We are baffled and confused by the proposal . . .[11]

The Congresswoman continued by educating all in the room that any so-called takeover of the schools in Milwaukee would be no small undertaking. MPS has its own budget, larger even than that of the city itself, Moore exclaimed! The school system has its own taxing authority, she noted. And finally, the mayoral takeover itself held no guarantee for precipitating the flow of federal dollars from the coveted Race to the Top funds being held in abeyance by the federal government. This critical point—no guarantee—was a key qualification which should have been a concern for the Race to the Top advocates. This obstacle was tellingly not reported by the mainstream paper of record, the *Milwaukee Journal-Sentinel*.

Congresswoman Moore concluded her prepared words sharing this sobering reality:

> We will not rectify the challenges facing MPS unless we talk about poverty, teen pregnancy, and the perverted policy initiatives that have exacerbated this problem for our city's public schools. Milwaukee Public Schools are working with a flawed state funding formula that sends our public dollars to private schools outside of the city. I fully believe that the governor and the mayor have the best intentions for MPS; however, I have yet to hear a credible explanation of how these difficult challenges get fixed by simply changing the way that our school board is chosen.

Next up to speak was school board President Michael Bonds, who had blown the whistle on the whole deal when he revealed that the mayor had asked him to move from his position as school board president to being a bit player on the mayor's newly appointed board of advisors. Bonds was lauded by Congresswoman Moore for holding accountable the businesses that held contracts in MPS, a sign she noted, that he was effectively curtailing the privatization of services that is all the rage in big city school districts like Milwaukee.

Bonds argued that the school district was overstretched and that resources were spread thin. Other key goals he sought were to make the school district in fact smaller, to standardize and enhance the curriculum and to maximize the use of resources. He spoke for Milwaukee parents and teachers, the majority opposed to dissolving an elected school board, and many of whom gathered outside of Congresswoman Moore's office when he said: "this school board is the most pro-student in years." Bonds proudly cited that reading and math scores had gone up, that improvements had been made with the preparation of students for college, and that an accountability office had been established to help facilitate information flow between the school administration and the board of directors in order for the board to make sound decisions.

But even more to the point, Bonds argued the mayoral takeover was about "power and control," simple as that. Given Milwaukee's economic problems, cost overruns, and racial discrimination, Bonds, drawing from a public letter to Governor Doyle, Mayor Barrett, and State Superintendent Tony Evers, questioned the wisdom of folding the district into the same city budget that parceled out and had to balance the expenses of maintaining parks and sanitation services:

> Do we really want to turn MPS over to mayoral control, given the city's current fiscal problems, governance issues, racial disparities in Milwaukee, and its recent history of corruption, its lack of expertise in education, and its lack of an educational reform plan?[12]

These concerns went unanswered.

Assembly Committee Doubts Mayoral Takeover Would Work

In order to make mayoral takeover a reality, a bill needed to be crafted and moved through the state legislature. Subsequently a hearing before the Assembly's Education Reform Committee was convened. This committee had been empowered statutorily to handle matters for huge urban districts like Milwaukee. State representative Leon Young, one of several members from Milwaukee, appeared puzzled, and reflected that there was indeed dissension between and amongst many in the Democratic Party over the plan given the go-ahead from the top Democrats in the state:

> You know what's surprising to me—because I've been in office for about 16 or 17 years—is that traditionally you would hear this type of [threat] from a . . . Republican Governor. What was surprising was that you've got a Democratic Governor that, you know—he [received] a lot of support from Milwaukee—for him to say "takeover" . . . that surprised me.[13]

In another stunning turn of events in this drama that was becoming a consistent pattern, the Committee on Education Reform happened to be chaired by none other than State Representative Annette "Polly" Williams, a key, if not *the* key, sitting Milwaukee Democratic Party member. Williams was well known by educational policy wonks as a Democratic iconoclast, and a maverick in her own party. As a staunch critic of public education in the early 1990s Williams had cut her teeth on education policy, launching the original privatization scheme, the so-called Milwaukee Parental Choice Program (MPCP). MPCP had national implications, well beyond Milwaukee, and in fact became the modern day prototype for the school voucher movement. Yet Williams, the former poster child for privatization, had now made a 180 degree turn, standing utterly in opposition to the takeover, suggesting that it was merely a cynical plot to strip power away from the large urban district in a bid (by Milwaukeean Tom Barrett, the presumptive gubernatorial candidate, no less) to appeal to conservative voters upstate. Like the rest of the committee, including the Republicans seated, she was quite suspicious of and opposed to this agenda.

Yet another Democratic Party State Representative from Milwaukee, Christine Sinicki, also was opposed. As the vice chair, Sinicki pledged she would block any bill that would change control of MPS to an appointed board. "If a bill is drafted, it'll die," Sinicki said. "If it doesn't die, I'll amend it to include all districts in the state."[14] In another move and what turned out to be a highly prophetic statement, Sinicki cautioned that the clamor around this debate was dangerous and could do more harm than anyone could expect. Ostensibly, Sinicki was speaking specifically to her fellow Democrats in relation to the harm that was being done to her party's candidate should he go down with the mayoral takeover ship.

As the hearing went on, it became well established by the committee gathered that day that mayoral takeover had less to do with fixing the schools, and more to do with political control. By any reasonable measure the school board under Bonds had certainly been making progress toward greater accountability and transparency. What else could this be, but a naked power grab? Bonds spoke at the hearing, lauding the work being done under his administration.

Several of the other Milwaukee school board members, including Larry Miller and Annie Woodward testified before the committee. Miller stated that he was working with the parents of Milwaukee to improve parental involvement, and he noted that the district was succeeding in reducing suspension through greater direct involvement with the students in the schools. Miller was the board member who would later ask the pointed question (in a public forum on October 1, 2009 at a Riverside High School) "how can MPS better educate the children of Milwaukee?" His own answer to the question was that mayoral takeover was hardly the answer, pointing out that the *Still Left Behind* report found that academic gains made by elementary students in the mayor-controlled Chicago Public Schools were illusionary: "[they] appear to be due to changes in the tests made by the Illinois State Board of Education, rather than real improvements in student learning." The study called the performance of Chicago's high schools "abysmal."[15] The same Commercial Club of Chicago that supported mayoral control in Chicago in the first place forwarded this information!

Speaking at the Assembly's Education Reform Committee hearing, Annie Woodward, a newly elected MPS board member and longtime social worker, wondered what mayoral takeover had to do with healing the long struggling Milwaukee community:

> If it takes everyone working together to help Milwaukee's public schools prosper and be accountable, to not only raise test scores but to meet the students' social and emotional needs, and to help teachers to be the best they can be, does it make sense to dismantle an elected body, placing the decision-making power for the entire school district in the hands of one elected official?

Duncan Lobbies for Mayoral Takeover in NY Legislature

The Milwaukee Public Schools faced (and still face) daunting challenges: 85% of their student body are on free and reduced lunch, and hail from impoverished homes. Yet as Peter Blewett, another of the school board members noted, Milwaukee still retains some of the state's very best schools! Despite the odds— well over 50% of the student population in poverty—an outstanding school like Rufus King High School could still achieve at the highest level. Blewett pointed out that while the aim was for 100% of the children to graduate, the Milwaukee Public School District's rate was only slightly below the state's average, 70%.[16]

All in all, as board members Blewett, Woodward, and Miller had demonstrated, MPS was steadily improving under the engaged stewardship of President Michael Bonds. The board at the time was actively in search of a new MPS superintendent, a position they believed would complete the vision: to shore up the finances, build out the "STEM" initiative (Science, Technology, Engineering and Math), guide the faculty and staff through professional development, and move students forward over the years ahead.

Given this commitment to success, why then a mayoral takeover?

The governor, mayor and state legislators Senator Lena Taylor and Representative Pedro Colon were actively pitching mayoral takeover as the only way to succeed, to become competitive, or at least eligible for the Race to the Top funds. But this proved not to be accurate.

Democratic Congresswoman Gwen Moore exposed the mischaracterization of the RTT criteria on two occasions. First, Moore asked Secretary Duncan point blank in a Washington D.C. June meeting, shortly after his original visit to Milwaukee, whether mayoral takeover was a precondition (like raising charter school caps was) for Race to the Top funds consideration. Begrudgingly Duncan said no, indicating that if a city and school district were already in partnership— like was the case of Milwaukee where the parks district worked with the school district—the mayoral takeover route need not be taken. Still, Duncan played coy; he made perfectly clear that his tenure would be a failure if mayoral takeover did not grow exponentially.

Duncan's support of mayoral control spoke louder than his equivocation when, in an unprecedented move, he positioned himself as a champion, lobbying in August, 2009, at the New York state legislature on behalf of continuing mayoral takeover and fortifying New York City Mayor Michael Bloomberg's agenda (Duncan also supported Bloomberg's re-election to office, which was focused on the "success" of the mayoral-run school system). Duncan did not mince words in expressing his espousal of 1) the need for a unitary executive for the schools and 2) dismissal of the democratically constituted school boards, characterizing being elected as being "unaccountable":

> If we believe that a system of mayoral control is the only chance we have of implementing real change in a school system like New York's, and I believe this strongly, then any kind of separate unaccountable decision-making body even if it will probably agree with the mayor most of the time is a step in the wrong direction.[17]

In August of 2009, I spoke with a Milwaukee social worker doing a residency with youth in New York City. Ursula, a graduate from Alverno College, had also attended the Creative Arts Elementary School, Roosevelt Middle, and the Milwaukee Theatre of the Arts High School, and was a lifelong Milwaukee South Side resident: "My dad is a public school teacher; my mom works at a community-based Milwaukee healthcare facility. I've spent my entire life in Milwaukee . . ." To Ursula, mayoral takeover failed to live up to the promise, despite all the media hype:

> If you talk with a lot of New Yorkers, most will say, "it's not working," parents do not have access. English Language Learner students have classes in staircases, there's overcrowding. Parents ask . . . how do we hold this system accountable? Due to mayoral takeover, parents have lost control over education. There is no way to make up for an elected school board . . .[18]

Furthermore, Ursula noted, when parents in New York City boroughs have a concern, they must travel far outside their neighborhood to engage city officials. Gone are the local school councils; newly constituted Educational Management Organizations (EMOs) have taken their place, with the result of

> Disenfranchisement. Parents are drifting away, not able to be involved in their child's education; there's no accountability. Lack of democracy in an appointed board can only create a parallel system of separation of parents from their children's education.

Concurring with Ursula's portrait, Deycy Avitia—NYC teacher and co-author with historian Diane Ravitch of a book on school reform —argued

> . . . there has been no significant improvement in any grade or subject tested by NAEP in NYC except 4th grade math, and in that subject, 25 percent of students were provided with "accommodation" or extra help, far higher than in any other city.[19]

> [Duncan] has consistently ignored the fact that the most credible measures of student achievement, the National Assessment of Education Progress, as provided by his own agency, the US Department of Education, show little or no improvement since Mayor Bloomberg's reforms were introduced in September 2003.[20]

Thus the New York success model, outside of Milwaukee, was hardly a success to the folks closest to its impact. Back in Milwaukee, the Coalition to Stop Mayoral Takeover continued to question the rationale that mayoral takeover must-be-implemented-with-all-due-haste-to-secure-RTT-funds.

The second and final time Congresswoman Gwendolyn Moore pressed further in a cover letter; Duncan finally caved in. In a formal letter, September 2009, he replied categorically with the following statement:

You asked about qualification and standards that states must meet in order to compete for Race to the Top grants. Although we have not yet released the final priorities and criteria for Race to the Top, mayoral control of the public schools was not a criterion included in the proposed priorities that we released for public comment in July.[21]

Locked Out

Despite Duncan's denial, the mayoral takeover advocates refused to give up the fight. Instead they opted to go down swinging against their progressive base, with the governor and the mayor playing hardball all the way. It was as if Governor Doyle and Mayor Barrett were stuck in a web of their own making: a two-time Democratic party Governor aiming to support his President's initiative and the mayor who expected to replace the sitting governor if he could only appear tough on his native Milwaukee, thereby appeasing rural, white, and likely conservative voters from across the rest of the state. It is hardly out of the scope of reason to suggest this political calculus as education policy legislation consistently had, after all, targeted Milwaukee, the urban center and home of the largest number of minority students from across the state. Getting tough on Milwaukee schools was a political move to carry favor with rural districts that frequently howled about spending too much money on the Brew City.

Thus on October 19th, 2009, a lame-duck Governor Doyle on his home stretch went on the offensive, making a choreographed, public visit to the Milwaukee YMCA to speak alongside the mayor and city council members. In order to *clarify* and insist that what Secretary Duncan *really* wanted (although Duncan didn't and wouldn't say this) was mayoral control of MPS, Doyle argued that this radical change would give Wisconsin a competitive advantage to secure the money. Never mind that the governor's math didn't hold up well in the weeks before, during, and after the community uprising: *the range of expected funding went from $200 million to $20 million in a few short months!* Instead, Doyle painted a picture that getting even modest funding was worth it, and apparently he saw as imperative the need for changing state law, dismantling what had been a cherished democratic institution, placing the school budget in the same pot as paying for roads and sanitation workers.

Several parents, unionists and community members didn't buy any of this, and picketed, holding a rolling rally outside the building. As the press conference was about to start they suddenly found theirselves locked out, denied entrance, despite the fact that many of them had already called in and reserved a seat at the gathering. In a scene reminiscent of Chicago teacher and rabble-rouser Margaret Haley's protests one hundred years ago to retrieve uncollected taxes, these folks—daycare, custodial, and food service workers—were excluded from the rehearsed proceedings inside. A group called People United for MPS (PUMPS), and Mothers for the Struggle nonetheless spoke out against the proposed mayoral takeover:

We don't want to go back to separate but unequal . . . the mayor has a lot of other things to do, like fixing the budget for the rest of the city.[22]

Other citizens who gained access to the gathering would later describe what had occurred inside:

> It was a horse and pony show . . . They have no plan . . . It's all about the Race to the Top funds . . . They want the money from the governor's supporters so the mayor can run for governor . . . They said that Milwaukee needed the takeover in order to develop more consistency . . . It seems like they have a shotgun sort of thing, they have plans, but they are kind of scattered.[23]

A Milwaukee area professor explained that the governor and mayor were playing the age-old game of changing the storyline:

> There's no condition [for mayoral takeover] at all and it [reminds me] . . . I teach history of the Vietnam War and we've all seen two wars in the Middle East, with both of the Gulf Wars and the Vietnam War, and this kind of reminds me [of that]. . . *the reasons for the takeover keep changing.*[24]

In recent months, the battle for recognition of the excluded citizenry was being led by an organization calling itself the *Coalition to Stop MPS Takeover.*[25] By raising an outcry that is being joined in other major U.S. cities where mayoral takeover had been instituted, Milwaukee had made itself one of the leaders in a growing storm that would succeed in tripping up the best laid plans of education's corporate privatizers.

Meanwhile, the political push moved forward. One week later, on October 27, 2009, Governor Doyle, flanked by five state legislators from Milwaukee, rolled out the idea of a proposed bill to allow the mayor to take over the Milwaukee Public School District. The bill would need to be introduced for a vote by the state legislature.

One week after the Governor announced his support for the proposed bill, on November 3rd in response, hundreds of Coalition to Stop MPS Takeover members occupied Milwaukee City Hall to protest.

On the Road to Reform Schools

The very next day on November 4th, following the protest against the still yet to be released—but soon to be expected—Mayoral Takeover Bill, President Barack Obama and Secretary Arne Duncan travelled to Wright Middle School, a premiere charter school, in Madison, Wisconsin. Speculation was that the visit was intended to support Mayor Barrett's bid for governor, but no one was talking. The President and the Secretary were officially there to push Race to the Top.

A peace protest, mostly ignored by the mainstream media, commenced a short block away from the event. This action drew hundreds of participants, largely citizens decrying the waste of taxpayer dollars on endless war, and calling for "Books not Bombs." Still other high school students rallied, calling for enactment of the DREAM Act. Finally, a handful of educators present denounced the expected Mayoral Takeover Bill and challenged it as a distraction from the real problem—inequitable school funding. Edgewood College instructor T.J. Mertz called this out most eloquently:

> What we're seeing in Wisconsin is lots of attention given to superficial and distracting reforms, like mayoral takeover, that may or may not be beneficial, and very little [attention] to how are we going to maintain the quality of schools that we value so much; we have a great tradition and the tradition is eroding.

Two days later on November 6th, 2009, foreshadowing the attacks that would openly erupt in the state in 2011, the *real* intent behind the concerted campaign to confiscate local administration of Milwaukee schools came out of its wrapping: namely removal from the teaching profession the right of collective bargaining. With the Wisconsin Educator's Association Council (WEAC, the teachers union) in tow, the State Legislature—acting under pressure from the President of the United States, Secretary of Education Arne Duncan, and Governor Jim Doyle—passed a law tying teacher salaries to students' standardized test scores. Finally it was leaked that State Senator Lena Taylor was planning, with her Milwaukee colleagues, Representatives Pedro Colon and Jason Fields amongst them, to sponsor "The Milwaukee TEACH Act" draft for consideration by the legislature in a special session. This was at long last the proposed and expected mayoral takeover bill.

The mayoral takeover seemed to have picked up steam. In retaliation, the Coalition's protests became more visible and desperate to turn the tide. On November 14th the Coalition upped the ante, forming a spirited picket line outside of Senator Lena Taylor's residence, demanding a public hearing on the pending legislation. The Coalition continued to meet weekly, largely co-chaired by longtime education activist and teacher, Bob Peterson, and Wendell Miller Milwaukee NAACP branch president. The meetings were in fact convened at the NAACP building, well attended, and evinced early struggles in Milwaukee for civil rights. Legislators were invited to attend the meetings and indeed several stopped by to fill the group in on the process. As stated before, a second bill by Senator Coggs and Representative Grigsby dubbed "The Race to Success Act." This bill, a seemingly reasonable compromise, was nonetheless unapologetically offered to preempt "The Milwaukee TEACH Act" calling for less takeover and more partnership.

Suddenly, against this backdrop of unexpected resistance to his planned smooth accession to school control of Milwaukee, the mayor ended speculation and declared his intention to run for Governor, while also indicating his intention to remain while campaigning in the office of mayor and while continuing all the while to push forward with his fight for mayoral takeover. In response the Coalition to Stop MPS Takeover continued the fight to sustain democratic control of the Milwaukee Board of School Directors. A second picket line formed, taking place on November 21st outside the home of Representative Pedro Colon, the pro-takeover legislator and Senator Taylor's cosponsor. This time the march stretched around the block.

By the middle of December 2009, with winter fast approaching, the battle did not lose any heat. Nonetheless, the Coalition itself almost splintered over its belief in what tactics would be appropriate to apply pressure on the Democratic Party; one wing opted out of protesting the mayor directly, the other wing having no reservation about showing up at "Barrett for Governor" fundraisers in Milwaukee and Madison with signs denouncing his plan. The Coalition did regain focus and come around to agree on the value of protesting in the street(s) and working the state legislators to support the mutually shared upon goal. To that end they set up "lobby days."

On the 16th of that month, several members paid a visit(s) to respective legislators, all of those that would see them—including Milwaukee Senator Jason Fields, a pro-takeover legislator who himself even attended one of the Coalition's own weekly meetings—to voice their concerns. In fact, Representative Polly Williams made her office hospitable to the group, even providing a full explanation of the legislative process and suggesting tips for the Coalition to win over other legislator support.

The lobbying day generated tangible results. The veil over the real political agenda of mayoral takeover was lifted when at one point the Coalition marched down to the legislative special session where it was expected that the bill would be introduced on the floor. On the way to the Assembly chambers, a pro-mayoral takeover group gathered in the front hall. Katy Venkus, a lobbyist for AT&T, clearly led the group in this instance as a lobbyist for Education Reform Now and paid for by the Democrats for Education Reform (DFER), a Colorado charter school advocacy group. In the days ahead, the *Milwaukee Shepherd Express* with a brilliant expose would shake the foundation of the so-called reform effort, pointing out that much of the funding structure and political advocacy behind which the mayoral takeover was conceived, came from this hedge fund supported, out of state group.

Mayoral Takeover Bid Stalls at Education Hearing

Despite putting on the best face, the mayoral takeover group, mayor, and governor attempted to ignore the turn of events. They instead fashioned what can only be called a propaganda show with orchestrated "press" events where with poker faces they attempted to sell their scheme. A few legislators stepped up to do the Governor's bidding, and S.B. 405, The TEACH Act (The Mayoral Takeover Bill) was launched with much fanfare from the city's public school-hating newspaper, the *Milwaukee Journal-Sentinel.* Yet the mayoral takeover side was dealt one setback after another, if not an outright defeat. The Coalition to Stop MPS Takeover led the charge, convening regular, weekly meetings, protesting the legislation sponsors, rallying at city hall, and generally keeping the heat on as the mayor and governor kept changing the storyline and rationale for the proposed takeover.

A stand up MPS Board of Directors under a dedicated President, Michael Bonds, continued their work, debated the Mayor and allies at public forums . . . *and won.* This school board composed of educators, social workers, and community advocates refused to sit quietly in the face of a proposed coup against democracy. They were joined by allies in this fight: Milwaukee's parents, teachers, social workers, special educators, concerned citizens, and other public education advocates . . . including the students. Having weathered the pain of a voucher and charter school system—in a word, privatization—which effectively had drained the public school coffers of sorely needed revenue, the Milwaukee citizens had finally seen a glimmer of hope in electing a truly proactive school board. They weren't about to give it up.

At the end of November, 2009, President Bonds authorized a special session where Milwaukee citizens overwhelmingly came out in opposition to the proposed dissolving of their elected MPS Board of Directors. Despite the omnipresent corporate interests and their lobbyists behind the scenes, the mayor and the governor's effort proved futile in the face of a resistant community of public school advocates.

Other key state legislators, Senator Spencer Coggs and Representative Tamara Grigsby offered a compromise to the mayor. They pitched alternative legislation, S.B. 462, The Race to Success Act (The Partnership Bill), which would have given the mayor the authority to approve the superintendent and to have an increased role over finances. It was basically intended to circumvent the original S.B. 405, The TEACH Act (The Mayoral Takeover Bill) by giving the mayor an opportunity to save face, while even increasing his power in the school district. But he wouldn't budge, nor would the rest of the mayoral takeover side.

Thus, on January 5th, 2010 the Senate Education committee held a full hearing at the MPS School Board room concerning not only S.B. 405, The TEACH Act, but also the compromise, S.B. 462, The Race to Success Act. With well over 2/3 of the testimony heard that day criticizing S.B. 405, it became abundantly clear that the mayoral takeover, so coveted by mayor and governor, the two top Democratic Party officials in the state, was dead on arrival. In fact it died without ever being introduced.

Shortly thereafter, the MPS Board of Directors hired their superintendent of choice, Gregory Thornton. Governor Jim Doyle's administration had to scramble; with other top officials they threw together the Race to the Top application without having secured their prized mayoral takeover bid. But the hastily assembled document was a loser.

Subsequently, Mayor Tom Barrett, having confused everyone about his political intentions, ran a lackluster campaign, ushering in a radical Republican: former Milwaukee County Executive, Scott Walker. Governor Scott Walker, barely into office, proceeded to give away millions of dollars in federal funds, slash the tax code so as to provide major tax breaks for the wealthiest individuals, citizens and corporations (at the same time putting up a sign about Wisconsin being "open for business"), and make promises to his millionaire and billionaire donors that he would indeed balance the budget by going after the public sector workers. He succeeded in doing just that, stripping away hard fought over collective bargaining rights of teachers and other state employees. A fifty-year precedent came to a crashing halt, massive protests ensued and ultimately, a recall effort in which Mayor Tom Barrett had the ignominy of running once again, and becoming a three-time gubernatorial candidate loser.

And Obama, who came to the Badger state—Madison to be precise—for

Race to the Top at the end of 2009, was a no show when Wisconsin workers were on the streets in Madison, 2011, demanding their rights to have a voice across the table from management. He had promised, during his first presidential bid, to put on his walking shoes, but he apparently forgot, preferring instead to push an ill-conceived race to nowhere. The mayoral takeover that never happened was emblematic, because like Obama, it never left a footprint.

Postscript

What had preceded is the accounting by an eyewitness to a history largely hidden from those from out of state of how a bumbling Democratic political leadership in Wisconsin, following a Master Plan laid out for them by the Democratic executive branch in Washington, split the state's electorate. provoking them to embrace the classically and unapologetically reactionary program of Republican Scott Walker for Governor and make the Wisconsin brand name an asset on the national stage in the eyes of those who selected Paul Ryan for a Vice Presidential candidacy in 2012.

Aspiring to follow the template of Chicago Democratic Mayor Rahm Emanuel's use of mayoral control of schools, that had been fashioned for him by Chicago schools C.E.O. Arne Duncan under previous Mayor Daley, the team of Tom Barrett and Jim Doyle wound up losing for labor and the Democrats not just Wisconsin but, potentially at least, paving the way for a national Democratic rollback as well. Thus has the idea of Democratic mayors of former urban/organized labor strongholds turning cities into a union-free, corporate paradise by handing whole school systems over to the business community wound up: with Chicago's dominant Nobel Street charter school chain naming its schools after living political donors, businessmen, and lawyers who have been called "billionaires, vulture capitalists, union busters, financiers and Republican operatives"[26] who adopt the schools much as the rich through the years have won celebrity for themselves by sponsoring racehorses and dogs in kennel shows.

Somehow with all its glitz, the Chicago mayoral magic failed to impress in Wisconsin, where mayoral takeover became dead in the water. As a result, while Chicago schools have names like DRW Trading College Prep, and where a child being tossed out of schools on a "one strike you're out" basis strictly controls student behavior, Wisconsin will need to come up with another educational model.

Notes

1. The United States Department of Education website for the application "Race to the Top Application for Phase 2 Funding CFDA Number: 84.395A." See http://www.2.ed.gov/programs/racetothetop/applicant.html (Last accessed July 14, 2012).

2. *The McKinsey Commission: The Economic Impact of the Achievement Gap in America's Schools.* April, 2009. See http://mckinseyonsociety.com/the-economic-impact-of-the-achievement-gap-in-americas-schools/ p. 47.

3. *The McKinsey Commission: The Economic Impact of the Achievement Gap in America's Schools.* April, 2009. See http://mckinseyonsociety.com/the-economic-impact-of-the-achievement-gap-in-americas-schools/

4. MTEA and WEAC, *Milwaukee Opportunity Plan: Ensuring Quality Public Schools.* October 2009. http://www.weac.org/issues_advocacy/resource_pages_on_issues_one/OpportunityPlan.aspx

5. "Exclusive: MPS President Bonds Resigns from Mayor's Advisory Council" the *Shepherd Express.* See http://www.expressmilwaukee.com/blog-4141-exclusive-mps-president-bonds-resigns-from-mayors-advisory-council.html; "Barrett aide Pat Curley on MPS Takeover" the *Shepherd Express.* http://www.expressmilwaukee.com/blog-4149-barrett-aide-pat-curley-on-mps-takeover-attempt.html

6. See http://www.jsonline.com/news/education/47001417.html

7. "Exclusive: MPS President Bonds Resigns from Mayor's Advisory Council" the *Shepherd Express.* See http://www.expressmilwaukee.com/blog-4141-exclusive-mps-president-bonds-resigns-from-mayors-advisory-council.html; "Barrett aide Pat Curley on MPS Takeover" the *Shepherd Express.* http://www.expressmilwaukee.com/blog-4149-barrett-aide-pat-curley-on-mps-takeover-attempt.html

8. Indeed having interviewed State Representative Jason Fields, it was acknowledged that Governor, Mayor and State Reps were unsure of who started the idea and whether the term "Mayoral Takeover" itself was unfortunate for rallying support.

9. Erin Richards and Larry Sandler, "Doyle, Barrett say mayor should pick MPS leaders." (*Milwaukee Journal Sentinel* August 13, 2009).

10. *The McKinsey Commission: The Economic Impact of the Achievement Gap in America's Schools.* April, 2009. See http://mckinseyonsociety.com/the-economic-impact-of-the-achievement-gap-in-americas-schools/

11. As Congresswoman Moore stated verbatim in the halls of the Milwaukee Congressional building.

12. Jay Bullock, *Journal of Politics, Music and Education. Folkbum's Rambles and Rants.* September 1, 2009. See http://folkbum.blogspot.com/2009/09/text-of-michael-bondss-open-letter-re.html last accessed August 20, 2012.

13. Price interview, *Education Reform Committee Hearing*, September 8, 2009.

14. Price interview, *Education Reform Committee Hearing*, September 8, 2009.

15. *Still Left Behind*, report of the Civic Committee of the Commercial Club of Chicago, July 2009.

16. *MPS Mayoral Takeover Opponents Say They'll Fight On Plus: Board President Bonds releases an accountability report.*

17. Deycy Avitia, et. al, *NYC Schools Under Bloomberg and Klein: What Parents, Teachers and Policymakers Need to Know,* (Class Size Matters, February, 2010)

18. Price interview of Ursula

19. Avitia, 2010.

20. Avitia, 2010.

21. Duncan to Moore: "Mayoral Takeover of MPS Isn't Necessary."

22. Ibid.

23. Ibid.

24. See http://www.youtube.com/watch?v=WZnjJt1ZJhU

25. See http://www.mtea.org/News/FeatureStories/coalition.nws

26. Jackson Potter, "Rahm Emanuel and Charter School 'Secret.'" See http://www.dailykos.com/story/2012/08/17/1121256/-Rahm-Emanuel-and-Charter-School-Secret

Chapter 8
The Privatization Pandemic:
Barbarians at the Schoolhouse Door[i]
Geoff Berne

In 410 A.D., Visigoth barbarians from northern Europe under their military leader Alaric sacked imperial Rome, trashing its museums and public buildings, vandalizing its art treasures, and driving its population out of the city and into the countryside.

Though there's been enough revisionism over the years to make it almost politically incorrect to use the word "barbarian," I have to admit that it's been an irreplaceable one for me as a term for the movement to privatize American education, a movement of hardened invaders right out of the movies treatments of the sack of Rome, uncouth in demeanor—and in tongue as can happen in unguarded moments when not expecting to be quoted— toward members of the education community not willing to play ball with their determined pursuit of profit.

Consider the language of combat used by, and about, rebels against the public education system such as Dennis Littky in *Teacher: Fight for a Better School.*[ii] For example, Littky's private remarks to Harlem charter schools entrepreneur Deborah Kenny in her book *Born to Rise*[iii] "Kids drop out because school is f***ing boring."[iv] Or consider the heroes in *Class Warfare*[v] by Stephen Brill, the words of the prominent Harlem charters founder-administrator Eva Moskowitz regarding teacher unions that create obstructive paper work: "This is the kind of crap I deal with every day."[vi]

Put off by the acrimony of the pro-privatization movement ever since being startled in my first brush with it in around 1990 as a parent of two young children who'd been attending perfectly acceptable, so I'd thought, public schools in East Windsor Township, New Jersey, I went from being first a student to a self-styled Truth Commission of One on the subject after moving in 1992 to the home district of then-Ohio state representative Michael A. ("Mike") Fox, 1974-1997, the father of Ohio's landmark vouchers experiment in Cleveland that had its startup in the 1996-7 school year.

Having been an eyewitness to the backlash that brought defeat to governors James Florio in New Jersey, 1989-1994, and Ted Strickland in Ohio, 2006-2010, both of whom had attempted to strengthen public education by complying with Supreme Court orders in both states declaring local property tax-based funding unequal and unconstitutional and demanding replacement with a statewide, income tax-based system, I've seen firsthand in the reaction against both governors the birthing of the contempt for the public system that's swept through the rest of the country to become the mantra that it is today.

And where that leaves me, after twenty or so years of writing and citizen action including membership in Ohio teacher union (OFT) president Tom Mooney's Citizens Against Vouchers group in the 1990s, is struck that—though the barbarians of privatization are indeed here inside the walls of the city with their firebrands held high, and nowhere so glaringly as in their attempted sack of the public school system in Milwaukee—there are signs that the pro-profit, anti-public movement may be losing some of its steam.

In Milwaukee an attempted sack of the public schools not only failed in its objective but ended the political ambitions of the city's Democratic mayor who had been in the lead of the sackers while also ending Democratic Party dominance of the pro-sack executive branch in Wisconsin.

Why, the average person might ask, was the confrontation of 2009-2010 over local versus mayoral control of schools in Milwaukee something that would seize the imagination of a distant observer like myself in Ohio; how did education in the rest of this country have a stake in the outcome of the Milwaukee battle, that upheld the claims of the upstart Milwaukeeans; finally, why would the removal of Board of Education control, followed by shutdown, and then privatization, of Milwaukee's public schools that the mayor had been seeking, have been such a bad thing?

Let me start by proposing that what happened in Milwaukee in 2009-2010 should be viewed as the equivalent of a civil resistance by a city population to an invasion of an unnamed yet quite material outside force, a confederacy acting in concert to usurp the rights, inherent in the existence of an elected Board of Education, of the citizenry to administer their own educational system.

This almost-consummated takeover of the functions of a city's elected school board, while under the ostensible generalship of the city's mayor, Tom Barrett, brought together in unity against Milwaukee's urban community a broad attacking phalange consisting of: Democrats biased for private rather than public education, from Wisconsin Governor Jim Doyle all the way up to President Obama and Secretary of Education Arne Duncan; Republicans across the nation with biases for private rather than public education; Wisconsin Republican officials and Wisconsin media—hostile to teachers unions and other unions in the government sector—who would two years later support the election of Republican Scott Walker in 2011 and then uphold his governorship against a recall challenge in 2012; and Foundations, PACs, and national columnists, broadcasters, and websites who hold a pro-privatization monopoly of the national media.

Considering the epic proportions of the force arrayed against them, the doughty underdogs of Milwaukee were facing an adversary comparable not just to a barbarian invasion but a pandemic plague as well!

And considering that they actually prevailed against these odds, kept doomed schools open, and upheld their Board of Education, the Milwaukeeans can be said to have mustered a defense of democracy that's worthy of recognition for the same reason that the Spanish Republic's resistance to fascism roused world interest in the 1930s: because that contest was obviously not just a local one taking place in a single nation, but rather a clash of ideologies and cultures that would soon spread to the entire world. Likewise in Milwaukee, the clash was between an ideology and culture of public ownership and democratic control and what Jonathan Kozol called "the worst, most dangerous idea to enter educational discourse in my lifetime," namely privatized, for-profit education.[vii]

The privatization true believers around Wisconsin and the rest of the country who leapt into action to decry the unruly Milwaukeeans saw the city as a beachhead that needed to be won for the future success of their privatization cause and its objectives, namely the selloff and outsourcing of publicly owned lands, services, and infrastructure to corporate domain.

Be it noted that federally grandfathered mayoral takeovers for the purpose of putting mayor-appointed leaders from the business community in charge of administering city school systems like Milwaukee's did not happen out of the blue starting in 2011; they culminated a "let business do it" trend that had become firmly ensconced in major cities like New York and Chicago since the 1990s but had originated even farther back.

Escorted by an honor guard of the two parties back to the seat of power it once held in the late 19th and early 20th centuries (and has sought to have restored ever since), a corporate camarilla bent on stripping the nation of its public capital and its public treasury has dragged us back to the 1920s, to 1921 when President Warren Harding and his cabinet members colluded with oil industry moguls in the privatization of federally owned lands in California and Wyoming's Teapot Dome. During this era the watchword of the U.S. Chamber of Commerce said it all: "more business in government, less government in business."[viii]

Then in the long liberal era of bi-partisan consensus around the basic policies of New Deal liberalism, the gospel of privatization with full government sponsorship has languished for want of a party voice.

That began to change, though, in the 1960s. By 1966, under Lyndon Johnson, the seeds of the selloff of government functions and services were being planted when the Office of Management and Budget issued Circular A-76, a directive for government to maximize the process of outsourcing under our "big government" President Lyndon Johnson who some historians have called the last of the New Dealers. This policy directive argued that:

> The competitive enterprise system, characterized by individual freedom and initiative, is the primary source of national economic strength . . . the government should not compete with its citizens.[ix]

Privatization picked up steam under Presidents Reagan and George H.W. Bush, whose presidential "privatization initiative" in his last year in office made the transfer of government services and capital to private ownership the official and declared policy of the United States:

> George H.W. Bush: Title 3 Executive order 12803 of April 30, 1992 57 FR 19063 / May 4, 1992
> Privatization initiative:
> To the extent permitted by law, the head of each executive department and agency shall undertake the following actions: (a) Review those procedures affecting the management and disposition of federally financed infrastructure assets owned by state and local governments and modify those procedures to encourage appropriate privatization of such assets consistent: with this order (b) Assist state and local governments in their efforts to advance the objectives of this order; and (c) Approve state and local governments' requests to privatize infrastructure assets.[x]

While the Bush directive laid out the game plan for massive asset sales, it was left to the Clinton Administration for implementation. According to Sheldon Wolin in Democracy Incorporated, the biggest private expansion into intelligence and other areas of government occurred under Bill Clinton. Wolin reminds us that during his first term, Clinton outsourced more than 100,000 Pentagon jobs, thousands of them in intelligence to private companies. By the end of his second term, he had cut 360,000 federal jobs and the government was spending 44 percent more on private contractors than it had when Clinton took office in 1993.[xi]

The Heritage Foundation typified the enthusiasm of the right for the Democratic Clinton's partnership in privatization. In 1996 then-House Majority Leader Newt Gingrich called Clinton's budget the "boldest privatization agenda put forth by any president to date."[xii]

Nowhere is the hold of private corporations over our national wealth more obvious than in the for-profit manufacture of arms, warplanes, ships and military hardware.

The Congressional Research Service in the U.S. reported that American weapon sales abroad reached $37.8 billion, or 68.4 percent of all global arms transactions. The next largest weapons supplier was Italy at $3.7 billion, less than one-tenth the U.S. amount. According to the Project on Governmental Oversight (POGO) database on Federal Contractor Misconduct, misbehavior by unaccountable and uncontrollable suppliers of arms and hired contract personnel, the top 100 defense contractors have cost the U.S. taxpayer billions in improper, illegal, unaccounted expenditures. The Commission on Wartime Contracting (CWC) released a "Special Report on Contractor Business Systems," exposing failures of Defense Department oversight of contractor business systems to prevent egregious "waste, fraud, and abuse" on a scale tantamount to "hemorrhaging."

Right now, taxpayers are vulnerable: the government can't effectively audit those systems and detect contractor errors, omissions, misstatements, and unsupported, unallowable, or unreasonable costs. As stated in the report, the

CWC found in an August hearing that "unreliable data from business systems produced billions of dollars in contingency-contract costs that government auditors often could not verify."[xiii]

Here are some of the more outrageous financial losses to the public treasury attributed to unmonitored corporations receiving government military contracts (since 1995). From a list of the top 100 contractors (instances of misconduct and dollars misappropriated or unaccounted for):

- Lockheed Martin: (50 instances of misconduct), $577.2 million
- Boeing (31 instances of misconduct), $1561.4 million
- Northrop Grumman (27 instances of misconduct), $790.4 million
- McKesson (8 instances of misconduct), $1356.7 million
- Merck & Co. (10 instances of misconduct), $5834.7 million
- GlaxoSmithKline (16 instances of misconduct), $4280.7 million
- In all there were 678 instances of misconduct run up by the 100 top contractors for total wasted dollars in the amount of more than $26 billion (26126.8 million).[xiv]

And then there is the military itself acting in its newer privatized guise. In Afghanistan and Iraq an estimated 180,000 private contractors employed by private for-profit corporations such as Blackwater/Xe are increasingly taking the place of members of our nation's own armed forces.

According to the Congressional Research Service, as of March of 2011, contractors made up 57 percent of the Pentagon's force in Afghanistan and a total of 65 percent if the past two years are averaged in. Congress appropriated $106 billion for contractors, earning salaries that are often triple or quadruple those of an American soldier or Marine in Iraq and Afghanistan from 2003 through the first half of 2008.

While as of March 31, 2008, there were still more uniformed military personnel—282,000 compared to contractors 242,657—it is not hard to imagine, if the trend continues, a future in which an American force will be sent into battle without swearing an oath to defend the U.S. Constitution and subordinate to the authority, not of an elected U.S. commander-in-chief, but to the dictates of their respective private corporations' CEOs.

One of the jewels in the crown of the new "let business do it" system of outsourcing public functions to private corporations is prison management. Private for-profit companies are increasingly running America's prisons. The Corrections Corporation of America, far and away the leading private corporation in the fast-growing incarceration industry known as "The Prison-Industrial Complex," operates a total of 65 facilities including 41 that it owns, and a total of 78,000 beds in 19 states and Washington D.C.

For 2007, CCA reported total revenues of $1,478,000,000 and profits of $266,300,000, an 18.4% increase over 2006. The net profit for that time period was $133.4 million, a 26.7% increase over 2006.[xv] When the dynamic of profit is allowed to enter into the field of incarceration, incentive is created to maximize the number of arrests and length of sentencing, a Pandora's Box opening the way to corruption of the justice system, what George Monbiot calls "the revolting trade in human lives."

In a *Wall Street Journal* article Monbiot described the use of guaranteed payments of public funds to private jails for a set number of inmates regardless of the number of cells that are full or empty. He also explained the rationale for and inducements to judges to counter declining crime rates by handing down disproportionate sentences just to keep jail cells full (and prison management companies' books in the black).[xvi]

So it is that vital functions of government such as arms manufacture, prisons, and the waging of war are increasingly being handed over to private corporations to be run for-profit.

So what is wrong with that? What is wrong with outsourcing government functions if private corporations can do a job more efficiently and cost-effectively than government itself?

What's wrong is that when corporations that operate for the purpose of maximizing profits perform functions on behalf of or as "partners" of elected government, policy is put at the service of profit and contracts between political entities and partnering corporations are necessarily filled regardless of changed circumstances such as diminished need or budgets.

When the dynamic that drives the system is privatization, gratuitous wars are waged for wantonly padded expenses, prisoner remediation vanishes and jails are stuffed to the gills by judges handing down inordinately extended sentences, medical insurers nickel and dime over coverage, and children are marched off to low-budget and non-union charter schools in desolate and abandoned shopping plazas and vacant industrial facilities for the sole purpose of making profit on investment and of maximizing profit yield for corporate investors.

Public School Districts under Siege

The next frontier for privatization is education. As with military manufacturing, military contracting and prison management, the federal government's education agenda under the leadership of Secretary of Education Arne Duncan was dead set on a policy of transferring the administration of public schools to private businesses. The secretary was giving evidence that his chosen means for accomplishing this handover was through putting mayors at the helm of entire (mainly urban) school systems. Under this process mayoral-appointed councils of business and retired military leaders would replace elected school boards. These new executive decision-makers would then go on to bring in for-profit corporations to manage the schools while drawing on budgeted money previously intended for public systems.

Duncan's "Race to the Top," a strategy of having states compete in a horse race for funds for education reform, made clear that only states making concrete efforts toward privatization would get the coveted funds. These efforts would have to include "fostering the growth of charter schools" plus taking steps to replace teacher tenure with procedures to make employment conditional on student test results, i.e. making both teacher retention and the continued existence of the schools they teach in as public rather than private entities conditional on performance measurement as in the world of business.

In these initiatives Duncan was setting for himself the roles of midwife, epigone, and chief factotum for the privatization doctrines first laid out by the "father of modern school reform," fellow Chicago luminary Milton Friedman. In a 1955 essay that he later incorporated into his landmark 1962 book Capitalism and Freedom, Friedman called for a wholesale "denationalization" of public education. Instead of public funds going to school systems, parents would receive vouchers on these funds to pay for "educational services" for their children at for-profit and not-for-profit schools that would be operated by education entrepreneurs and managers. This new breed of school administrators would be free to set teacher compensations as low as a dog-eat-dog market for teaching jobs could bear. Government's role would be reduced to "insuring that . . . schools met certain minimum standards, such as the inclusion of a minimum common content in their programs, much as it now inspects restaurants to insure that they maintain minimum sanitary standards."

In true survival-of-the-fittest purism, Friedman believed that parents should, if they decide to have children, be prepared to pay for their education.

In a prescient prophesy of the state of education today Friedman depicted that the downfall of public schooling would be smoothly accomplished in a piecemeal fashion with a slowly mushrooming privatized sector coexisting with the shrinking and declining public sector for a transitional period of time. "Since governmental units . . . would continue to administer schools, the transition would be gradual and easy." An educational regime change would be accomplished before people realized it had happened.

Though at present only 20 states have established voucher-type subsidies for private schools, Friedman smelled victory for his idea of free-market education reform in an interview conducted for *Reason Magazine* in 2005 on the 50th anniversary of his 1955 vouchers essay and two years prior to his death. Friedman stressed that the proof that the tide had turned for privatization was the growing favor being shown by the capitulation of the teachers unions. Their "dam is buckling," he waxed proudly, "and will shortly break . . . The basis of the National Education Association's and the American Federation of Teachers' power is crumbling."[xvii]

At present the privatization process with its union-disabling subtext, is being promoted to the public as a rescue effort to "turn around" schools in impoverished and struggling urban neighborhoods ASAP. States are being pressed as in Wisconsin to give mayors of major urban centers the powers to effect the same transformation Duncan presided over in Chicago. In the Windy City, mayoral control under Richard Daley Jr. had existed since 1995. Succeeding Paul Vallas, who later went on to help dismantle most of the public schools in New Orleans, Duncan made a name for himself by closing 75 schools and replacing them with smaller schools shorn of union contracts and community governance and run with business-inspired managerial approaches.

Typically, when mayors need management for the schools that have been put under their direction, they make appointments from the business community and/or turn to ready-made education management corporations that are waiting for a call.

So why should what works for the urban schools not work for suburban, small-city, and rural schools? Starting with the cities, the precedent will have been established for America to be left, in education as in healthcare without a "public option."

In other words, education privatization is not just about mayors "turning around" underperforming urban districts. It's ultimately about opening the whole education sector to for-profit management.

First, however, the public has to be sold on the need for "turnaround." First, the public has to be whipped into frenzy over a crisis in our schools, that is, in our urban schools, a crisis requiring urgent "reform." And then in the name of reform the way is paved for business to be brought in on a white horse as reformers.

In the guise of reformers celebrity tycoons from the world of business, opportunistic social advocacy personalities, ambitious public officials and the new education managerial class emerging from graduate schools of education and corporate institutions like the Broad Foundation's New Leaders for New Schools seek to make a name for themselves as advocates for corporate interests. These groups have been the leading players in the new world of investment and career opportunity around privatized education. Regardless of having no professional training as pedagogues or published works or other credentials as education theorists, researchers, or analysts, the current barons of finance for no discernible reason other than their enormous wealth have been elevated to the status of venerated education mavens and saviors of our children's futures.

Prominent in this category are entrepreneurs like Microsoft's Bill Gates who, notwithstanding his record of epic business success, also happens to have dropped out of college (Harvard) in his sophomore year rather than go to the top of the educational stepladder that is held out as model and paradigm for America's schoolchildren.

Secretary Duncan, an administrator whose advancement came from endearing himself to Chicago's corporate community by his policy of shutting down public schools and opening charter schools, has no hands-on experience as an educator other than a period of time spent working in his mother's tutoring school.

African-American charter school advocate Al Sharpton and his "action organization" has been the beneficiary of generous residuals for his public appearances at the White House and around the country in support of opening charter schools that would supposedly put minority children on a college prep track, while he, himself, dropped out of Brooklyn College in his sophomore year. Two illustrious business names who have been ceded a national megaphone on the subject of education in spite of having zero credentials in education are former financier Michael Milken and real estate and nursing home entrepreneur Eli Broad.

Milken parlayed a career of reaping high returns from low-yield junk bonds. As a result of these buyouts he created almost a one-man recession by throwing the whole workforces of "bought" companies out on the streets. In the process he became the 458th richest man in the world. Still his only experience as an educator came in three years of community service teaching math to minority children in Los Angeles in fulfillment of a ten-year sentence for securities and financial reporting felonies for which he served 22 months in federal prison.[xviii]

By 1999, only three years following his release from prison, Milken had amassed an empire of companies catering to every possible facet of the education industry. His corporate network looked as though it might someday rival his former scale of operations as a financier.

Today, Milken heads a foundation purporting to set the standard for the training of quality K-12 teachers. He uses money incentives for teacher candidate recruitment and sends his graduates out all armed with math skills and fluent in the use of computer technology. Yet, other than the conferences his foundation sponsors in order to affirm the superiority of private over public education, there is no evidence that Milken, this towering colossus of the age of for-profit education, has a holistic educational philosophy of how one actually inspires a young person to want to read, study, and achieve.

Eli Broad rose from the status of 19-year-old prodigy in the field of accounting ("the youngest in Michigan history") to founder of one of the nation's biggest networks of assisted care facilities. Broad has devoted a significant portion of the $5.8 billion net worth (number 42 on the list of 400 richest Americans) to the cause of totally privatizing American education. To this end, Broad has contributed $10.5 million in startup funds to the Green Dot charter schools network in Los Angeles. In 1999, he and his wife Edythe established the Eli and Edythe Broad Foundation and joined the ranks of family foundation empires like those of Bill & Melinda Gates and Michael and Lowell Milken. A flagship program of the foundation is the Broad Superintendents Academy that identifies and trains executives with experience of leading large service organizations including the military. He then places the graduates in urban school districts.

But is there any evidence—if one looks beyond their sales promotion slogan that American education needs to be run more "like a business"—that this group of indisputably wealthy and successful individuals has a conceptual clue about how to cultivate and motivate the mind of a child?

These businessmen may be part of that group that historians once called Captains of Industry and Finance. They may be builders of unparalleled monopolies in the fields of software, finance, real estate, insurance, etc.—world-straddling economic players in the mold of the successful businessman that Theodore Dreiser portrayed in *The Financier*[xix] . . . *The Titan*[xx]—but they hardly fit the profile of "educators." As far as education is concerned, they are "barbarians at the gates," untrained and uncouth in the arts of shaping the lives and intellects of children.

Yet here they are, the nation's prime movers in the raging battle to replace public education with a system in which the schools are outsourced to for-profit businesses, businesses that are not accountable to government financial oversight and that are free from union contracting that protects the job security of teachers.

Do American parents want schools to be run like businesses and their children to be treated as employees? Will they accept the idea of delivering their children into the hands of specialists in financial deal-making and cutthroat competition who may or may not have completed college themselves and who view students strictly as "human capital" to be schooled in skills narrowly tailored to niches in today's ever-so-transient corporate job market? Do they want education to be made over in the model of privatized industries like military manufacturing, military contracting and prison management - industries that have taken advantage of the less-government, anti-oversight policies of federal administrations of the past three decades to pile up a record of fraud and financial abuse unmatched by any era in American history?

Or are parents now getting a little tired and put off by the endless blizzard of promotion[xxi] for "education reform" as the panacea for all that ails our economy, job market, and society? While far from a political tidal wave, it is clear from reported anti-shutdown activities in Chicago, New York, and other locales that Milwaukee's stand against federal turnaround designs and mayoral handover of public schools to private, for-profit business has sounded the cry, laid down the glove, and pressed the ignition switch of what could become an assertive new trend around the nation.

Notes

i. Reprinted from Counter Punch, Dec. 4, 2009.

ii. Susan Kammeraad-Campbell, and Susan Kammeraad-Campbell, *Teacher: Dennis Littky's Fight for a Better School.* (New York, N.Y., U.S.A.: Plume, 1989).

iii. Deborah Kenny, *Born to Rise: A Story of Children and Teachers Reaching Their Highest Potential.* (New York: Harper, 2012).

iv. Kenny, 2012, p. 76.

v. Steven Brill. *Class Warfare: Inside the Fight to Fix America's Schools.* (New York: Simon & Schuster, 2011).

vi. Brill, p. 428.

vii. Interview with Lisa Kaiser, *Milwaukee Shepherd Express*, 3/4/09.

viii. "At the time this was . . . an official slogan of no less an institution than the U.S. Chamber of Commerce." Thomas Frank, *The Wrecking Crew: How Conservatives Rule*, (New York, 2008) p. 29.

ix. See http://www.whitehouse.gov/omb/rewrite/circulars/a076/a076.html

x. Title 3 Executive order 12803 of April 30, 1992 57 FR 19063 / May 4, 1992 http://www.naftasuperhighway.info/uploads/Executive_Order_12803.pdf

xi. Sheldon Wolin: *Democracy Incorporated*, (Princeton University Press, 2008) p. 73.

xii. Wolin, p. 87.

xiii. See http://www.wartimecontracting.gov/ The *Commission on Wartime Contracting (CWC)*

xiv. Project on Government Oversight, Federal Contractor Misconduct Database, http://www.contractormisconduct.org/

xv. "Corrections in the 21st Century," *Corrections Corporation of America Company Profile*, August 14, 2008.

xvi. George Monbiot, "The Revolting Trade in Human Lives," (*UK Guardian*, March 3, 2009). http://www.guardian.co.uk/commentisfree/2009/mar

xvii. Nick Gillespie, "The Father of Modern School Reform: Fifty years ago, Milton Friedman introduced the idea of school vouchers. Now he looks back on his legacy." *Reason.com*, December 2005. See http://reason.com/archives/2005/12/01/the-father-of-modern-school-re/1

xviii. Milken was punished after pleading guilty to the following crimes: 1. Aiding and abetting another person's failure to file an accurate 13d statement with the SEC since the schedule was not amended to reflect an understanding that any loss would be made up; 2. Selling stock without disclosure of an understanding that the purchaser would not lose money; 3. Aiding and abetting another in filing inaccurate broker-dealer reports with the SEC; 4. Sending confirmation slips through the mail that failed to disclose that a commission was included in the price; 5. Agreeing to sell securities to a customer and to buy those securities back at a real loss to the customer, but with an understanding that he would try to find a future profitable transaction to make up for any losses; 6. One count of conspiracy to commit the other five violations. See http://en.wikipedia.org/wiki/Michael_Milken#Education]
For a definitive profile of Milken's post-prison education activities and investments, see Ross Baker, "The Education of Mike Milken, From Junk-Bond King to Master of the Knowledge Universe," (*The Nation*, May 3, 1999).

xix. Theodore Dreiser, *The Financier*. (Champaign, Ill: Project Gutenberg,1999). http://search.ebscohost.com/login.aspx?direct=true&scope=site&db=nlebk&db=nlabk&AN=1085515.

xx. Theodore Dreiser, *The Titan*. (Cleveland: World Pub. Co. 1946).

xxi. For example, government employees unions AFSCME and AFGE; also environmental and watchdog organizations: See, respectively http://www.afge.org/Index.cfm?Page=Privatization http://www.sourcewatch.org/index.php?title=Privatization

Chapter 9
Clash Over Charter Schools in Ohio:
Ted Strickland's Challenge to the
Obama-Duncan Wrecking Ball
Geoff Berne

On May 1, 2009, Michigan's Board of Education—like boards in most states across the U.S.—issued a resolution "recognizing that teachers are vital to the very fabric of our society" and declared the week of May 4th through the 8th Teacher Appreciation Week. Three days later President Obama issued a proclamation designating May 3rd through May 9th as National Charter Schools Week. Rather than honor the contributions of American teachers in our 95,000 plus public schools and teaching as a profession, as had become customary, the president chose instead to salute only the personnel of the 3,500 charter schools. These rapidly expanding alternatives to traditional neighborhood schools are publicly financed, but are frequently allowed to operate like private businesses, independent from and competitive with the public school system. In his address Obama praised charters saying:

> I commend our Nation's successful public charter schools, teachers, and administrators, and I call on states and communities to support public charter schools and the students they serve.[1]

How ironical, then, that in Ohio, called the "School Choice State" for having been one of the founders of today's charter education trend with its Cleveland vouchers program introduced in 1996-7, a bristling backlash against the privatization concept was being led by none other than the state's governor since 2006, Ted Strickland.

In the direct line of sight of the governor's regulatory charge was Ohio's nation-leading total of charter schools, 330 in all. While Strickland's administration had set itself on a course to strengthen public schools and reduce the role of charters—that would be cut short with his defeat by Republican John Kasich in the 2010 gubernatorial election—the precedent created by his campaign to hold private schools to the same standards as the public schools opened a breach in the wall that had previously insulated the performance and operations of the charters from scrutiny—and policing.

Strickland—one of nine children in the family of a coal-mining father from eastern Ohio, an A.B. in history and psychology, M.A. in guidance and counseling and M.A. in divinity, former professor of psychology at Shawnee State University, Minister in the United Methodist Church, prison psychologist, and Democratic U.S. Congressman—was first elected governor in 2006 on a platform pledging to remove the exemptions from government oversight and academic accountability requirements that had been preferentially granted to Ohio charter schools. This dispensation had provided charters with a decisive advantage in allowing them to market themselves as a superior alternative to traditional public schools with zero in the way of evidence to support the claim.

Now Strickland was vowing to shut down charter schools that were taking state funds but delivering a substandard education. Following his landslide election, not only did he not renege; he vigorously pursued his crackdown pledge.

Showdown at Schottenstein

In a full demonstration of his commitment to uphold the state's obligation to sponsor and pay for public education, the governor on May 8, 2009, hosted a mass rally on the Ohio State University (OSU) campus grounds outside the Schottenstein Center in Columbus that capped a sixteen month-long "listening tour" he had conducted across the state to promote his plan to restore Ohio to its once-top place among state economies through a renewal of public education.

At every stop on the tour Republican leaders and newspapers friendly to them denounced the plan for its reliance on federal stimulus money that they said would require replacement with new state taxes within two years. To which Strickland persisted in calling for increasing state funding, expanding programs connecting education to work, supporting creativity and curricular innovation, and ending the open door policy that had allowed charter schools to obtain state monies without oversight or accountability.

Indeed, flying in the face of a decade and a half of pro-charters consensus and following through on his campaign pledge to do so, Strickland introduced procedures to shut charter schools found to be mismanaged and academically substandard.

So, there was audacity to spare in Strickland, who had criticized the making of profit off of low income children by charter schools as "immoral," extending an invitation to U.S. Secretary of Education Arne Duncan, the known spokesman for President Obama's staunch commitment to charter education, and past prolific charterizer himself in his seven years of heading the public school system in Chicago, to speak at this partisan rally for public education!

What came into view as the Secretary looked out from the speakers platform on that beautiful spring day in America's heartland was a vast array of public education celebrants including union leaders, teachers, parents, students, legislators, and administrators, all there on the campus of America's biggest public state university to let their voices be heard in celebration of "Teacher Appreciation Week."

Left to appear as the final speaker on the program, Duncan had been made to wait patiently through a succession of speeches resolutely supporting public education. When he finally spoke, he used the occasion to explain how states and districts that had previously obtained federal education funding as outright grants would now have to vie for a funding in the form of a limited number of awards strictly tied to student performance on tests under the newly-announced Race to the Top competition.

A key requirement for Ohio to have a chance at obtaining a fair share of the mere five billion dollars in federal money that he was offering as an incentive to all 14,000 American school districts would be for the state to show the Department of Education in Washington that she was strongly committed to the kind of education "reform" that was sanctioned by the Administration.

Translation: evidence of that commitment to reform would be the degree to which the state could show it favored expansion of charter schools.

The President's Emissary: A Man on a Mission

Could there have been a more incongruous speaker at a public education rally than Secretary Duncan? His record as head of Chicago public schools for seven years prior to his 2008 cabinet appointment had consisted of shutting down 20 public elementary schools and six high schools and converting them to mostly privatized, charter schools, and replacing them with new academies.

Named CEO of Chicago Public Schools in 2001 with no significant prior administrative experience other than his apprenticeship to his school-slashing predecessor Paul Vallas—who had gone on from Chicago first to Philadelphia where he shut 40 schools in five years, and then to New Orleans—Duncan had not worked in schools at all, other than as a tutor helping minority children with their homework in his mother's tutoring program in Chicago.

The replacement of 100 of Chicago "underachieving" and predictably underfunded public schools—15 percent of the city's total—with new experimental schools in gentrifying neighborhoods, was the goal of the Renaissance 2010 education plan created by a business association: the Commercial Club of Chicago.

Building on what he started in Chicago, and in the face of massive evidence, such as the Stanford Study of 2009, refuting the notion of the academic superiority of charter schools, Duncan has made charter education the idée fixe of the Department of Education in the Obama era. In doing so he gives every appearance of credence to the idea promoted by his longtime supporters in the Commercial Club of Chicago, that if business is involved, it's good and children will excel; if unions are involved, it will be rife with mediocrity and student failure will follow.

The objective is to shut down so-called "underperforming" public schools, schools that are almost without exception located in minority urban neighborhoods, and replacing them with publicly funded chartered schools that with their status as independent business enterprises are freed to purge faculties of union members and union protections.

So here was Duncan coming to make a debut appearance as Secretary of Education to proclaim how Race to the Top would advance the goals of education reform, when as most of his Ohio audience knew, when the Secretary used the words "education reform," what he specifically meant, to quote the Associated Press's Libby Quaid, was "closing public schools, firing their staffs and principals, and "turning the school over to a charter operator."[2]

One can imagine that this maiden appearance as U.S. Education Secretary at Governor Strickland's rally in Ohio was to have been Arne Duncan's shining moment, the symbolic kickoff of his bringing to the country as a whole his "Chicago" get-tough policy of raising quality of schools by threatening to shut them down.

But it was not to be. What happened instead can be put in one word.

Upstaged

Preceding Duncan on the program was Governor Ted Strickland. But before Strickland began to deliver his address, the former psychology professor artfully yielded the stage to two individuals who would turn out to overshadow all other speakers including Strickland's guest dignitary from Washington and even Strickland himself.

These two larger-than-life personages were Dale DeRolph and Nathan DeRolph, the father and son who had come to symbolize the struggle for educational improvement in Ohio.

Starting in 1991, the DeRolphs had persevered through eighteen years of litigation and advocacy which had culminated in four successful Ohio Supreme Court challenges to the state's grossly unequal education system since that had attracted national attention—and embarrassment.

For the audience at Schottenstein the DeRolphs needed no introduction. As though for maximum effect, their names seemed purposely to have been left off of the rally program, with the result of thunderous acclamation descending on them from an audience surprised by their unexpected appearance on stage.

The DeRolphs had been asked to be there to tell the story of their intervention that had started with an effort to change the primitive conditions of the schools in their home area of southeastern Perry County. Their pursuit of all legal avenues to force improvement had spearheaded a crusade by a coalition of teachers, parents, and school administrators to reverse the state's neglect of schools in low-income areas. Their advocacy culminated in four favorable Ohio Supreme Court judgments between 1997-02 in which the Court repeatedly ruled that Ohio school funding based on local tax levies was unconstitutional.

These rulings helped end the hold on the public of Republican indifference and inaction towards Ohio's school inequalities that had reigned in the state through the 1990s and early 00s and paved the way for Ted Strickland's education-themed campaign and eventual election as governor in 2006.

Here at the Schottenstein rally for public education, Dale DeRolph, the quiet-spoken hero of the funding crusade, told the emotional story of discovering his son taking a final history examination while sitting cross-legged on the Sheraton High School gymnasium floor. At that moment, even though young Nate found nothing out of the ordinary or wrong, Dale was outraged and vowed he would seek legal help to change this deplorable situation. He went on in his speech to describe the Perry County schools at the time saying they had

> . . . split classes in elementary, [relied on] reusable textbooks, labs without equipment or working equipment, and buildings that were under constant repair; teachers (who were often) our third and fourth choices of teacher applicants.[3]

Nate DeRolph, in whose name the court challenges had been waged, and who was a fifteen-year-old high school freshman at the time of the initial filing, spoke next. He confided that

> Once my dad and I got involved . . . we traveled to some of the wealthier districts in Ohio and some of the poorest. I think I can speak for both of us when I say we were shocked. The wealthier schools had every college prep class you could imagine and extracurricular activities I thought only colleges offered. They had facilities and learning materials rivaled by none, then we visited some of the poorest schools and it was like being in a Third World country. Buildings falling down, textbooks from the 60s and 70s, and minimal college prep courses, if any.[4]

The younger DeRolph then confessed amazement at the failure of four Supreme Court decisions to budge the Republican-controlled state legislatures of the 1990s and early 2000s toward making a more equitable school funding system. Nate speculated, saying:

> I hate to think what would happen if you or I ignored the Supreme Court. I thought with each ruling that they would have to fix school funding. How could they say no to the children of Ohio? But with each ruling came more backlash and more politics. More people saying that school funding couldn't be fixed and that there was no good solution.[5]

Finally, Nate DeRolph reminded the crowd that his suit "was originally filed 18 years ago," how the class that was born when the lawsuit started had since graduated. He then remarked that

> I'm now 33, married, with two kids of my own.[6]

Strickland's Crusade

Another Strickland believer is Sue Taylor, Ohio Federation of Teachers president, who we, Todd Price and myself, spoke with after the rally: we asked her to "tell us about the Governor; who is he, and why did he have this education reform rally?"

> Taylor: His background, you know, is being a minister [note: in the United Methodist Church], and when he feels passionately about something you know

he really does use it as his bully pulpit! He obviously is very passionate about improving education and very frustrated by the wall that's up in the Senate and whether or not we can get through that wall.

Taylor reflected on her own frustration with the Obama administration:

> I don't understand it. The president and Arne Duncan are breathing new life into the charter movement because it's clear that its failed in Ohio . . . yet they do want to breathe new life back into it and I'm not sure why. If they had some plans to improve them in a clear set of strategies, ok, but they're just espousing them.

Prior to the rally, on May 6th, Taylor had forwarded a letter[7] on behalf of the OFT to President Obama in an attempt to explain the union's position on educational reform. In the letter, which she handed me at the outset of our interview, she called Ohio's $3.4 billion investment in charter schools "experiments that have wasted $3.4 billion of taxpayers' money and have failed thousands of our children." Documenting this glaring failure of charters to show the dramatic improvements claimed are the data she offered:

> Two out of three charter schools earned failing grades from the Ohio Department of Education on last year's state report card; 64 percent of charter schools that received state report cards earned Academic Watch and Academic Emergency ratings . . . Statewide, traditional public schools outperform charter schools in each tested subject at each tested grade level; the difference in pass rates ranges from 5 to 10 percent. Traditional public schools experienced gains in proficiency levels that are from 2.2 to 4 percent a year higher than those of charter schools.[8]

Thus it was made clear, by this union president and Strickland supporter, that there was an emerging schism in the Democratic Party over the issue of education reform.

Strickland aims to fix school funding, and place a cap on charters

From Ted Strickland's first days in office in 2007 until his election defeat by John Kasich in 2010, the traditional Ohio attitude that "school funding can't be fixed and that there is no good solution" kept coming back with a vengeance.

To a great degree it was fired by the pro charters/anti-public education editorial bias of virtually all Ohio news media. Across the state influential voices in the press, on radio and television seemed determined to help restore Republican ascendancy and break the momentum of the governor's unprecedented pro-public education campaigning. Cox Newspapers, a national newsgroup of 43 newspapers including *The Dayton Daily News, Hamilton Journal-News,* and six other papers in Southwestern Ohio saw the Republican majority in the state Senate as an opposition too formidable to overcome.

Cox and other elements of the Ohio news media through their repeated failure to hold the state's entrenched Republicans' accountable for fixing the unconstitutional school funding formula had provided political cover to the opponents of public education.

"Governor Ted Strickland is not going to get his way on changing how Ohio pays for schools. Nor should he,"[9] Cox proclaimed in its syndicated editorials. They went on to rebuke Strickland for placing education above other equally compelling funding needs of the state, such as prisons. Acknowledging that Strickland had won backing from Ohio business as well as labor, Cox media still turned its thumbs down on Strickland's formula for arriving at a per-student funding number. The requirements, they insisted, may fit some schools in need of improvement but not others who are already strong.

Strickland's philosophical position on school funding was in the opposite direction (in the Cox papers' publishers' eyes, at any rate) that a good part of the state, those parts for whom Ohio Republicans speak, wanted to go—toward charter rather than public schools.

So, the Republicans gave no quarter toward Strickland on education reform. His goal of leading Ohio citizens against the continuation and expansion of charter schools was a direct challenge to how they saw the future of education reform. Indeed, during their party's fifteen years in Ohio's political majority they had themselves staked out an identity as school reformers. In the name of "reforms," they had wrapped and packaged initiatives that would further weaken and threaten the existence of public education.

Their answers to the challenges facing public schools that they promoted as "reforms" were vouchers, charters and competition from an alternative system of school privatization. As Cox concluded, in its statewide editorializing:

> they [Ohio Republicans] think that if anybody should be credited with changing the rules in a profound way that fosters genuine reform, they have had—and still have—the better changes.[10]

A Line in the Sand

In Ohio in the 1990s and early 2000s, then-Congressman Ted Strickland and other strong supporters of public education had drawn a line in the sand and pledged to build on the good elements of the public system and stop the bashing of schools and teachers that had endured for 15 years under Republican rule.

The attack on public schools and craze for publicly funded private charter schools in Ohio that had started with the experiment with vouchers for education in Cleveland was the capstone of a national phenomenon. It was the peaking of a mindset that had become a gospel in this country in the years of the two Bush, Clinton, and Obama administrations that the public education system was in an incurable crisis and needed to be replaced by schools run like private business, and by private businesses themselves.

However, the championing of public education by the irrepressible Governor Strickland changed that narrative; the people—in all corners of the state—all of a sudden were hearing stories of charter school failures . . . coming straight out of the governor's office.

His message was that, looking soberly at the data, performance of the state's charter schools, far from being a path to academic improvement, had been more like a scandalous failure. Thanks to Ted Strickland, for the first time the Ohio charter movement was being placed on the defensive.

Also for the first time since the introduction of Ohio's first income tax by John Gilligan in the 1970s, a governor was holding out the tantalizing hope that Ohio public schooling would restore the state to the haven it had once been for development and manufacture.

In the two short years following his election, Strickland was making the debate over Ohio's educational future a two-sided rather than one-sided argument and brought hope of a reprieve for a public system that prior to his arrival had seemed to be headed for Death Row.

Death Row

When Ted Strickland took office as governor in 2006, Ohio was ranked nationally as 11th in job layoffs, 48th in new company startups, 3rd in home foreclosures, 2nd in bankruptcies, 50th in job growth, and 44th in Real Gross State Product. In education the state was 46th in equity of school resources, 50th in students per computer, 42nd in schools with unsatisfactory heating, and tuition at public universities was 46 percent higher than the national average.

From 1999 through 2008, the legislature, embarrassed by the Supreme Court's rulings exposing the state's grossly deficient school environments, increased their investment in existing schools and new school structures by 47 percent.

However, the Strickland plan called for funding to increase even more with investment of an additional 45 percent in the decade ahead. Just as importantly for ensuring a strong future for public schools, Strickland's plan of increasing still further the money given to public education would not be compromised or diverted to proliferation of charter schools whose record of student failure, financial and academic mismanagement, and lack of oversight and control were being put under a microscope and held accountable as never before by an American governor.

The handwriting was on the wall when soon after taking office in 2006, Governor Strickland pledged to require that those charters performing significantly worse than the public schools lose their public funding. In doing so, Strickland was riding a tide of realism as some voices in the national media began reporting the real results of America's charter school experiment.

A May 10, 2006, *New York Times* editorial, "Reining in charter schools," cited a study showing that states with charter programs dominated by for-profit education companies have poorer results for those schools in terms of performance and accountability.[11] A July 15, 2006, Times article by Dianne Schemo reported an Education Department study documenting that children in public schools generally performed "as well or better in reading and mathematics than comparable children in private schools."[12]

So it was that revelations of the misreporting of student academic performance and of financial mismanagement by a significant percentage of Ohio charter schools fueled the Strickland pro-public education fire. None of these revelations, or Strickland intention to act on them, however, changed the fact that already 43 percent of the students in the Dayton school district were attending private or charter schools, nor did they enable Strickland to slow down the Ohio choice movement's single-minded goal of breaking up the public school system and privatizing the entire system of the state's schools.

Strickland Upended

On May 11, 2009, as predicted by those who have watched him in Chicago, Duncan wasted no time in announcing in an Associated Press interview the intention to close 1,000 so-called "underperforming" schools in each of the next five years, a total 5,000 schools. With the arrival of Duncan and the Obama administration, the "war" against public education that many had seen coming for more than two decades was declared in the open and now obviously bi-partisan in its political support.

However, accelerating the introduction of a market model into education at this unpropitious time—when the market model had brought down the national and global financial house on people's heads in the U.S. and worldwide—Obama and Duncan could not be assured of smooth sailing. In Ohio Ted Strickland staked his administration on the success or failure of a campaign to target publicly funded education from pre-school through graduate school as the make or break goal for turning around the limping state economy.

Then, as the state encountered record job losses and the emigration of the young working age population in the aftermath of the financial crisis of 2008, a demand for quick fixes put an end to voter tolerance for the Strickland scenario of long-term reconstruction through education. Democratic losses in Ohio as well as nationwide contributed to the squeaker victory of Strickland's job-promising opponent Republican John Kasich who embodied the privatization agenda.

Kasich, a former Contract with America congressman, Fox TV channel host, and managing director of Lehman Brothers, the disgraced and defunct firm, had made the campaign statement of hoping to "break the back" of organized labor in the schools. To that end he did not disappoint; his endorsement of Senate Bill 5 which aimed to do just that by stripping collective bargaining rights from all public employees, not only teachers, lit a fuse in the public sector.

Privatization's Overreach?

Barely a year later following one Ohio governor's exit and another's inauguration, the tide turned again. In October, 2011 Ohioans boomeranged, only this time it was against Governor Kasich, in a landslide vote to reverse the Republican effort to destroy unions in the notorious campaign around Senate Bill 5/Issue 2.

To be certain, even a significant number of Republicans voted against what was largely seen as a major overreach. All told, however, as a defeat for the forces seeking to crush unionization of public employees the callback of Senate Bill 5 was a setback for the virulently and quintessentially anti-union movement for school privatization in the very state in which, with its leading-the-nation percentage of charter schools, it had been making its strongest stand.

It was also a vindication for Ted Strickland, who had quickly put his 2010 election defeat behind him to throw his weight and voice behind the Senate Bill repeal initiative in which voters who had once backed the Democratic Strickland for governor came back to shock the state so close on the heels of his loss.

Another test in Ohio followed soon on the heels of the Issue 2 recall/defeat in the form of H.B. 136 which proposed to extend Ohio's vouchers program from urban areas to the entire state. Slowed by lack of support, this already notorious legislative effort has been called by one Ohio school financial official "The Death of Public Education Bill." In promptly coming out against this new attack on public education, Ted Strickland showed that his retirement from office looks to be anything but a quiet one.

As disenchantment builds, even among its former staunchest champions, with the movement for replacement of public education with for-profit "school choice," Americans will look back at the Profile In Courage of the Governor of Ohio from the first decade of the 21st Century, Ted Strickland, who defied the pro-choice consensus in American political leadership including the President and Secretary of Education from his own party in trying to stuff the genie of education privatization back in the bottle.

Notes

1. Proclamation 8372 of May 4, 2009, National Charter Schools Week, 2009, by the President of the United States of America A Proclamation. See http://edocket.access.gpo.gov/cfr_2010/janqtr/pdf/3CFR8372.pdf
2. Education Sec. Arne Duncan interviewed by Libby Quaid, AP and Michele McNeil, Education Week. Washington, DC Sunday, February 22, 2009.
3. These words delivered in speech at the Ohio Education Association education rally on Ohio State University campus grounds are documented on a video: See DeRolph http://youtu.be/akNWYNMzAnM
4. Ibid.
5. Ibid.
6. Ibid.
7. Sue Taylor's May 6, 2009 letter to President Obama: "This article is unpublished and currently unavailable" according to the Ohio Federation of Teachers website. http://oh.aft.org/index.cfm?action=article&articleID=666f4264-1f83-4d17-a6c8-ae79c4e 0fda9
8. Ibid.
9. See "Editorial: Strickland school commission bad idea Dayton Daily News, Tuesday, May 26, 2009, 12:00 AM and Dennis Willard, "Strickland steals from poor, gives to rich schools," *Akron Beacon-Journal Columbus Bureau.* (Published: March 16, 2009 - 10:26 PM).

10. Ibid.
11. *New York Times* editorial, May 10, 2006.
12. Dianne Schemo, "Public Schools Perform Near Private Ones in Study," *New York Times*, July 15, 2006.

Part III
Neoliberalism: The Ideology of For-profit Public Education

In Chapter 10, "The New Corporate Agenda: Austerity, "Shared" Sacrifice, and Union Busting", Jack Gerson presents a political analysis arguing that the attack on public education is a central feature in the efforts of corporate and financial interests to consolidate and expand control of the American economy. Gerson ties the attacks on public education to the failed U.S. financial system, the injustices of American labor policies, a grossly inequitable tax system, and the ongoing drain on resources by a permanent state of war. He traces how earlier attacks on teachers have been accelerated under the Obama administration, and shows how business interests with bi-partisan political support have shifted the burdens of the bank bailouts away from Wall Street and onto to the public sectors and the backs of public workers. Into this political-economic cauldron, Gerson introduces the leadership of the two national teacher unions, the American Federation of Teachers and the National Education Association. He shows how key union leaders have acquiesced in and even aided the corporate attacks on public education and teachers. In the final section of his analysis, Gerson presents a counter discourse taken up by rank and file teachers and other unions like the California and Wisconsin Nurses Associations. It is a story that has finally caught the attention of the national media. It is a struggle through which teachers and other workers now are aggressively challenging corporate defined economic austerity and the scapegoating of union workers and fighting back to defend the rights of workers and to reorder our larger political economic system for democracy and justice.

In Chapter 11,"Recovering Schools and Classrooms in the Recovery School District", Karen Roth reclaims the highly effective teacher from a narrow behavioristic frame, re-inscribing on teacher education the idea of ethics, identity, doing good deeds, perseverance, and dedication to the craft. Her story is one of teachers developing the knowledge, skills, and dispositions through service learning trips to upside down urban centers such as the New Orleans Public School District (NOPSD). Roth and her service learning team make a real difference in the lives they touch, going beyond 'AYP' or raising test scores. The power of her essay is that the alternative clinical experience, afforded through the service learning experience, can be effective—even amidst privatized spaces—in fostering a broader social space where community might yet flourish and teachers may truly become "highly effective" by reconceptualizing their own profession.

Chapter 12 has co-editor John Duffy describing "Four Hundred Years of Chartering" in the Americas and why the penchant to charter in the 21st century should come as nothing new, no surprise.

In Chapter 13, "Rationalizing Standards, Rationing Opportunities: Neoliberalism and the Paradox of Success in Haitian and U.S. Education" by Baudelaire Ulysse, the author describes further the Neoliberal condition, one wherein the Commercial Club Curriculum having originated in Chicago, has now moved to New Orleans, the White House, and Port Au Prince, Haiti. Haiti and New Orleans share a common ancestry from French dominion, the author notes, and neoliberalism shares some common lineage with neocolonialism. In the forward to this chapter, John Duffy offers a short history and review on just what neoliberalism means to public education . . . and to the public citizenry.

Chapter 10
The New Corporate Agenda: Austerity, "Shared Sacrifice" and Union Busting
Jack Gerson

For nearly three decades, public schools and teacher unions have been battered by a relentless assault financed by corporations and the super-rich. This chapter focuses primarily on the most recent phase of this assault, the severe policy of structural readjustment (austerity) imposed since the near-meltdown of the world financial system and ensuing Great Recession of 2008-9. However, it is crucial to understand the austerity campaign, and the response of labor to it, in the context of the corporate war against public education that began a quarter of a century earlier. Therefore, we begin this chapter with an overview of the corporate war against public education as it has unfolded since 1983.

The War Begins:
"A Nation at Risk" and the Business Roundtable

Berliner & Biddle (1995), Emery & Ohanian (2004), and Bracey (2003) demonstrated convincingly that the current and ongoing corporate war on public education began in earnest with the publication of the "A Nation at Risk" report (1983).[1] "A Nation at Risk" claimed that U.S. public education was declining rapidly relative to other advanced industrial countries, threatening the nation's economy and national security.[2] Emery & Ohanian (2004) show how the ensuing media blitz and lobbying campaign was largely coordinated and funded by the Business Roundtable (BRT).[3] The BRT campaign claimed that veteran teachers, protected by intransigent teacher unions, would not or could not teach basic math and literacy skills. Its proposed remedies were: adopt skill-based, uniform standards; base curricula on these narrow standards; enforce teaching to these standards by frequent administration of multiple choice tests; hold students, teachers, schools accountable based on student test scores (test-based accountability). Emery & Ohanian (2004) demonstrate that much of the No Child Left Behind legislation of 2001 was developed from the BRT's "National

Education Goals" (1989) and "Nine Essential Components of a Successful Education System (1995).[4]

The years of heavily funded propaganda and lobbying from the Business Roundtable paid dividends, as NCLB sailed through Congress with broad bipartisan support in 2001—its main Congressional sponsors were the liberal Democratic Senator Ted Kennedy and the liberal Democratic Representative George Miller—and was signed into law on January 2, 2002 by George W. Bush.

No Child Left Behind

NCLB wrote the Business Roundtable's education agenda into federal law. Among its requirements:

- Schools receiving federal funding must annually administer statewide standardized tests.
- Schools receiving Title I funding that do not make "adequate yearly progress" (AYP) are designated as in need of "Program Improvement" and subject to progressively harsher punitive sanctions:
- Schools that fail to make AYP for three consecutive years must use Title I money to provide third-party after-school tutoring;
- Schools that fail to make AYP for six consecutive years must either close, hire a private company to manage the school, convert to a charter school, or be run directly by the state education department.[5]

NCLB encouraged privatization and commercialization. Its requirement of mandatory testing guaranteed profits for the textbook companies that created the state standards, created the tests based on those standards, and published the textbooks based on the standards and the workbooks that prepared students for the standardized tests they had created. Its punitive sanctions against schools that failed to make AYP guaranteed contracts to test preparation mills that ran the mandatory after-school tutoring programs and to private school management organizations that ran the reorganized schools.

NCLB's AYP requirement was ludicrous. The legislation required that by 2014 every student score at or above grade level! This is Lake Woebegone, where "every child is above average." But what this ludicrous clause did do was to guarantee that there would be a large and growing number of schools subjected to privatization and commercialization as they failed to meet the ridiculous AYP criteria.

Finally, the law restricted local control of public schools by externally imposing punitive sanctions, including bringing in private companies to run low-scoring schools, and by opening the door for the proliferation of charter schools, since charter schools receive public money but are run by private boards.

The Venture Philanthropists

While NCLB was being molded into its final form, several of the wealthiest individuals in the country emerged in leadership of the corporate education reform movement, most prominently: Bill Gates, Eli Broad, the Waltons (Walmart family), and Donald Fisher (the Gap). These venture philanthropists (VPs) brought more money to the education table-outspending the older foundations by more than two to one. The organization and deep pockets of the VPs provided the leverage and the money needed to fully promote the NCLB high stakes testing and privatization mandates:

- School reorganization: between 2000 and 2008, Bill Gates poured $2 billion into breaking thousands of comprehensive high schools into smaller schools (Ravitch, 2010).[6]
- Charter schools: Walton, Fisher, Gates and Broad collectively provided hundreds of millions of dollars to underwrite a huge expansion of charter schools (e.g., between 2002 and 2008, charter school enrollment in Oakland quadrupled from 2,000 to 8,000; charter schools took over New Orleans education; by 2009 74% of New Orleans schools were charter schools; in Houston, Gates funding allowed the KIPP charter chain to open forty schools, multiply enrollment by more than ten-fold, and present itself as an alternative school system; and as this is written, more than half of Detroit public schools are being closed, many slated to be replaced by charter schools). Nationally, charter school enrollment nearly tripled between 2000 and 2010.
- Test-based accountability: The VPs took test-based accountability to a new level. They demanded high returns on their "investments", using student test scores as the unit of measure. Saltman (2009) reports that the Broad Foundation partnered with the U.S. Department of Education on the School Information Partnership and the Data Partnership, providing more than $25 million in funding.[7] The explicit objectives of these projects are to track and identify teacher performance based on whether and how much their students' standardized test scores increase or decrease, and to force out "bad" teachers by reporting results to parents.

In addition, the VPs set out to recruit and train cadre from outside education to take over teaching, school administration, and district management.

- Teachers: Broad and Gates heavily funded Teach for America and the New Teacher Project, providing a reserve army of teacher interns to make those "bad" veteran teachers expendable.
- Site administrators: Broad funded the national New Leaders for New Schools program as well as various local "Principal Leadership Academies". Many of the recruits to these programs had no educational experience other than a two-year stint in Teach for America.
- "Professional" managers: Broad recruited and indoctrinated hundreds of school superintendents and other high-level school district managers, most of them ex-military officers and corporate executives. They were trained in Broad's Urban Superintendents' Academy and Broad Residency

programs to provide the backbone for imposing the "business model for education. At the time of writing, Broad-trained executives lead 21 of the 75 largest school districts, and are in high-level positions in the three largest districts: New York, Los Angeles, and Chicago.[8]

Corporate Reform Agenda Fails

The corporate reform agenda has been a washout. S. Sparks summarizes the National Academy of Science's rigorous study which concluded that high stakes testing has not increased student learning.[9] The National Center on Performance Initiatives' large-scale study of performance-based pay for public school teachers found what others had found before: "merit pay" doesn't work.[10] Studies repeatedly find that charter schools are if anything, outperformed by public schools, a result most recently observed by Stanford University researchers in a multi-state study funded by the Walton Foundation.[11] In several cities, the "professional managers" have been fired or forced to resign after having attempted to steamroll the community, teachers, local school boards, and school/worker unions.[12]

Berliner (2006) provides overwhelming evidence that U.S. student test scores typically rank in the top five on international comparisons; when the comparisons are adjusted for the effect of poverty.[13] There is no question that inner city public education is overall in a woeful state. Indeed, it is the very grim reality that student learning in high-poverty areas is unacceptably low that makes the promises of the corporate reformers so attractive. But, sadly, the corporate reforms have made things worse:

- Kill 'n' drill, teach-to-the-test destroys students' natural curiosity and eagerness to understand. It is a sorting mechanism to find and nurture submissive obedience and to isolate and punish inquiry and rebelliousness. By the same token, it stifles teacher creativity and discourages teacher initiative.
- School closures make already unstable high-poverty communities still more unstable, by eliminating one of the few enduring institutional anchors.
- High teacher turnover adds to the instability. It is worsened by the campaign to weaken due process and replace veteran teachers with two-year-and-out Teach for America recruits.
- Charter schools, because they are exempt from large parts of the protective regulations in state education codes, make students and teachers more susceptible to arbitrary harassment, discipline, and dismissal.[14]

Poverty: The Root of the Problem

In fact, the real barrier to student learning is no mystery. It has been known for decades that socioeconomic status is the best predictor of student achievement. Nearly half a century ago, the Coleman Report (1966) established that "out-of-school" factors—primarily poverty and its consequences—are twice as important as "in-school" factors in predicting academic success.[15] Numerous other researchers have confirmed this. Berliner (2006) provides an excellent survey, going into detail on the debilitating effects on student learning of untreated illness, hunger, homelessness, absence of positive role models, and drug-ridden neighborhoods.[16]

This is not to say that what goes on in school is unimportant. Certainly, we should strive to improve pedagogy, resources, etc. But until this society expends the money and the will to eradicate poverty and overcome its effects—i.e., the effects of class and race—a yawning "achievement gap" will persist. Indeed, poverty negatively impacts "in-school" factors, too: schools in high poverty areas generally have inferior facilities, fewer resources, larger class size, and higher teacher turnover than schools in affluent areas. Sadly, rather than making eradication of poverty their main focus, the billionaires and their allies in both political parties have blamed teachers, teacher unions, and the poor themselves for the failure of education in high-poverty schools. They roll out their agenda beneath the banner of "Don't try to use poverty as an excuse. No excuses. The problems of schools must be solved in the schools. It's not about money."

The fact is that the corporate foundations and billionaire venture philanthropists are instrumental in deciding where and how much capital and associated resources to invest. Specifically, it is they, together with the politicians of both parties over whom they hold so much sway, who decide whether or not to make the investment in social infrastructure—housing, jobs, health care, counseling, nutrition, as well as education—that could dramatically reduce poverty. But they have not made such investments.

Instead, they have dramatically increased their share of wealth and income at the expense of workers and the poor.[17] They have relentlessly sought to burst the dam between public and private education, downsizing, privatizing and wherever possible eliminating or limiting the public's control over their schools. Alongside, and indeed motivating the high stakes testing and test-based accountability has been a relentless drive to increase the share of economic assets of corporations and the super-rich at the expense of working and poor people. Karp (2011) puts this well: What's ultimately at stake is more basic. It's whether the right to a free public education for all children is going to survive as a fundamental democratic promise in our society, and whether the schools and districts needed to provide it are going to survive as public institutions, collectively owned and democratically managed—however imperfectly—by all of us as citizens. Or will they be privatized and commercialized by the corporate interests that increasingly dominate all aspects of our society?[18]

Enter Obama and Duncan

The 2008 elections should have been the salvation of public education. For years, teacher unions and parent organizations had fervently hoped, prayed, and lobbied for the day when there would be a Democratic president and a large Democratic majority in both houses of Congress. But when that day arrived, it was no salvation at all. Barack Obama, despite the rock-star adulation he received in the 2008 campaign, is a proponent of the corporate agenda for education. He advocates uniform standards, test-based accountability, and more charter schools. Obama announced the key planks of his educational policy well in advance of his election. In 2007 and again in 2008, he addressed the National Education Association's Representative Assembly (its national convention), and twice told the delegates of his advocacy for test-based accountability, charter schools, and getting rid of "bad teachers".

For those who hadn't yet gotten the point, Obama's selection of Chicago Public Schools CEO Arne Duncan for the job of U.S. Secretary of Education should have been the clincher. Duncan is closely allied with Eli Broad and Bill Gates.[19] While Duncan was at the helm in Chicago, he focused on closing "failing schools" and firing their teachers, expanding the number of charter schools, and outsourcing services.

In Obama's first major policy address on education, in March 2009, he essentially outlined the corporate agenda for education and called it his policy. The corporate reformers observed and approved. In the words of Tom Vander Ark, former education director of the Gates Foundation:

> But yesterday, Eli [Broad] won. Obama's speech sounded like Eli wrote it. It was about choice and charter schools, human capital and performance pay. It was right on message from pre-school to college. We've never had a Republican president that so clearly articulated a Republican strategy. Only it's the *new* Democrat strategy. It's Eli's strategy. He finally won.[20]

Duncan quickly put Obama's message into practice, announcing that his newly introduced "Race to the Top" funding program would only accept grant applications from states that agreed to loosen restrictions on charter schools and to base teacher evaluations on student standardized test scores. By awarding far fewer grants than there were applicants, Duncan forced states to compete against one another in promoting charter schools and increasing test-based accountability. To compound this, the Gates Foundation was allowed to bias the competition by offering awards of $250,000 to states that would agree to incorporate Gates' eight key criteria in their Race to the Top applications.[21]

It is not an exaggeration to say that under Obama and Duncan, the venture philanthropists dictate education policy. Indeed, the Department of Education's newsletter has said as much. Barkan (2011) cites the following passage from The October 29, 2009 issue of that newsletter, *The Education Innovator*:

> . . . the Department has truly embraced the foundation community by creating a position within the Office of the Secretary for the Director of Philanthropic Engagement. This dedicated role within the Secretary's Office signals to the philanthropic world that the Department is "open for business."[22]

Duncan has indeed fully opened public education to business. He surrounded himself with Broad and Gates veterans as his assistant secretary, assistant deputy secretary, chief of staff, and general counsel. Today, the corporate agenda proceeds in full force: test-based accountability is expanding, as more and more cities and states adopt pay-for-performance, often with union support.

Privatization and commercialization is expanding so rapidly that it is hard to keep tabs on it. For example, on June 2, 2011, a new consortium headed by retired tennis star Andre Agassi, former Los Angeles Mayor (and Eli Broad ally) Richard Riordan, and Los Angeles investment bankers announced that they were launching a for-profit investment fund to finance $750 million in new charter school construction.[23] The very next day, the *Financial Times* reported that "Shares in private education companies soared after the U.S. Department of Education put forward guidelines for the industry that were less strict than had been expected."[24] And one week later, New Jersey Governor Chris Christie announced a program that will allow private companies to run public schools in some of the state's "underperforming" school districts.

Bad as this has been, it's now getting worse. The Obama/Duncan/Gates policy does not merely continue the overall thrust of the corporate reform agenda. Rather, it extends that policy, using the economic turmoil in the aftermath of the financial panic of 2008 as both the reason to impose harsh austerity cuts to public services and public workers and as an excuse to push the corporate reform agenda harder and demand more privatization, more charter schools, more test-based accountability, more victimization of veteran teachers, and more disenfranchisement of the public as more school systems, and even whole communities, are put under state or private management.

Austerity

Two years ago, amid the near-meltdown of the world financial system following the collapse of the housing bubble, it was evident that the big banks and Wall Street brokerages were responsible for the crisis. Yet over the past three years, the financial industry has managed to transform its huge private debt into public debt. Now Wall Street, politicians, and the media insist that public workers and public services caused this debt, and that there's just no alternative to harsh austerity cuts to public programs and to the jobs, wages, and benefits of public workers.

Overall, the global financial services industry was handed a bailout exceeding $20 trillion.[25] The U.S. government alone disbursed nearly $14 trillion of that amount: $4.7 trillion in loans, $9.2 trillion in loan guarantees.[26] Of the $4.7 trillion in outright loans, nearly $2 trillion has not been repaid. Two trillion dollars just happens to be the estimated cumulative total of all U.S state debt and municipal debts.[27] No wonder McNally (2010) says that Wall Street has taken its private debt and transformed it into public debt:

> In short, the bad bank debt that triggered the crisis in 2008 never went away . . . it was simply shifted on to governments. Private debt became public debt. And as the dimensions of that metamorphosis became apparent in 2010, the bank crisis morphed into a sovereign debt crisis. Put differently, the economic crisis of 2008-9 did not really end. It simply changed form. It *mutated*. With that mutation, the focus of ruling classes shifted toward a war against public services. Concerned to rein in government debts, they announced an age of austerity—of huge cuts to pensions, education budgets, social welfare

programs, public sector wages, and jobs. In doing so, they effectively declared that working people and the poor would pay the cost of the global bank bailout.[28]

This has had a devastating effect on state and municipal budgets, which were already under severe stress from the Iraq and Afghan wars' siphoning of federal money away from public services[29] and from changes to federal and state tax policies since the late 1970s that have sharply decreased taxes on corporations, capital gains, and the highest incomes.[30] State budget deficits now total in excess of $200 billion (excluding pension liabilities), and states have responded by making across-the-board cuts to public programs. County and city programs can't compensate for the cuts to state programs, because cuts in state funding and decreased tax revenue have triggered sweeping cuts in local programs. The pressure for more punishing cuts to local programs continues to increase: nationally, more than 100 cities are on the verge of declaring bankruptcy.

The implications for education and the achievement gap have been profound. Rather than bolstering programs aimed at mitigating poverty, the austerity cuts fall disproportionately on programs that deliver services to high-poverty communities. Thus, the crucial "out-of-school" factors are stacked even more against children in low-income families. To compound this, the "in-school" factors are being similarly affected. Thus, more than 100,000 teachers have been laid off nationally. In spring 2011, 19,000 California teachers and every teacher in Detroit were given layoff notices.

Arne Duncan and Bill Gates see this ongoing catastrophe for poor and working people as an opportunity to better pursue their education reform agenda. On November 17, 2011, Duncan, speaking at the American Enterprise Institute (a prominent Washington free market think tank), announced "The New Normal" is "Do More With Less".[31] Duncan told his audience that schools and teachers had better get used to doing more with less, because funds for public education had dried up and budget cuts were here to stay. Duncan said this provided an "opportunity for dramatic improvements in educational productivity" by introducing "smart" reforms like merit pay, larger class size, and deferring school maintenance and new school construction.[32]

Two days later, Gates told the Council of Chief State School Officers that reduced funding for public education was permanent. Gates recommended saving money by eliminating teacher seniority and changing teacher compensation—that is, by forcing out higher-paid veteran teachers and adopting merit pay schemes to pay "effective teachers" more while cutting average compensation. Like Duncan, Gates advocated increasing class size (he urged an average increase of 4 students per class), and paying "effective teachers" extra to teach the larger classes. (Gates thinks effective teachers can handle much larger classes. But what would actually happen is that most would rapidly become far less effective.) In addition, Gates urged the state school chiefs to rapidly align all instruction and testing with the Obama Administration's new "common core" standards, arguing that this would improve teaching and achievement by allowing more accurate and sweeping use of standardized test data.[33]

The approach advocated by Duncan and Gates sounds chillingly like what Klein (2007) called "disaster capitalism". Klein described how catastrophic events have been used repeatedly as a pretext for imposing harsh austerity programs prepared in advance of the disaster, citing, among others, New Orleans after Hurricane Katrina and Chile after Pinochet's coup.[34] Duncan and Gates see the huge public deficits induced by the $14 trillion Wall Street bailout and the multi-trillion dollar war spending as their "opportunity" to fast track large parts of the program they have been advocating all along: to impose more standards, more test-based accountability based on those standards, more cuts in pensions and health benefits, and to weaken teacher unions by getting rid of seniority and forcing out veteran teachers.

In reality, eliminating or cutting essential public services exacerbates poverty. Thus, "do more with less" austerity will inevitably make the failure of education in the inner city much worse for many more. There is more hunger, more homelessness, and more untreated illnesses. There are fewer libraries, fewer youth programs, and fewer jobs.

"Do more with less" sounds an awful lot like Senator Jim DeMint's recent comment about withdrawing government funding from National Public Radio: "It's about two simple facts. We can't afford it, and they don't need it".[35] Perhaps for this reason, a less offensive rationale is frequently used. We are told, "there is no alternative" to "shared sacrifice". Thus, Democrats and Republicans alike, in states across the country, insist that there is no alternative to the shared sacrifice of cuts to public programs and concessions on pensions, health benefits, and (often) compensation.

This is Barack Obama's justification for a multi-year wage freeze for federal workers. It is the rationale of New York Democratic governor Andrew Cuomo and of California Democratic governor Jerry Brown for budgets that cut back on medical care and welfare for the poor, home services for the disabled, assistance for seniors, and funding for education. It is the excuse given by Wisconsin Republican governor Scott Walker for program cuts, for economic concessions from state workers, and for effectively eliminating collective bargaining for state worker unions (and it's also the excuse given by Wisconsin Democrats for agreeing that the program cuts and economic concessions are essential.) It is the reason given by Michigan Democrat and then-governor Jennifer Grantholm for giving Robert Bobb dictatorial power over Detroit schools, the reason given by Bobb for closing down more than half of the city's schools and increasing class size to over 60, and by Michigan's Republican governor Rick Snyder for pushing through legislation allowing the state to put cities in receivership and thus disenfranchise the public from control of their community (this is happening to the city of Benton Harbor).

In fact, the Democrats have a dual slogan: "there is no alternative to deep program cuts and economic concessions from public workers, unions, and pensions—but the Republicans' proposal is even worse than ours." Thus, in California, Jerry Brown's budget calls for $12.5 billion in cuts and an equal amount from extending for *another five years* a "temporary" package of regressive taxes adopted under his predecessor (Republican Arnold

Schwarzenegger), while the state's Republicans propose to get the entire $25 billion from cuts. Along these same lines, Wisconsin Democrats go along with Republican Walker's proposals for economic cuts and concessions, but balk at his union-busting proposals. In state after state, variants of this scenario are being played out (Indiana, Ohio, Tennessee, Idaho, and Oklahoma, to name a few) as Democrats advocate program cuts and wage and benefit concessions while Republicans push for more onerous cuts and stripping unions of collective bargaining and job protections.

Ominously, in several states the Democrats are beginning to initiate union-busting legislation—just slightly less onerous than the Republican proposals. In liberal Massachusetts, the Democratic majority in the state assembly voted to restrict health care bargaining rights for public workers. In Connecticut Democratic leaders in the state legislature supported a bill that would strip college faculty of bargaining rights by reclassifying them as managers. In Illinois the Democratic-dominated state legislature proposed and adopted legislation restricting teachers' bargaining rights, seniority and job security, and right to strike.

We are not Broke

Despite the ubiquitous calls for shared sacrifice, it is hardly a secret that not everyone is sacrificing. Certainly not the "financial services industry" (aka Wall Street and the big banks) whose pre-tax profits are now 60% higher than they were before the onset of the 2008-9 Great Recession (which hasn't stopped them from holding onto $2 trillion of the bailout loans). Not the rich, as Obama and Congress extended the Bush tax cuts that lower taxes for the wealthiest 2% and exempt estates worth as much as $5 million from inheritance tax.

Indeed, by 3rd quarter 2010 corporate profits soared to an all-time high of $1.7 trillion (Moody, p. 14). Corporations are virtually choking on the dough that's rolling in at record rates. "There is a cash crisis in America", Jason Zweig observes in the May 29, 2011Wall Street Journal, "although it comes not from a shortage of the stuff, but from a surplus." Zweig (2011) explains:

> In the first quarter, the five companies with the greatest cash hoards—Microsoft, Cisco Systems, Google, Apple, and Johnson & Johnson—added $15 billion in cash and marketable securities to their balance sheets. Microsoft alone packed away roughly $9 billion, or $100 million a day. All told, the companies in the Standard & Poor's 500-stock index are sitting on more than $960 billion in cash, a record . . . Cash is piling up faster than most industrial giants can possibly find a prudent use for it.[36]

Even before the 2008-9 recession, public workers' real wages were falling. Thus, between 2000 and 2006 teachers' salaries fell 3% behind inflation (Moody, p.14). Indeed, as Lawrence Mishel (2011) shows in an Economic Policy Institute briefing paper, the sacrifices have been borne entirely by working and poor people:

Business income [profits] is now 21.7% above the level reached before the recession. Yet the total compensation paid to workers in the corporate sector remains 5.7% below pre-recession levels, reflecting the reduced employment levels and hours worked in the sector.[37]

So although profits are up, wages are down and unemployment is higher. And still, we are told that more "shared sacrifice" by working and poor people is mandatory:

Quite remarkably, the category of spending that has received the most attention (and been targeted for cuts) has been non-security, appropriated domestic funding—frequently called discretionary spending. These programs include all federal spending on transportation, education, health research, the environment, parks, energy, and other domestic matters . . . The current spending in these areas is historically low . . . Between 1980 and 2010, the per person spending on domestic discretionary programs actually fell by $195 . . . *This is not an area of spending that has been breaking the budget.*[38]

The implication should be obvious: The austerity cuts are not inevitable. They result from priorities and policies that favor corporate profit and personal wealth at the expense of essential public services, jobs, and income for the working class. Mishel concludes:

There is an old joke about the Lone Ranger, who turned to Tonto and said, "We're surrounded by Indians," and Tonto responds, "What do you mean by 'we,' kimosabe?" The same logic applies to policymakers who claim that "we're broke." It matters who is included in "we" . . . so are we broke? Only if we choose to be.[39]

Governments are broke because of the priorities they have pursued: the $14 trillion Wall Street bailout and consequent transformation of trillions of dollars of private debt into public debt, the huge and wasteful war budget, and the inverted tax policies that over the past 30 years have grossly lowered taxes on corporate and private wealth.

How has Labor Responded?

For several years, demonization of teacher unions has been the leading edge of the private sector's effort to increase its profitability at the expense of the public sector. Such scapegoating was under way well before 2008, although it has qualitatively increased since the onset of the Great Recession. Since education in the inner city has failed so many for so long, it has been crucial that those responsible for the failure—the corporations and politicians who decide on the priorities of how capital and resources are allocated—find a scapegoat for their failed policies. Teachers, entrusted with the education and well being of the nation's children, are in an especially sensitive and vulnerable position.

Teacher unions are potentially an enormous obstacle to the campaign against public workers and public programs. Test-based accountability requires teachers to surrender academic freedom and control of how to teach in favor of teaching to the test. Performance pay requires teacher unions to abandon their historic opposition to merit pay. Polices that facilitate dismissal of veteran teachers require teacher unions to agree to weaken due process and abandon seniority.

Consequently, obtaining the acquiescence of teacher unions and/or eliminating their ability to resist is now a top priority of the Gates Foundation and of Arne Duncan's education department, who campaign to eliminate seniority and due process rights for teachers at the lowest-scoring 10% of U.S. public schools. The corporate reformers, with their control of the mass media and heavily funded lobbying, have at least partially succeeded in convincing the public that "bad teachers" protected by powerful teachers unions are largely responsible for the "achievement gap" in test results between low-scoring and high-scoring schools.

Teacher unions have the size and the resources to organize an imposing campaign in defense of public education. More than half of all organized public sector workers belong to teacher unions—the 3.2-million member National Education Association (NEA) and the 1.5-million member American Federation of Teachers (AFT). The NEA and AFT have deep war chests and the demonstrated ability to mobilize their members to campaign and lobby. Finally, many parents and other community members still respect and support their children's teachers.

Teacher Unions: From Compromise to Retreat

Unfortunately, under relentless pressure from the bottomless bankrolls of the billionaire venture philanthropists, teacher unions have given ground. Their concessions have turned to full-scale retreat since the financial collapse and especially since Obama took office in 2009. AFT and NEA have markedly weakened or abandoned their historic opposition to pay-for-performance and test-based accountability through a series of agreements that use student test scores as a basis for teacher pay, teacher evaluations, and teacher promotion and firing.

This has been especially true of the AFT. AFT president Randi Weingarten has negotiated a series of contracts that weaken due process and eliminate seniority protection in "low-performing" schools. This accepts test-based accountability, since schools are designated as "low-performing" based on student scores on standardized tests. In fact, Weingarten has explicitly agreed to performance-based pay and evaluations in several agreements she negotiated since fall 2007.

Randi Weingarten (AFT) and Dennis Van Roekel (NEA)

In October 2007, Weingarten (at the time president of AFT's New York affiliate, the United Federation of Teachers) agreed to a pay-for-performance scheme that awarded bonus pay based on student test scores, with funding provided by Eli Broad. Many teacher unionists expressed shock and dismay at Weingarten's about-face on AFT's longstanding opposition to "merit pay". But Weingarten had only just begun.

In November 2009, Weingarten, by then president of AFT, helped broker a contract in New Haven, Connecticut that made major concessions on pay-for-performance, test-based accountability, and charter schools. The contract includes provisions for basing pay bonuses, evaluations and promotions on student test scores. The union agreed that schools with high-test scores could be given some autonomy, while schools with low-test scores could be converted to charter schools. Randi Weingarten hailed the agreement: "I rarely call something a model or a template for something else, but this is both."[40]

It didn't take long for Weingarten to improve upon her "model" and enhance her "template". In December 2009, Weingarten collaborated with Detroit's state-appointed school boss, Robert Bobb, on a contract that included a two-year wage freeze (and a one percent raise in year three), pay-for-performance, weakened seniority rights, and forced loans from teachers to the state via $250 per paycheck deductions *to be returned only when the teacher is no longer employed by Detroit public schools*. This contract was so unpopular that in March 2010 an opposition coalition swept all twenty Detroit Federation of Teachers (DFT) delegate positions to the 2010 AFT national convention. Weingarten hailed the contract as "historic".

Shortly thereafter, in a January 2010 speech to the National Press Club, Weingarten announced plans to weaken due process protection. Weingarten told the audience, "We recognize that too often due process becomes glacial process. We intend to change that." In the same speech, Weingarten reiterated her commitment to basing teacher pay and evaluations "in part" on student test scores.[41]

In May 2010, Weingarten reached agreement with notorious teacher-basher Michelle Rhee on a contract for Washington DC teachers. That contract includes a particularly insidious pay-for-performance clause that allows "better" teachers to trade job security for higher pay.

Also in 2010, Weingarten facilitated similar agreements in Pittsburgh, Pennsylvania and Hillsborough County, Florida (Tampa). In Hillsborough County, the union agreed to allow the firing of the "lowest-performing" five percent of teachers to be fired solely on the basis of their students' test scores. This agreement was instrumental in Hillsborough County winning a $100 million grant from the Gates Foundation (part of Gates' $335 million "teacher effectiveness" initiative). When the Florida legislature passed a bill making dismissal of "low-performing" teachers mandatory statewide, Hillsborough County was explicitly exempted because it had already agreed to such measures. Hillsborough was the only school district so exempted.

In July 2010, Bill Gates was the keynote speaker at the AFT national convention, held in his hometown, Seattle. Gates told the delegates that teachers are the most important factor in student achievement, and therefore it is critical to focus on how to improve "teacher effectiveness". Gates explained that his teacher effectiveness project would be videotaping thousands of teachers to better analyze teaching. This is a nice way of saying, "We intend to slice and dice you, develops a set of metrics on which to score and rank you, and then harass and fire the bad (i.e., low-ranked) teachers." (Gates neglected to explain how thousands of videos could possibly be thus micro-assessed, and by whom. In the end, it turned out that untrained contractors would assess them.)

Nevertheless, Weingarten hailed Gates' initiative and soon signed on to it. Her enthusiasm may have been stimulated by the more than $3 million in grants that the Gates Foundation awarded the AFT shortly before the convention.

NEA leadership has been more reluctant than Weingarten to formally commit to test-based accountability, and it has been far more hesitant to openly abandon due process protection. However, its opposition has been passive, when not just muted.

During the Bush administration, despite the fact that NCLB was adopted with overwhelming bipartisan support, NEA leaders insisted that the only way out of the NCLB nightmare was to elect a Democratic President and a Democratic Congress. Then, the November 2008 elections put in office a Democratic president and an overwhelmingly Democratic Congress. But NEA ought to have known in advance of the elections that Barack Obama wasn't going to be the solution.

When candidate Obama told the 2008 NEA national convention that he supported merit pay, getting rid of "bad teachers", and more charter schools, his remarks barely made a dent in the huge and orchestrated elect-Obama pep rally on the convention floor. Then-NEA president Reg Weaver had warmed up the 10,000 delegates for Obama's speech by leading chants of "O! O! O!" from the podium. A few delegates booed Obama's remarks (that, after all, was what Obama wanted—he was "getting tough" with teacher unions), and then the delegates resumed the pep rally, with groups of teachers snake dancing through the aisles in t-shirts announcing NEA's support for Obama's election.

The next morning, I walked into the California caucus to hear California Teachers Association (CTA) president David Sanchez and executive director Caroline Doggett criticize Obama's speech. They told the delegates that Obama and his advisers were taking California for granted and were unresponsive to the point of being insulting. Sanchez and Doggett emphasized that Obama's education policies were at odds with NEA's opposition to merit pay. The CTA leadership threatened to pull out all stops to pressure Obama—but in the same breath pledged that CTA's support for Obama in the presidential race was unconditional, because "there is just no alternative".

CTA's disgruntlement with Obama did not go very far. For them, as for NEA, the Democrats are the only show in town. Back home in California, CTA has gone out of its way to accommodate its business allies in the California Education Coalition. For example, in the spring of 2008, when pressed to explain why they did not campaign to close a notorious tax loophole that essentially freezes property taxes for large California corporations far below their assessed values, CTA staff and leadership explained that if CTA campaigned to eliminate the loophole, then big business would heavily fund a campaign to eliminate dues check off. (This exchange took place at an expanded meeting of CTA State Council's Financing Public Education committee in Spring 2008. I was there, as a member of that committee and a State Council delegate from Oakland.)

Thus, intimidated from campaigning to raise adequate funding by increasing taxes on corporate wealth, months before the housing bubble burst CTA was already reduced to supporting "shared sacrifice". They settled for vigorously lobbying in support of a proposal by Democratic state legislators to cut the state budget by "only" $1.7 billion from K-12 education and $5 billion overall. (Only six months earlier, CTA had insisted that any cuts would be unacceptably harmful to public education. They were right.)

Fast forward to April 2010. We have a Democratic President. We have a Democratic Congress. But Barack Obama, working through Arne Duncan, has delivered what he had promised in 2008: charters, competition, standards, and test-based accountability. NEA's Van Roekel leadership stood on the sidelines, applauded politely, and even praised these programs that their organization opposed on paper:

- In April 2010 Duncan announced that Delaware and Tennessee were the lucky winners of first round Race to the Top competition. Despite NEA's opposition to RTTT, Van Roekel's press release said "NEA applauds selection of Race to the Top Winners: Department of Education sends clear message that collaboration of all stakeholders is key."[42] However, the awards were for teachers collaborating with administration around pay-for-performance and test-based evaluation. Such collaboration is not a solution. It is a big part of the problem.

- Two months later, at the 2010 NEA convention in New Orleans, Van Roekel was on the hot seat because of his ongoing praise for Obama and Duncan. Van Roekel had been strongly criticized by local and state leaders in preconvention gatherings. So in his opening remarks to the convention, the preternaturally passive and meek-sounding Van Roekel made an effort at a fire-and-brimstone denunciation of the administration's policies, calling it "the worst environment for teachers in his memory". He blasted Obama for his support of pay-for-performance and charter schools. He acknowledged that the Obama administration had put the needs of banks ahead of the needs of public education. As a delegate to the convention, I listened for the disclaimer that had to be coming. Sure enough, Van Roekel devoted the last several minutes of his speech to insisting that, bad as their policies were, "there is just no alternative to supporting the Democrats".

- On July 27, three weeks after the NEA convention, Duncan announced RTTT Phase 2 winners. Van Roekel applauded again.[43] Duncan spoke of a "quiet revolution" and said his funding programs have "unleashed an avalanche of pent-up education reform activity at the state and local level."[44] Commenting on the speech, Van Roekel said that "NEA members have been at the forefront of the 'quiet revolution' taking place in the nation's public schools for a long time" and commended the secretary "for urging so-called reformers to stop blaming educators for everything that ails public education."[45] However, the text of Duncan's speech makes clear what he meant by "quiet revolution": "I was surprised to learn that some states had laws prohibiting the use of student achievement in teacher evaluation. Because of Race to the Top, those laws are gone." Duncan's speech also effusively praised charter schools.

Thus, it should come as no shock that in October 2010, Van Roekel, Weingarten and Duncan announced a joint call for a national education reform conference on labor-management collaboration. But as fate would have it, that conference convened four months later, just as mass protests against austerity erupted in Madison, Wisconsin.

Wisconsin: February-March 2011

The events in Madison caught everyone flatfooted—labor leaders, politicians, and even the participants themselves. They began when the American Federation of State, County, and Municipal Employees (AFSCME), in conjunction with the Wisconsin NEA and AFT affiliates, called for a February 15 day of lobbying against Republican governor Scott Walker's proposed austerity legislation. Walker's proposal called for severe program cuts, an 8% wage cut for Wisconsin public workers, and three provisions aimed at breaking the state's public employee unions: eliminating dues check off, imposing annual recertification votes, and virtually eliminating collective bargaining.

But February 15 went far beyond what the labor leadership had anticipated. As two active participants wrote recently,

> Union leadership was forced to follow its rank and file into mass protest, as the vivacity of the popular movement made their lobbying day appear not only conservative but absurd.[46]

In the days that followed, tens of thousands poured into Madison. Madison high school students staged mass walkouts and marches from their schools to the capitol building. Within a week, thousands packed into the capitol by day and hundreds occupied the capitol building at night. The day of lobbying had snowballed into a true mass movement.

Although Walker had created the budget deficit by handing out $140 million in corporate tax breaks, and although Wisconsin state workers hadn't had a raise in three years, within two days labor leaders agreed to agree to all of Walker's economic demands, including the 8% wage cut. In effect, they threw in the towel. But Walker threw it back out.

In short, Wisconsin's labor leaders did not break from "shared sacrifice". Despite the massive outpouring of support from all corners of the state, they did not budge from this position. When the National Nurses Association and others organized a march of 10,000 in an attempt to launch a "No Cuts, No Concessions" movement, the labor leadership discouraged participation and expressed its disapproval.

Caught off-guard by the size and power of the mass protests which seemed to come from out of nowhere, it took the top labor leaders weeks to corral the movement and lead it off the streets. They finally accomplished this with a dual strategy: first, stick to "shared sacrifice" and continue to accept all of Walker's economic cuts; second, urge protesters to focus their energy on gathering signatures calling for elections to recall Republican legislators and replace them with Democrats. Here we see a major reason for the labor bureaucrats' insistence on capitulating on making all the economic concessions: the Democrats were, naturally, all in agreement with the need for "shared sacrifice", and labor continues to pin all its hopes on the Democrats.

By the time I visited Madison at the end of March, petitioning was in full swing. The movement was off the streets. Walker's legislation had passed.

Nevertheless, fourteen Democratic legislators who blocked the legislation for three weeks by fleeing to Illinois were considered heroes. Without doubt, they had shown some courage. But certainly, their backbones had been stiffened by the movement's strength. And they, like the labor leaders, never budged from their support for shared sacrifice.

California: The May 2011 Week of Action

On the evening of Monday, May 9, 68 Bay Area college students, public school teachers, and their supporters, chanting "Tax the Rich! That will fix the deficit!", were arrested for occupying and refusing to leave the Rotunda of the State Capitol building in Sacramento, California. Although this happened on the first day of a "Week of Action" called by the California Teachers Association (CTA) to protest cuts to state funding for K-12 education, CTA leadership walked away from the occupiers and pulled members out of the Rotunda, saying that the protesters were "not on message". Yet three days later, CTA president David Sanchez and several other CTA leaders were arrested for sitting in at the offices of Republican state legislature leaders Robert Dutton and Connie Conway. In the words of CTA's press release, "CTA members refuse to leave capitol and demand passage of tax extensions to keep deeper cuts away from schools, colleges and essential public services."

Last year, California labor unions contributed $20 million to Jerry Brown's gubernatorial campaign. CTA was one of the biggest contributors. However, as soon as Brown was elected, he started talking up the need for shared sacrifice. Brown has proposed an austerity budget that includes about $12 billion in cuts to essential public programs (($1.7 billion from medical care for the poor; $1.5 billion from welfare, $1.4 billion from higher education; cut hundreds of millions from programs for the disabled, for home assistance for the elderly, etc.) and an equal amount from extending regressive taxes set to expire this year (among them increases to state sales tax, vehicle license fees, and a decrease in tax deductions for dependents). Brown's cuts have already been approved by the legislature, but Republicans are blocking extension of the regressive taxes. So the argument in Sacramento has been between Brown—who wants to extend Schwarzenegger's soak-the-poor taxes for another five years—and the Republicans—who call for more program cuts instead of more taxes. Two rotten choices. But CTA leadership stridently demands immediate approval of Brown's tax package. That was why they sat-in at the offices of Republicans Dutton and Conway on Thursday. They tried to break up the Monday sit-in because its message was "tax the rich", not "pass the tax extensions" (i.e., "tax the poor").

However, in California the falseness of the "shared sacrifice" slogan is particularly apparent. The state is home to 95 billionaires. The highest-earning 1% of Californians have an average gross annual income of $1.8 million, yet the state's income tax rate is nearly 2% lower than it was five years ago. California is the only oil-producing state without an oil extraction tax. More than half of all profitable California companies pay no state income tax. And this just scratches the surface of the state's inequity and of its inverted tax structure.

In fact, the Brown/Sanchez call for "shared sacrifice" has been so hollow that even many long-time supporters of the CTA leadership (and of the Democrats) have bridled. At CTA's early April state council meeting, the 800 delegates forced the leadership to revise their plans for the May "Week of Action". The call that emerged from this meeting added support for a Capitol occupation and for "long term" progressive taxation in addition to the CTA leadership's "short term" solution of extending regressive taxes.

CTA leadership never had any intention of a massive mobilization to Sacramento, leave aside a weeklong occupation. CTA has over 300,000 members. It has hundreds of paid staffers. CTA State Council alone has 800 members. CTA leadership could have turned out thousands to Sacramento without even trying. But that wasn't their plan. Their plan was to keep everything small, mild, and most of all under their control. Had thousands shown up on Monday, the Rotunda occupation might have turned into a sustained occupation, and the calls for "Tax the Rich" might have grown in substance and appeal. Things might have gotten out of hand. And so there were well under two hundred at the leadership's Monday noontime "mass rally", where the speeches were all about supporting Brown and his regressive taxes.

The leadership's attempt to squash the Monday occupation and their late-week "on-message" tame action emphasized the same message: unambiguous support for Brown's budget and total emphasis on targeting the Republicans for blocking the regressive tax extensions. CTA leadership's focus was strictly on the "short term".

But Brown's proposal is for a five-year extension of the regressive taxes. If five years is short term, what is long term? Furthermore, vague calls for "long-term" progressive taxation are already congealing into proposals for modest increases to high-end income taxes and equally modest adjustments to corporate taxes.

The fact is, CTA leadership's short-term and long-term strategies are identical. They are to co-opt dissent and channel it into the Democrats; provide massive funding for Brown and Democratic politicians; phone-bank for Democratic candidates; usher incipient mass movements off the streets and into lobbying, phone banking, fundraising, etc. And the Democrats' strategy—short-term, long-term, and in-between-term—can be summarized in one word: austerity.

We have seen that this is more than just a California strategy.

Why Won't They Fight?

In May 2011, in a major policy shift, NEA's Board of Directors announced that they would propose that the 2011 NEA convention recommend the use of "valid, reliable, high-quality standardized tests" of student learning for evaluating teachers, in combination with multiple other measures.[47] At nearly the same time, the New York City Department of Education announced it will substantially increase student testing by introducing a new series of tests to be taken by students but whose sole purpose will be to grade teachers, not students.[48]

NEA decided to throw in the towel on opposition to test-based evaluation, and New York City chose to qualitatively expand its test-based accountability, just when a blue ribbon panel appointed by the prestigious National Academy of Sciences determined that nearly a decade of test-based accountability has not improved student achievement and has encouraged gaming the tests.[49] This confirmed what was already well known to the NEA and AFT leaderships. Why then have they chosen to abandon their historic opposition to merit pay and test-based evaluations? Why, for that matter, has AFT abandoned due process and seniority protections for teachers in low-performing schools (who need it the most)?

They've done this for the same reason that the labor leadership has signed onto "shared sacrifice" and voluntarily agrees to make major economic concessions. They know "shared sacrifice" means sacrifice by workers and the poor, not corporations and the rich, just as Van Roekel knows over testing is harmful and just as Weingarten knows all teachers need due process protection. But they don't believe they can fight and win.

Throughout the postwar period, most of organized labor has had a strategy of relying exclusively on Democratic Party politicians. The "labor movement" has become a combination of ad agency, lobbyist and fundraiser for the Democrats. But the Democrats are not a party of labor. They overwhelmingly represent corporate interests—and this has been increasingly so over the past several decades.

Indeed, it is evident that the Democrats, with only a few exceptions, are convinced that the big banks really are "too big to fail"—i.e., that the alternative to the present financial system is chaos. This locks them into the priorities of bailing out the banks, and more generally of sustaining corporate profitability, and the labor leadership is locked right in with them. Thus, when the economy turns down and banks and corporations feel the squeeze, Democrats and Republicans agree that austerity and sacrifice are needed to right the economy (read: bail out the banks, restore corporate profits). That's why for the past three years the argument between Democrats and Republicans has been over the pace and scope of austerity cuts; they both agree on their necessity. Likewise, there has been broad bipartisan support for the war machine budget—and when the chips are down, the labor leadership is in lockstep here as well.

As long as there is no mass pressure from labor and/or other social forces to do otherwise, there will be no alternative. And for decades, there was no such pressure. To the leadership, austerity is the only show in town. Or, as Gore Vidal told Bill Maher, this country has one political party with two right wings.

What Next?

Terence Yancey, a San Francisco State University student who was among the 68 arrested in the Rotunda on May 9, poignantly summarized where things stand and the challenge before us:

> Instead of using the opportunity to fight for what education in California should be, the CTA decided to lobby for the governor's proposed extension of a series of regressive taxes that disproportionately impact poor and working class Californians. While this plan would stop further cuts to education, at least for the next year, it does nothing to restore the billions of dollars that have already been cut from public education, not to mention the many vital social services children and college students rely on. Further cuts to education would be devastating, but the cuts that have previously been made are already devastating the state.
>
> The CTA chose to focus on four Republican legislators, but the problems facing education in California are much bigger and much more complex than a handful of legislators. The CTA also failed, more accurately they did not attempt, to build the broad coalition necessary to deal with such a critical issue. They played right into the divide-and-conquer strategy Brown has used to try and divide K-12 and higher education.
>
> If this division is successful, both groups will fail. What is most important to remember, though, is that an entire generation of young Californians are on the verge of losing access to the opportunities their parents and grandparents, and that many dedicated people fought and gave their lives for during the early part of the 20th century, and during the late 1950's and 1960's. All sectors of the state's population need to come together to do everything in their power to reverse this.
>
> Anything less is a betrayal of California's youth.[50]

Yancey's comments apply equally to the rest of the country. The austerity attacks will deepen . . . unless working and poor people, within and without the unions, are able to build a mass and united response. But there is hope. Many of the young people and the veteran unionists who formed the backbone of the mass movement in Wisconsin will have learned volumes from their struggle. They will be back. The same applies to many of those who participated in the 2009-10 movement against budget cuts in California, and to many of the hundreds of thousands who took to the streets to demand full rights for immigrants on May Day, 2006.

Indeed, there are signs that a national movement to reverse social priorities and attack austerity at its roots may be stirring. The $14 trillion Wall Street bailout, with its transfer of private debt onto the backs of the public and the consequent "shared sacrifice" austerity attacks, did not take place without leaving deep tracks. Just beneath the surface, there is bitterness and anger at the Great Rip off and the foreclosures, evictions, unemployment, and shredding of social services that followed in its wake. Over the past several months, across the country there have been more and increasingly larger demonstrations demanding restitution from the banks, ending foreclosures and rescinding the cuts and layoffs. This movement is still embryonic, but it is alive and it is growing.

Here's an example close to my home and heart: On Thursday May 12, the same day that CTA leaders staged their pro-Jerry Brown protest at the Sacramento Republican leaders' offices, several hundred Oakland teachers, college students, and community supporters staged a two-hour militant protest outside Wells Fargo Bank's downtown Oakland branch. Inside the branch, I and six other Oakland teachers refused to leave and were arrested for trespassing. The protesters chanted "Bail Out Schools and Services, Not Banks", "End Foreclosures", and "Jail the Real Criminals". Rather than dispersing after the arrests, the protesters marched a quarter of a mile to City Hall to protest the closure of approximately half of Oakland's libraries.

The following week, in Ohio, close to one thousand demonstrators crossed a moat to confront JP Morgan Chase management at the company's annual shareholders meeting. Similar demonstrations have been organized in New York, Chicago, Los Angeles, Seattle, and other cities across the country.

In late May, Wells Fargo agreed to meet with representatives from the Oakland teachers' union and from anti-home foreclosure organizations. At the meeting, Wells Fargo's Regional President for the greater Oakland area categorically refused the demands that his bank take the lead in getting the financial sector to adequately fund education and end foreclosures. Responding to the demand for education funding, he said, "If we were to do that for Oakland, we would have to do it for every other school district. We won't take responsibility for the public debt." But, as was pointed out at that meeting, the bank bailout transformed trillions of their debt into public debt. They are responsible for the public debt, and awareness of that fact is continuing to grow.

Fighting austerity requires a mass movement that rejects the whole notion of "shared sacrifice" and insists on rolling back all the cuts and all the layoffs and getting the money that's needed from the banks, from the corporations, from the war machine, and from wealth (earned and inherited). The sacrifice is not shared. The country is not bankrupt. The priorities are upside down. They will not be turned right side up by heeding the labor bureaucrats' advice to continue to stay on the sidelines and off the streets, nor by continuing to fund, lobby, and vote for Democratic Party politicians. Rather, what's needed is a movement that builds mass direct action and mass political action to defend and expand public control of the society and the basic right of every citizen to get what's needed to live a decent life.

The old slogans still apply: People before profits! Make the bosses pay!

Notes

1. See David Berliner and B. Biddle, *The Manufactured Crisis.* New York: Basic Books. 1995; Kathy Emery and Susan Ohanian, *Why Is Corporate America Bashing Our Public Schools?* Portsmouth: Heinemann. 2004; Gerald Bracey, *What You Should Know About the War Against America's Public Schools,* Boston: Allyn and Bacon, 2003; United States. 1983. *A Nation at Risk: The Imperative for Educational Reform: A Report to the Nation and the Secretary of Education, United States Department of Education. Washington, D.C.:* National Commission on Excellence in Education. Also, for a blueprint for business type education reform, see National Council on Education and the Economy. *Tough Choices or Tough Times.* San Francisco: Josey-Bass. 2007.

2. Ibid; *A Nation at Risk,* United States, 1983.

3. See Kathy Emery and Susan Ohanian, *Why Is Corporate America Bashing Our Public Schools?* Portsmouth: Heinemann. 2004.

4. Ibid.

5. *The Elementary and Secondary Education Act, 2002.*

6. Diane Ravitch, *The Death and Life of the Great American School System,* New York: Basic Books. 2010.

7. See Kenneth Saltman, "The rise of venture philanthropy and the ongoing assault on public education: The Case of the Eli and Edythe Broad Foundation." *Workplace* 16, 53-72. 2009.

8. Christina Samuels, "Broad academy's growing reach draws scrutiny." *Education Week.* 30(33) 1, 12-13. June 8, 2011.

9. S. Sparks, "Panel finds few learning gains from testing movement." *Education Week.* 30(33) 1, 14. June 8, 2011.

10. M. Springer, Ballou, D., Hamilton, L., Le, V., Lockwood, J., McCaffrey, D., Pepper, M., and Stecher, B. *Teacher Pay for Performance: Experimental Evidence from the Project on Incentives in Teaching,* Nashville, TN: National Center on Performance Initiatives at Vanderbilt University, 2010.

11. See *Center for Research on Education Outcomes Multiple Choice: Charter School Performance in 16 States*: Stanford: Stanford University, 2010.

12. Samuels, 2011.

13. David Berliner, Our impoverished view of educational research, *Teachers College Record,* 108:6 June 2006, pp. 949-995.

14. Ibid.

15. James Coleman and E. Campbell, C. Hobson, J. McPartland, A. Mood, F. Weinfeld, and E. York. *Equality of Educational Opportunity.* Washington, D.C.: U.S. Department of Health, Education, and Welfare, Government Printing Office. 1966.

16. Op. cit. Berliner. 2006.

17. See J. Hacker & P. Pierson Winner-take-all politics. New York: Simon & Schuster, 2010.

18. See Stan Karp, "Who's bashing teachers and public schools and what can we do about it?" *Rethinking Schools,* 25(3), 28-33. Spring, 2011.

19. Jitu Brown, Rico Gutstein, & Pauline Lipman, "Arne Duncan and the Chicago success story: myth or reality?" *Rethinking Schools,* 23(3) Spring, 2009.

20. Tom Vander Ark. "Eli finally won." *Huffington Post.* March 11, 2009. See http://www.huffingtonpost.com/tom_vander_ark/eli_finally_won_b_174152.html

21. J. Barkan, "Got dough? How billionaires rule our schools." *Dissent,* Winter, 2011. See http://www.dissentmagazine.org/article/?article=3781

22. Ibid.

23. R. Vincent. "Agassi to invest in charter schools." Los Angeles Times. June 2,

2011. See
http://articles.latimes.com/2011/jun/02/business/la_fi_agassi_fund_20110602
    24. D. Gelles, "Guidelines boost private education groups' shares," *Financial Times*. June 3, 2011. See http://www.ft.com/intl/cms/s/0/33fac542_8d78_11e0_bf0b_00144feab49a.html#axzz1Owiyduyh.
    25. D. McNally, *Global Slump: The Economics and Politics of Crisis and Resistance*, Oakland: PM Press. 2010.
    26. Center for Media and Democracy, "Total Wall St. Bailout Cost," *Madison Center for Media and Democracy*. 2010. See
http://sourcewatch.org/index.php?title=Total_Wall_Street_Bailout_Cost.
    27. E. Moya. "$2 trillion debt crisis threatens to bring down 100 U.S. cities." December 20, 2010. See
http://www.guardian.co.uk/business/2010/dec/20/debt_crisis_threatens_us_cities
    28. Op cit. McNally. 2010.
    29. See J. Stiglitz, & Bilmes, L. *The Three Trillion Dollar War*. New York: W.W. Norton. 2008.
    30. Op. cit. Hacker & Pierson. 2010.
    31. See Arne Duncan, "The New Normal: Doing More with Less – Secretary Duncan's remarks at the American Enterprise Institute." Washington DC: U.S. Department of Education. November 17, 2010. See
http://www.ed.gov/news/speeches/new_normal_doing_more_less_secretary_arne_duncans_remarks_american_enterprise_institute
    32. Ibid, 2010.
    33. See Bill Gates, *Bill Gates: Prepared remarks to Council of Chief School Officers,* Seattle: Bill & Melinda Gates Foundation, November 19, 2010. Available online at http://www.gatesfoundation.org.
    34. Naomi Klein, *The Shock Doctrine: The Rise of Disaster Capitalism*, New York: Metropolitan Books, 2007.
    35. L. Mishel, "We're not broke nor will we be," EPI briefing paper #310. Washington DC: *Economic Policy Institute*. 2011. p. 13.
    36. J. Zweig. "What will it take for companies to unlock their cash hoards?" Wall St. Journal, online edition. May 29, 2011.
http://online.wsj.com/article/SB10001424052702303654804576349282770703112.html?mod=WSJ_PersonalFinance_PF2
    37. Op. cit. Mishel. p. 7.
    38. Mishel. pp. 10-11, emphasis in original
    39. Mishel, p. 12.
    40. T. Carroll. "New Haven's Teacher Contract a Model? Not So Fast", *Huffington Post,* October 21, 2009. See
http://www.huffingtonpost.com/thomas_w_carroll/new_havens_teacher_contra_b_328950.html
    41. See S. Sawchuck. "AFT Chief to Revise Teacher_Dismissal Process." *Education Week*. 29(18). January 12, 2010.
    42. *NEA*. "NEA applauds selection of Race to the Top Winners" (press release). March 30, 2010.
    43. Ibid. NEA 2010. See
http://www.edweek.org/ew/articles/2010/04/21/29dccontract_2.h29.html
    44. Arne Duncan, "The Quiet Revolution: Secretary Arne Duncan's remarks at the National Press Club," Washington DC: U.S. Department of Education. July 27, 2010. See http://www.ed.gov/news/speeches/quiet_revolution_secretary_arne_duncans_remarks_national_press_club
    45. NEA, ESEA/NCLB update 93 August 6, 2010.

46. T. Echeverria, & C. Donegan, "From Deference to Direct Action: An Account from Madison," *Against the Current* 152, 8-9. Spring, 2011; also for more background, see K. Moody. "Wisconsin and Beyond."*Against the Current.* 152, 13-17. Spring, 2011.

47. S. Sawchuck, "NEA proposes making a shift on evaluations." *Education Week.* 30(31) 1, 18-19. May 26, 2011.

48. S. Otterman, "Tests for pupils, but the grades go to teachers." *New York Times.* p. A1. May 24, 2011.

49. Op. cit. Sparks. 2011.

50. T. Yancey. "CTA's state of complacency." *The Organizer Newspaper,* May 28, 2011. See
http://www2.socialistorganizer.org/index.php?option=com_content&task=view&id=445
&Itemid=1

Chapter 11
Recovering Schools and Classrooms in the Recovery School District
Karen Roth

The self is not something ready-made, but something in continuous formation through choice of action.—John Dewey

Foreword by John Duffy

The political and financial interventions of federal, state and corporate interests in New Orleans public schools following Hurricane Katrina offer a classic application of the central thesis from Naomi Klein's book, *Shock Doctrine: The Rise of Disaster Capitalism*, (2007). In a brilliant and disturbing expose Klein documents both the domestic and global efforts of U.S. corporate elites, with the support of national and international institutions like the CIA, World Bank and International Monetary Fund to privatize vast swaths of publicly owned property while undermining democratic institutions and public sector social support structures. She describes compelling examples of how catastrophic natural and political crises are seized upon by those wishing to bring about major transformations of public and democratic institutions. Advocates of privatization work to end government control and regulations while bringing public capital assets under corporate domination. Such efforts dominated outside interventions in New Orleans following Hurricane Katrina.

Most interventions in New Orleans, we suggest, also demonstrate the extension of Commercial Club Curriculum with its privatization schemes, support for chartering public education and the elimination and/or drastic weakening of teacher unionism. When Katrina devastated New Orleans state and national proponents of privatization swept down on New Orleans and with Bush administration and Louisiana government manipulation turned the majority of formerly public schools into charter schools. According to a retired teacher Richard Flesher—who went to Washington to advocate for the public schools as the assistance promised New Orleans through federal funds for public schools were drastically reduced from earmarked totals—charter school creation funding surged. Flesher states in a personal correspondence that:

> The Reconstruction School District (RSD) promised principals of the NOLA public schools various amounts but what they received was far less. Not one person, of those I met in DC, was willing to find out why funds were missing. The NOLA public school principals were certain the funds were diverted to the RSD system by Paul Vallas and the Louisiana Superintendent of Schools Paul Pastorek. Needless to say if funds are being diverted away from the public schools, in the various programs, the tasks of teaching and learning become much more problematic.

Even as these privatization efforts were underway thousands of citizens and students mobilized across the nation to aid the school children of New Orleans. Many of these efforts made no distinction between aiding surviving public schools or supporting the rapid proliferation of new charter schools in the Reconstruction School District headed by former Chicago Public Schools CEO Paul Vallas. Vallas, as we relate earlier in this book, spearheaded corporate reform designs in the revival of Commercial Club Curriculum in Chicago during the 1990s.

It is important to also point out that one volunteer group from the Chicago area, Schools Count, a non-profit network founded by retired teacher Richard Flesher in the suburb of Hinsdale, went to New Orleans to consciously support only public schools. As a lifelong union teacher and citizen activist involved in local, national and global efforts in support of democracy and human rights, Flesher critically understood that the voluntarism he organized was taking place within a larger political context dominated by others, who in collaboration with the Bush administration, were out to dismantle public schools and the local democratic traditions that supported them.

In the following chapter our friend and colleague Karen Roth shares stories of herself, her colleagues and teacher education graduate students working in NOLA schools. While they did not frame their work with the political perspective that Flesher has used to guide Schools Count, Roth, her colleagues and students, as you will see, still learned life altering lessons through their heartfelt work on behalf of the children of New Orleans.

City Submerged

When the new school year began in 2005, Hurricane Katrina slammed into the city of New Orleans (NOLA). Katrina's intensity ripped roofs off of buildings, battered historical public structures and trampled the levees that held at bay the waters of Lake Pontchartrain and the Mississippi River. If the structures weren't beaten up, they were flooded. Nothing was spared, not even the schools, public and private, in and around the city parishes. Nearly all of them were brutally affected by the rushing waters from the broken levees, with water rising to the second floors of more than half of them. Over all, approximately 200 child-care centers and K-12 schools were impacted by the after effects of the storm.

As the media portrayed in those following days, weeks and months, little was left that resembled the "Big Easy" so memorialized in literature, movies and songs. Nearly 1,500 citizens perished, including young children, who refused to leave their homes until their parents arrived from work. Thousands were eventually dispersed all over the United States, living in hotels and community shelters and enrolled in local public schools, from elementary to college age. They lived anywhere, with families eager to assist, while anxious about their children missing out on their academic experiences.

When the city opened for re-entry, New Orleans became the epicenter for volunteerism and civic service. Tulane and Loyola Universities, founded on the principles of civic engagement and community service, sustained extensive damage to their campuses, and were unable to admit students until the fall of 2006. Thus the numbers of local volunteers was depleted, leaving the city ripe for outside assistance. Non-profit organizations such as *Habitat for Humanity* and *Common Ground* and others from around the United States converged on the city to begin the process of rebuilding. Some of the assistance came in the form of tearing down structures destroyed by wind and flooding, clearing out mold and water-damaged homes, and building new dwellings for the homeless and destitute, who struggled even before the hurricanes forced the levees to break. Many of the residents who fled the state returned to live in FEMA trailers on their personal properties or in makeshift trailer camps, usually located in empty parking lots of closed down shopping malls and now abandoned public parks.

Devastated Schools and Students

Public school teachers and administrators were hit with a double-whammy. Immediately upon the closure of the city, public school employees were notified that their contracts had been nullified. With the uncertainty of the public schools reopening at any particular time, the New Orleans Public School District (NOPSD) sent electronic "pink notices" to over 4000 of its employees. It was quickly learned that no NOPSD employee was guaranteed a future position, let alone a position in the last school they worked. Within months after NOLA public school teachers, principals and parents settled into temporary accommodations, all over the US, with Internet and social media availability, a nation-wide movement began to write charters to reopen the NOLA public schools.

National Louis University (NLU), a school with a tradition of training teachers for over 125 years, responded to the needs of New Orleans in a manner that best supported its heritage. Just 3 days into the first week of school, children, teachers, staff and administrators of the 140 public and private schools in and around the New Orleans Parish School District were sent home to weather out the storm, and await instructions from the city's governing officials. No one could have predicted the outcomes of the effects of the Hurricane on the schools of NOLA, nor its impact on what was learned from it.

Since the summer of 2007, over 100 pre-service and in-service teachers from NLU have traveled to the city to assist the reopening of their public schools. Teams of college students, alumni and faculty joined efforts with newly hired, and in some cases, rehired, administrators and staff, to prepare the school buildings and classrooms for the children of returning families focused on rebuilding their neighborhoods and their lives. What members of NLU's *NOLA Schools Project* encountered, and came away from their experience, was more than they had anticipated. What they discovered of the impact of the devastation to the city, the lives of the people and to the system of education surpassed the scope of what they had learned from the multitude of newspaper articles, TV documentaries and government reports released. What they learned about themselves went beyond the service they performed.

A Bridge from Theory to Practice

In higher education today, particularly in colleges and universities that prepare candidates to teach in public schools, scholars in the field are rethinking the way pre-service teachers are prepared to meet the growing challenges of working with children from pre-kindergarten through high school. Current research continues to probe the questions: What makes a great teacher? How much does disposition, theoretical knowledge and practice impact highly effective practices and student learning outcomes within the classroom?

There is also a growing movement to re-examine how pre-service teachers are engaged in clinical experiences, both through traditional and alternative routes. This "rethinking" the way pre-service teacher candidates develop into highly effective classroom teachers speaks to the issues addressed by Darling-Hammond and Bransford (Eds.) in *Preparing Teachers for a Changing World: What Teachers Should Learn and be Able to Do (2005)*. In their chapter *"Theories of Learning and Their Roles in Teaching"*, researchers Bransford, Derry, and Hammerness, highlight *innovation* as a core element of teacher training. Innovation, they claim, is "the ability to unlearn and let go of previously held beliefs to try new strategies." [1] The researchers go on to recommend that faculty who prepare future teachers

> must help prospective teachers prepare themselves for these new tasks. A major way to prepare teachers for innovation is to help them develop inquiry skills that support ways to look at student learning and adapt accordingly. [2]

Bransford, Derry and Hammerness further explain that it is beneficial for new teachers to "make sense of learning" by developing a "conceptual framework of influences on learning" through questioning learning assumptions. [3] The domains of teacher learning, according to Bransford, Darling-Hammond and LePage, consist of understanding "development and learning in a social context; subject matter, skills and social purposes of schooling; and designing classrooms that enable diverse students to learn challenging content." [4] Specifically, pre-service teacher candidates must acquire and process the skills required to work with a diverse population of students, with unique languages and learning styles, within a space designed to support the wide ranges of experiences, responses and cultural backgrounds and beliefs. Research on learning appears to indicate that much more than facts are necessary to become a "responsible, responsive and reflective "practitioner".

Engaged experiences, conducted in meaningful and reciprocal learning environments, are essential aspects of the learning process. In an engaged experience, additionally, the concept of "space" and the development of "teacher identity" come into question. Education researchers note that "crafting identities is a social process, and becoming more knowledgeably skilled is an aspect of participation in social practice."[5] Furthermore, "much of the work within teacher education has relied on traditional behaviorist notions" that, "ignore the social, dynamic and generative quality of learning that can support the development of competencies needed in urban schools."[6] New Orleans schools are definitely reflective of the need for highly effective teachers, engaged in meaningful experiences, continuously examining templates for social practice.

Cochran-Smith and Lytle illustrate in "*Relationships of Knowledge and Practice: Teacher Learning in Communities* (1999) three concepts of teacher learning: knowledge for practice, knowledge in practice and knowledge of practice. Knowledge for practice addresses the study of "best practices". The teacher candidate learns how "to solve problems by implementing certified procedures rather than to pose problems based on their first-hand observations and experiences."[7] How do we know what is effective and in what context of use? Knowledge in practice refers to the use of practical knowledge in the day-to-day operations within the school community. Pedagogic beliefs are practiced, reflected upon and altered to best meet the needs of the learner. The whole process is one of collaboration and socialization as the practitioner defines and refines ones professional style and behavior.

Even more important is the third concept of teacher learning, especially for urban school districts like NOLA. Through *the knowledge of practice*, "teachers make problematic their own knowledge and practice as well as the knowledge and practice of others and thus stand in a different relationship to knowledge."[8] Teachers, at various points of their profession, develop critical views of their practice, and begin to question their own beliefs. This approach, however, does not distinguish between the veteran teacher and the novice to the field. Therefore, if we believe that how we come to the experience is a compilation of our perceptions, feelings, thoughts, understandings, interpretations and personal beliefs, and formed by the way we learn, communicate and engage within that experience, then we must recognize that the environment/space in which the learning occurs factors into the outcomes of all we encounter within the scope of our teaching practice.

NOLA School Project Participants

For the past 5 years, pre-service teacher candidates engaged in the *NOLA Schools Project* dedicate a week in July and August, before the school year begins, to work in newly reopened, and newly chartered, elementary schools.

There is usually no set agenda as to what the work will be. When the NLU teams arrive, they meet with newly hired teachers of the NOLA schools, who usually find their new classrooms empty, bare walls and bulletin boards, lacking of materials and supplies. Books for school libraries are packed in boxes from the publishing companies, and school supplies are stacked in hallways awaiting distribution and storage. Building administrators, anticipating the arrival of the student volunteers, generate a list of various duties, ranging from sorting books and supplies, organizing classrooms, and preparing materials for the first day of school, to identifying homeless children, communicating with parents and coordinating bus routes.

Teacher educators are interested in learning who the highly effective teacher candidates are, why they become interested in service learning as an alternative practice for professional development and what they hope to gain from the experience. The pre-service teacher candidates on this particular service-learning trip come to the *NOLA Schools Project* with varied backgrounds, personally and academically. Prior to the actual service work, student participants attend a pre-trip orientation, where they learn about the unique history of the charter school landscape in NOLA, the expectations of the service experience, and a brief lesson on the distinction between service-learning and volunteerism. Examples of previous service work and testimonials from former participants allude to assumed expectations ahead.

A pre-trip survey, completed as part of the registration process, indicated that all of the participants are either currently teaching, retired teachers or enrolled in college degree programs. More than half of the 100 who have traveled to New Orleans with the project are enrolled in teacher preparation programs. Approximately three-fourths of the team members are of Caucasian descent, with 15% Hispanic, 5% Asian and 5% African American. Male students make up about 10% of the overall group. Pre-service teacher candidate participants are products of both the urban and suburban public school systems, with some volunteer experience.

Pre-trip survey results, from the pre-service teacher candidates, also indicated a variety of motivational reasons:

> Volunteering has played a major role in my life. My goal is to pursue working in the educational field as a counselor or teacher. When I saw (the *NOLA Schools Project* service trip) I thought what a better way to get an understanding than to work with students and teachers and not only gain experience and insight, but also give something back as well.

Many were "interested in learning about new people and cultures". Others find working with children enjoyable and are "often inspired by the classrooms and curriculum". Still others find a personal satisfaction in "helping make a difference and the opportunity to gain more life skills knowledge in the process".

When the NLU teams arrive in NOLA the skills they bring to the work experience are as varied as the participants themselves. Student teacher candidates represent certification programs in early childhood, elementary and middle school, high school and special education. Nowhere else in these student's schools calendars do they interact in an educational setting together. Theoretical and practical experiences acquired from their unique program coursework, blended with the knowledge and skills gleaned from previous service work, integrated with their own personal interpretations and learning from life experiences, develops an individual who is a creative, resourceful and flexible thinker. Working together toward the same goals, with pre-service teacher candidates trained in pedagogies different from theirs, brings a greater understanding of collaborative and empathic learning to the whole experience.

Defining Service-Learning

Understanding the pedagogy of service-learning is essential to embracing its benefits to teacher development. As stated above, research supports community service as a methodology for bringing knowledge to life. The National and Community Service Trust Act of 1993 defines service-learning as

> a method under which students—Learn and develop through active participation in thoughtfully organized service that: is conducted in and meets the needs of the community and is coordinated with—an institution of higher education—and with the community; helps foster civic responsibility; is integrated into and enhances the academic curriculum of the students—and includes structured time for the students—to reflect on the service experience.[9]

Scholars and practitioners of the pedagogy generally agree that service experiences seamlessly integrate leaning goals with academic goals, challenges critical thinking skills, structures reflection in a more meaningful way, and enhances the relationship between the learner and the experience.[10] Regardless of the outcome, the learning/results are almost always reciprocal. The "server" and the recipient of the service agree on the need and course of action. Reflection is ongoing. As a result of reflection, the scope of the action and goals may change. Both the participant and the community agent(s) engage in a relationship that is mutually satisfying and rewarding.

Service-leaning offers a "broader appreciation of the discipline and an enhanced sense of personal values and civic responsibility".[11]

Alternative Clinical vs. Traditional Clinical

Service-learning is not new to teacher education. John Dewey encouraged meaningful classroom experiences for teacher development.[12] What is new is the idea that a service learning experience could serve as an alternative to traditional clinical placement(s). Current debate continues between the idea of alternative certification versus more traditional teacher preparation routes.[13] Traditional clinical approaches to student teaching usually take the appearance of a pre-determined setting, arranged by a placement coordinator, in a classroom with a seasoned teacher, often with an advanced degree and tenure in the district. The classroom space is well managed by the mentor teacher, and candidates are expected to be in the classroom every day as they "practice" the skills to becoming an effective teacher. Placements generally follow a prescribed agenda for advancement through the experience. Pre-service teacher candidates are measured, assessed and evaluated by a set of described behavioral expectations, by both the mentor teacher and a college appointed supervisor, whose responsibilities are to coach and assist the candidate to meet both state standards and program requirements. Additionally in most teacher preparation programs the candidate is actively involved in their own evaluation process through the submission of daily and weekly reflective journals, lesson plans and self-assessment documents. Upon successful completion of their experience and program, candidates are expected to be ready to take on a teaching position in their own classrooms.

In alternative clinical experiences, pre-service teacher candidates have the option to participate in service-learning experiences to fulfill required clinical hours. Students engaged in service experiences as a component of their teacher preparation program do so intentionally. They work in traditional public school classrooms, collaborate with classroom teachers and are expected to be in the classroom on a regular basis, but may follow a more flexible, less predictable route. They are encouraged to participate in activities beyond the parameters of the experience. Usually students are aware, but may not be fully cognizant, of the risk presented when one moves from a place of familiarity and comfort to one that is unknown and challenging. Yet it is this movement to the unfamiliar that could encourage and support pre-service teachers drawing on knowledge, skills, and dispositions they might not otherwise know they have. Virginia Jagla believes, "service-learning can be a meaningful variable affecting student learning" and "is a powerful pedagogy which engages the use of academic skills to address and solve real-life problems in the community."[14]

Sonia Nieto in chapter one of her book, *What keeps teachers going?* examines the evolution of teaching. Reflecting on her own teacher preparation experiences, Nieto simply but insightfully concludes that "teaching is hard work" and that "becoming a good teacher takes time". This is so, she states, because so much of teaching is all about social justice:

> This means tackling educational problems not just in the classroom and community, but at the highest policy and ideological levels as well, in other words, becoming active agents for change. But even if they work only in their classrooms—a difficult enough job—teachers *can still* make a difference in their schools and in the lives of their students.[15]

Service learning builds connections between the service experience and teaching for social justice.

Another valuable aspect of the service experience is the impact on disposition and values. Hammerness, Darling-Hammond, (et all) explain that the makeup of the candidates observation experience is critical to the whole learning experience of becoming a teacher.

> Prospective teachers come to the classroom with preconceptions about how the world, and teaching works. These preconceptions developed in the "apprenticeship of observations", condition what they learn. If their initial understanding is not engaged, they may fail to grasp the new concepts and information, or they may learn them for purposes of a test but revert to their preconceptions outside the classroom.[16]

In *Service-Learning in Teacher Education: Enhancing the Growth of New Teachers, their Students and Communities,* editors, Anders, Swick and Yff (2001) define service as "an approach to teaching and learning in which service and learning are blended in a way that both occur and are enriched by the other."[17] In relationship to the pre-service teacher candidate, Anderson et all sites that service "addresses an actual, recognized community or school need" and allows students to "take an active role in choosing, planning, implementing and evaluating" the experience.

In addition, the authors enhance the collaborative gains as "all partners benefit from the service project and contribute to it."

Traditional, practical experiences typically measure the pre-teacher candidate's academic competencies and intelligences. How well does the student teacher demonstrate an understanding of pedagogical theories and research learned in class? To what extent are *best practice(s)* and *developmentally appropriate practice(s)* observed in the development and implementation of lessons? In addition, how well does the teacher candidate utilize the pre and post assessment data?

Assessment of practice, reported by student teaching supervisors, often does not address the emotional connection to the learning experience. *Emotional Intelligence (EQ)*, a behavioral model introduced by Daniel Goleman (1995), identifies five basic tenets: self-awareness, self-management, responsible decision-making, social-awareness, and relationship skills.[18]

The more competent the pre-service teacher is in using these skills, the better able she/he will be to succeed. Alternative learning experiences provide a strong foundation for growing, and evaluating, these social-emotional abilities. Real world challenges and conflicts are integral, not detrimental, to the learning process and the consequences of the student teaching outcome. The focus becomes learner-centered, less training-centered.

In sum, through thoughtful contemplation teacher candidates' learn how actions and choices are influenced by the way they think and feel, learn ways to manage emotions when dealing with personal and professional obstacles, and, as they build collaborative relationships, understand how the perceptions and feelings of other's may impact the learning outcome. Through service, the individual grows from the inside out.

Learning through Reflection

Ongoing reflection is an essential element of service-learning. Maintaining a daily diary or journal, contributing to a group blog, and/or contributing to group discussions, pre-service teacher candidates think critically about their practice, learning outcomes, and the relationships they are building in the classroom. Whereas in traditional clinical settings, reflections are often limited to issues within the classroom setting, contrary to this, candidates engaged in alternative practices, for example service-learning, also reflect on issues beyond the classroom.

Pre-service teacher candidate participants of the *NOLA Schools Project* used a variety of methods to record the details of their work and their affective relationship to the work.

Overall, participants expressed a change in their attitudes and perspectives. Daily meetings, a trip blog and a post-trip survey were utilized to collect data. Morning meetings allowed participants to share what they learned from the previous days' work. Topics included arranging the classroom for the most impact on learning, best practices in working with students with special needs, for example helping children adjust to being homeless post-Katrina, and lesson planning. Conversations more often centered around the impact of the neighborhood on the children's development and learning, the lack of accessible nutritious food sources and the many ways a student could be labeled as homeless. Post-trip surveys indicate that the experience changed and reshaped their thinking. Trip participants often find themselves paired with newly hired teachers, fresh from teacher preparation programs. Together they set up classrooms, select and assess grade level curriculum and organize resource materials. Trip participants described their experiences as transformational: "This service trip gave me hope for this country and our school system. Every person I talked to experienced tragedy—everyone was positive, grateful and extremely respectful".

Through the group blog, participants reflected on their personal pedagogical beliefs: "it changed my way of teaching and thinking."

Others felt their experience reaffirmed their educational philosophy:

> It broadened my thinking about education and helped me notice how dedicated I am to the—field—I feel more informed and experienced about my career in an urban district.

and

> I learned about myself. I am always looking to be a better me and this trip helped me to do even more personal reflection. This trip always makes me think about the teacher I want to be as I enter the new school year. I know I want to be the positive teacher that makes every child happy to enter [classroom] 206

Still others, already valuing the hard work in education, felt their experience moving and inspiring: "[the experience] made me even more humble and appreciative of the job that teachers do . . . I am sparked to move, to teach and mentor youth."

Traditional experiences stress the importance of developing relationships, whereas service provides the opportunity for authentic relationship building:

> I expected to enjoy this (experience) but I did not expect to make the bonds that I have made. I realize that there is always a hidden layer to every situation, and that you need to go into every conversation and encounter with open eyes and an open heart,

and

> I value hard work and I value building relationships while working hard toward goals that merit hard work. Now that this fact is more crystallized for me, I feel I have more focus in terms of the projects I take on, the service opportunities I am likely to take on in the future, and the way in which I plan to run my own classroom, with close relationships and clear purpose.

One participant was able to express how service can be utilized to better understand the child's relationship to the school experience: "I left the (experience) feeling more committed to education and to using education as a tool of social development for the young people who come to school every day".

Others responded to the cultural inequities observed in previous clinical experiences:

> It made me realize that clean, well maintained and comfortable classrooms are not a 'given' for all schools in the USA, now instead of just talking or complaining about it, I realize I can actually help do something about this problem.

Becoming a Highly Effective Teacher through Service

As the participants of the *NOLA Schools Project* conversed with the NOLA teachers, the children and their families of the schools where they worked, and the people they met on the streetcars while traveling to and from the school, opportunities emerged beyond their makeup of the service trip. Several conversations focused on the growth of charters in NOLA and triggered deep debate on the national charter school movement and subsequent federal support. These conversations often spilled over into their work environment as the *NOLA Schools Project* partners with newly reopened charter elementary schools. Some participants were given the task of welcoming new parents to the school and assisting them with first day information and materials for their children. Learning first-hand how important that school-family connection is, one student reflected

It gave me a greater understanding of the types of challenges students in inner city and urban communities faced, as a teacher in Chicago Public Schools. I needed that information. It also showed me how communities and schools support one another.

Finally, these "future educators" learned that their willingness to become involved in assisting New Orleans impacted more than the school experience itself, but ultimately impacted their own growth beyond the classroom: "although the school wasn't perfect it helped me realized that it's truly the teachers and staff that make the school. Not the location, not the surroundings." Overall the teacher's main goal was to help the students learn and do whatever they could to get things ready in the best way possible. It made me realize how important the teacher is, not only the curriculum. And as one participant, reflecting on her service experience in the classroom, so poignantly writes:

In the end, you recognize that you have the choice of knocking persistently, asking for favors, savoring snow balls, and singing in the rain with new friends, and that this place and time and circumstance are only temporary, the waiting perhaps made more bearable and easily tolerated just because you know you can leave soon and go back to your more comfortable home and life. It dawns on you that this has been a blessed time and most welcomed experience shared with a wonderful and spirited team—and yet there is this little voice telling you that those people who live in this neighborhood don't always have a choice of whether or not to wait or to leave. Knowing that, you understand that you can't really go back to the way you were before.

Notes

1. See Linda Darling-Hammond and John Bransford, *Preparing Teachers for a Changing World: What Teachers Should Learn and be Able to Do.* (San Francisco, CA: Jossey-Bass, 2005) p. 77

2. Ibid. 77

3. Ibid. 79

4. Ibid. 31-38

5. See Jean Lave, "Teaching, as Learning, in Practice," *Mind, Culture, and Activity.* 3(3) (1996) p. 149-164

6. Jeannie Oakes, *Becoming Good American Schools: The Struggle for Civic Virtue in Education Reform.* (San Francisco, Calif: Jossey-Bass, 2002)

7. Marilyn Cochran-Smith, & S. L. Lytle, "Relationships of Knowledge and Practice: Teacher Learning in Communities. *Review of Research in Education*, 24, (1999) p. 259

8. Ibid. p. 273

9. *The National and Community Service Trust Act of 1993*

10. See Barbara Jacoby, *Service-learning in Higher Education: Concepts and Practices.* (San Francisco: Jossey-Bass Publishers, 1996); Virginia M. Jagla, Antonina Lukenchuk, and Todd A. Price, "Imagining a Better World: Service-Learning as Benefit to Teacher Education," *Journal of Research on Service Learning & Teacher Education* Vol. 1(1), (Fall 2010); Jeffrey B. Anderson, Kevin J. Swick, and Joost Yff, *Service-learning in Teacher Education: Enhancing the Growth of New Teachers, their Students,*

and Communities. (Washington, D.C.: AACTE Publications, 2001); Karen Meaney, Kent Griffin and Heidi Bohler, "Service-Learning: A Venue for Enhancing Pre-Service Educators' Knowledge Base for Teaching," *International Journal for the Scholarship of Teaching and Learning*. Georgia Southern University Vol. 3, No. 2 (July 2009).

11. See Robert G. Bringle, Julie A. Hatcher and Rachel E. McIntosh, "Analyzing Morton's Typology of Service Paradigms and Integrity." *Michigan Journal of Community Service Learning*. (2006) 13 (1): 5-15.

12. John Dewey, *Democracy and Education: An Introduction to the Philosophy of Education*. (New York: Macmillan, 1916)

13. Amanda Ripley, "What Makes a Great Teacher? How One Organization, Drawing on Two Decades of Observation and Research, May Have Found The Answer." *(The Atlantic Monthly, 58, 2010)*

14. See Todd Alan Price and Elizabeth A. Peterson, *The Myth and Reality of No Child Left Behind: Public Education and High Stakes Assessment: A Report Issued on Behalf of National-Louis University, 2008*. (Lanham: University Press of America, 2009) p. 152.

15. Sonia Nieto, *What Keeps Teachers Going?* (New York: Teachers College Press, 2003) p. 22
http://www.netlibrary.com/urlapi.asp?action=summary&v=1&bookid=98795.

16. Hammond, p. 366

17. Anderson, Swick, and Yff, 2001.

18. See Daniel Golman, *Emotional Intelligence: Why it Can Matter More than IQ*, (Bantam Books, 1995)

Chapter 12
Four Hundred Years of Chartering
John Duffy

Over four hundred years ago, the first entrepreneurial ventures carrying forth the European invasion of North America were licensed as charters. These emerging corporate organizations of venture capitalists sanctioned by the British monarchy made it possible for investors to undertake exploration, conquest and occupation of native people's lands. In the pursuit of profits to be shared with the British crown and other investors, these market driven organizations waged war against, removed, enslaved and exterminated indigenous people in pursuit of gold, silver, iron, furs, tobacco and other raw materials and crops prized in England and Europe. A similar wave of racial genocide preceded this North American brutality with the British occupation of Ireland in the 16th century. In both contexts, the Irish and North American peoples responded with hundreds of years of resistance to white European exploitation. The African slave trade and genocide soon followed. Eventually many people including white indentured servants, African American servants and slaves, as well as religious dissenters like the Quakers joined in the opposition to the racial order being created in North America during the colonial conquest and then later after the formation of the American Republic.

It is often said that history repeats itself in a manner where the lyrics may be new while the melody remains old and quite familiar. Today, we maintain that the chartering of American education reproduces a melody established long ago with the first charters in North America. Like then, the current chartering of education, the accelerating transfer of socially controlled resources (public education) into a business as a profit venture, privately owned and undemocratically operated. Modern chartering and the seizing of social capital for private gain still largely targets people of color and those socio-economic groups with little political clout in mostly poor, urban communities. Under the Obama administrations' education policies and despite their problematic and mixed results, charter schools continue to expand with powerful corporate, foundation and venture capitalist support. This expansion attempts to replace more communal, local and democratic conceptions of public education, as the authors of this volume have argued. These charter schools have yet to be held to accountability standards being imposed on traditional public schools.

While the development and expansion of charter schools have several causes, as we have shown in the preceding chapters, much of their growth follows a general pattern of undermining democratic institutions, seizing public capital investments, sponsoring ruthless competition and supporting new forms of private capital acquisition. These key aspects of charters have been virtually unreported as the mainstream media showcases examples of the so-called 'miracles' as traditional school structure and governance, including teacher collective bargaining rights, are dumped. In 2011 the Illinois State Assembly created Illinois State Charter School Commission with members appointed by the governor. As yet the assembly has did not provide funding for the body. The new commission in a slap at local community democracy has been empowered to grant local school charters to proponents who had been turned down by democratically elected local school boards. A similar authorization board as TJ Mertz describes in *This Is What Democracy Looks Like: Learning By Numbers* was recently defeated in Wisconsin. In Illinois clear documentation of how involved corporate backers are in the chartering of public education stands out. In lieu of state funding, the new Illinois State Charter School Commission has received over a million dollars from the Walton Foundation to initiate its work. And through all of this, state officials incredulously claim there is no compromising of civic democracy, while maintaining the foundation has asked for nothing in return for its substantial donation.[1]

The dominant media analysis of the chartering of public education has been equally hesitant to expose the conversation among neoliberal and neoconservative elites from government and business who understand and see that public education represents a massive publicly capitalized area of American life. It is this major portion of shared public life, up until now socially owned, that corporate interests and their allies in major foundations linked to Wal-Mart, Microsoft, Dell and other giant corporations now work to privatize in their quest to have schooling resemble any other part of the vast consumer market system that dominates our civilization. These interests seek to open this vast arena of socially controlled capital to new avenues for private capital accumulation. This is a vital part of the story that we have described throughout the volume—the ascendancy of *Commercial Club Curriculum*—by way of our teaching, advocacy, analysis, resistance and research. It is a story that has also been richly documented by others[2] who offer an equally revealing and critical description and analysis of how Neoliberal ideology and policies subvert democracy and undermine equity while doing little to address systemic injustices that have hindered the American promise of equal education for all children.

The context surrounding the struggles over public education that have been related in the preceding chapters emerged and accelerated with the conservative political restoration beginning in the post-Civil Rights Era over thirty years ago. The attacks on public education arose simultaneously with opposition to racial equity and truly equal opportunity for all children being sought by the Civil Rights Movement. The assault on public schools gained ideological support with the release and popularization of the supposed independent governmental and scientific report *A Nation at Risk* in 1983. Public school deficiencies, then, as is the norm today, became the primary scapegoat in explaining the relative weakening of the American economy vis-à-vis our global competitors. It was out of a long emerging set of beliefs, values, ideology and public policies we and others call neo-liberalism that the transformation of education received its strongest leverage. Once the U.S. domestic political, economic and global decline were tied to shortcomings of public schools, the path to our current situation was laid clear, though it certainly would meet opposition every step of the way, especially from those who worked daily to help all students regardless of their race, class, gender, sexual orientation or ability realize the idealistic promises that equitable public school could offer.

The solution for struggling schools, fostered by business and political elites in the late 1980's was an increased standardization of both school content and teacher preparation. A rapidly growing standardization movement around school curriculum and teacher education gained strength in the 1990's during the Clinton years and became full blown in a bipartisan manner during the George W. Bush administration with NCLB and its suffocating blanket of high stakes standardized testing. And now in the last four years the acceleration of turnaround policies for schools that failed to meet NCLB targets and the mantra of school choice as a local option under NCLB have opened the flood gates for the rapid expansion of public school chartering. And as we have told through the many perspectives and varying personal, social and political contexts stretching from Ohio, through Chicago, Wisconsin, down to New Orleans and out to California, Race to the Top has intensified this undermining of public education and given unprecedented support to the proponents of privatization. We have told stories of resistance to the most recent developments of this effort to transform public education because it is a critical narrative that should inform and urge on those committed to preserving public education. These stories can also offer a counterpoint to many in the education establishment who have too often allied themselves with the corporate agenda through their silence, acquiescence, collaboration and positioning themselves for professional advantages or even personal gain.[3]

Perhaps the most important and overlooked evidence for the replacement of public education with private for profit market driven schools, as discussed earlier by Jack Gerson, came with the release of *Tough Choices or Tough Times* (2007), funded largely by the Hewlett, Gates, Lumina, and Casey Foundations, and authored, at least signed off on, by a wide range of academics, business leaders, and government officials ranging from individuals like John Engler, former Michigan Governor, to Richard Riley, President Clinton's Secretary of Education.

The 250 pages report, in a spirit resembling the alarm sounded by *A Nation at Risk*, stopped nothing short of calling for a revolution in school organization. The plan it unfolds is to replace public education as we know it, arguing that the traditional system has failed to lead Americans forward into the new millennium of global economic competitiveness.

Tough Choices or Tough Times boldly and unapologetically asserts that it is time that the public school structure, ownership and governance be replaced altogether.[4] Though not always perfectly coordinated, *Tough Choices or Tough Times* like so many other corporate sponsored efforts also seeks to end teacher unionism and collective bargaining rights by stressing the anti-union mantra of the privatization and chartering crowd and re-imagining teachers as individual entrepreneurs, who like physicians, alone or with added capital investors, might develop their own privately owned schools, which of course would have access to public capital now supporting public schools.

As threatening as the attack on public education is to the very nature of American civic and social foundations, it is important to note that the chartering and privatization efforts have developed unevenly both in the United States and globally. Local historic social and economic conditions, the class and racial composition of schools and the ability of local school leaders to succeed or fail at creating conditions for substantive school improvements all impact how the discourse and policies that play out locally and when they play out. While there may be little talk of chartering and privatization in affluent suburban districts in the United States, the growth of an audit culture across the public school landscape has spilled over into these districts as more and more states adopt value added measures (tied to test scores) as part of teacher evaluation. The corporate sponsoring of chartering and its imposition of more student and teacher surveillance, the diminishing of collective bargaining, renewed attacks on tenure, the implementation of merit pay, and a narrowing of curriculum reaches beyond the network of charters located primarily in urban poor communities. Schools and teachers everywhere have been impacted by the proliferation of Commercial Club Curriculum.

In the chapter that follows Baudelaire K. Ulysses, a Haitian American teacher and scholar, describes and analyzes how business dominated American school reform has been carried by U.S. and other global interests into Haiti. Here as you will see, school reform is replete with the tensions and contradictions that have accompanied public schools whenever they are developed in new communities. As is the case across the American landscape, in Haiti the vital questions always come back to who will control these schools, whose interests will the curriculum serve and in what ways will education transform or reinforce long established conditions of inequality.

Notes

1. Chip Mitchell, "Charter-school agency's funding raises questions: A new Illinois commission can authorize charter schools rejected by local officials. Its money comes from a foundation that backs charter schools." (*WBEZ*, December 15, 2011). http://www.wbez.org/story/charter-school-agency%E2%80%99s-funding-raises-questions-94919

2. Danny K. Weil, *Charter School Movement: History, Politics, Policies, Economics and Effectiveness.* Amenia, N.Y.: Grey House Publishing, 2009; Lois Weiner and Mary Compton, "Teachers' Unions and Social Justice" in *The Routledge International*

Handbook of Critical Education, edited by Michael W. Apple, Wayne Au, and Luís Armando Gandin. New York, NY: Routledge, see http://site.ebrary.com/id/10280041; Pauline Lipman, *The New Political Economy of Urban Education: Neoliberalism, Race, and the Right to the City.* New York: Routledge, 2011; William H. Watkins, *The Assault on Public Education: Confronting the Politics of Corporate School Reform.* New York: Teachers College Press, 2012.

3. Diane Ravitch, *The Death and Life of the Great American School System: How Testing and Choice are Undermining Education.* New York: Basic Books, 2010.

4. See National Center on Education and the Economy (U.S.), *Tough Choices or Tough Times: The Report of the New Commission on the Skills of the American Workforce.* San Francisco: John Wiley & Sons, 2007.

Chapter 13
Rationalizing Standards, Rationing Opportunities: Neoliberalism and the Paradox of Success in Haitian and U.S. Education
Baudelaire K. Ulysse

> *NCLB represents what has been called the politics of "conservative modernization"—the complicated alliance behind the wave after wave of educational reforms that have centered on neo-liberal commitments to the market and a supposedly weak state, neoconservative emphases on stronger control over curricula and values, and "new managerial" proposals to install rigorous forms of accountability in schooling at all levels.[1]*—Michael W. Apple

Do Adam Smith and Karl Marx have something in common? What is the likelihood of Haiti and New Orleans being conjunctively mentioned in the same sentence for reasons other than their shared colonial link to Napoleon's France? Why do some schools from across internationally distant spaces subscribe to common standards? The above questions may not dominate the discussion; nonetheless, they are pertinently related to the central subjects of this chapter—neoliberalism and education—and as such, beautifully preface the ensuing discussion.

In particular, the first question reminds us of the clairvoyance of the two foremost political economy thinkers whose ideas cannot be ignored in any global economic discourse and, by association, global education. Many economists, including the late Milton Friedman (1912-2006), one of the leading and influential figures of the last century, have credited Adam Smith (1723-1790) with the fundamentals of capitalism and the free market[2] By contrast, although Karl Marx (1818-1883) is considered one of the most influential thinkers of human civilization, his social and economic ideas are widely viewed as the philosophical underpinning of the emergence of socialism. Like capitalism, socialism is theoretically an economic system, but the proponents of socialism have touted it as a political alternative, if not a replacement, to capitalism. Although the juxtaposition of capitalism and socialism does not intend to reduce the discourse exclusively to these economic philosophies, it does, however, intend to emphasize capitalism and socialism as two major competing and concurrent political paradigms, which have relevance to and ramifications for the discourse of neoliberalism.

The last two questions are similarly significant: restated, how are Haiti and New Orleans, Louisiana similar? In an article passage by Seattle public school teacher, Jesse Hagopian, the author makes the case that:

> Haiti and New Orleans have an inextricably linked history, including the 10,000 refugees that left Saint-Domingue (present-day Haiti) and arrived in New Orleans in 1809, doubling the population of the city. They brought with them the Creole culture and voodoo religion, elements of which persist in the bayou to this day.[3]

Assuming they do share a history, do they also share common standards for education?

In answering both questions, Haiti and New Orleans are distinct geographical and geopolitical locations, whose recent educational reforms, with an emphasis on standardized tests as determinants of success, nonetheless, mirror a very similar neoliberal agenda. This neoliberal agenda is manifested literally in the personage of one school reformer, Paul Vallas:

> Meet Paul Vallas. The 58-year-old Vallas is the former CEO of the Chicago and Philadelphia public school systems and was hired in the aftermath of Hurricane Katrina as superintendent of the Recovery School District of Louisiana that oversaw the transformation of the New Orleans school system. Vallas' legacy in these cities of privatizing schools, reducing public accountability and undermining unions made him a shoo-in to take charge of the Inter-American Development Bank's (IDB) education initiative in Haiti.[4]

Karen Roth, in the chapter "Recovering Schools and Classrooms in the Recovery School District", provides an insightful portrait of educational initiatives that have taken place in New Orleans, LA (NOLA), addressing the need for a reconceptualization of pre-service teacher training that will effectively meet the educational needs of students in that region. Thusly, I will refrain from discussing NOLA, instead focusing on the geopolitical landscape of Haiti as it pertains to neoliberalism and the initiative to privatize the Haiti's school system.

Early Years, My Haitian Education

I grew up in Haiti, and as such, I am intimately acquainted with its social, political, and economic aspects.

The state of public education in Haiti has been, not surprisingly, dismal. Access, or the lack thereof, is a perennial issue. The lack of incentive for teachers and the scarcity of resources have likely made matters worse. I should note that private schools in Haiti are very popular and profitable as well; while Haiti's private schools tend to be exorbitant, they attract a significant portion of the population. The reason is that these private schools are widely believed to be better alternatives to state-sponsored schools.

Personally, I obtained my primary, secondary, and high school education in Haiti, and I spent only two years in the public school system. Those two years were to my mother's chagrin, for she was adamant about her children attending private schools for the reasons mentioned earlier. Overall, I consider the education I received in Haiti to have been above average; but that was fifteen years ago, and things have dramatically changed since then.

Haiti and the Making of a Neoliberal Neophyte

Neoliberal efforts are not new to Haiti, but Haiti is a neoliberal neophyte; in fact, foreign private interests have been trying to convince Haiti to convert to neoliberal market approaches as early as mid-1980s.[5] Such efforts by foreign private interests were renewed in the early 90s at the advent of Aristide's ascendency to power, especially upon his return from his first exile as president. Klein (2005) reports:

> Washington's negotiators made one demand that Aristide could not accept: the immediate sell-off of Haiti's state-owned enterprises, including phones and electricity. Aristide argued that unregulated privatization would transform state monopolies into private oligarchies, increasing the riches of Haiti's elite and stripping the poor of their national wealth.[6]

Having been placed on hold by Aristide's refusal, neoliberal efforts did not gain significant traction until after the end of Aristide's term and the eventual election of Rene Preval. Preval then capitulated and catered to the demands of private interest groups a move that was virtually inescapable. The capital funds Haiti needed would not have been disbursed without the unequivocal commitment and movement by Preval's administration, as Girard notes:

> Foreign demands that companies be privatized prompted aid delays that resulted in acute budgetary shortages. By the summer of 1996, public employees complained that they were owed month of salary arrears.[7]

The privatization initiatives were eventually set in motion during Preval's first term, but later were interrupted by Aristide's re-election to a second term in 2000. With Aristide being overthrown once more and sent to exile in South Africa, Preval was re-elected for a second term in 2006. This shift of power effectively resumed the privatization process, which ensured formerly government-owned companies such as Haiti's telecommunications, flourmill, cement mill, and sugar mill, to name a few, were sold to the private sector.[8]

The privatization of these state-owned companies was part of a sweeping neoliberal project aimed at, as the International Finance Corporation (IFC) bills it, catalyzing private sector development through an integrated approach providing investments and advisory services. Since 2000, IFC has committed $51 million to Haiti's private sector. IFC's strategy in Haiti seeks to promote job creation and increase access to basic services.[9]

IFC is the private branch of World Bank, which oversees implementation of neoliberal reforms in developing countries,[10] particularly privatization. Such reforms are being more aggressively pursued in Haiti since the 2010 earthquake debilitated the already dysfunctional infrastructure. Shortly after the earthquake, while humanitarian efforts were mounting among private citizens from everywhere around the world, particularly in the United States, it was reported that a few world leaders, including Secretary of State Hilary Clinton, were meeting to discuss how neoliberal reforms in Haiti might be accelerated. MacDonald reported on this meeting while quoting Cannon, the host of the meeting, make these welcoming remarks:

> We also have with us today some members from the private sector who have given generously to the humanitarian appeal but will also play an important role in Haiti's future. Singling out several publicly owned sectors of the Haitian economy, they [members from the private sector] will be accompanying and supporting us in rebuilding the national infrastructure of ports, roads and power generation and in re-establishing essential services from electricity to banking and communications.[11]

MacDonald prefaced her report by mentioning the names of the people in attendance including key representatives from the World Bank and International Monetary Fund. Also worth noting is the ubiquitous private sector that is ever ready, not only to support the rebuilding of Haiti, but also to transform publicly run entities into privately owned and economically profitable treasure troves. As such, IFC has been very involved in purchasing negotiations of Haiti's public services, which also may include the public school system.

Privatization and Haiti's Public Schools

With Haiti's economy being stagnant for the most part and unemployment rising at a very high rate, the quality and the affordability of education have certainly gone down. Recent initiatives would seem to warrant such conclusion. In 2007, the World Bank, through the Global Partnership for Education, approved a $25,000,000 grant for educational initiatives in Haiti, aimed at providing access for poor children. Announcing the grant, the

Director of the World Bank for the Caribbean, Caroline Anstey, made the following remarks:

> This project directly supports the Haitian Government's efforts to strengthen governance and deliver visible benefits to the Haitian people. Expanding access to education in Haiti is not only essential to improve human development and reduce poverty, but also to increase hope among the population, particularly among the poor, whose children will be the main beneficiaries of this program.[12]

Ms. Anstey's remarks are revealing, not only on what is being done to help Haiti but also on what is not functioning. The educational system has certainly not been functioning well and it could use significant reforms. But will the Haitian public education system eventually be privatized with the money that is being poured in?

While the private sector is bent on privatizing state-owned or government-run institutions, the privatization of the Haitian public education system seems subtle and less forthcoming at the outset. This perspective is due in large part to a recently approved agreement between the Haitian government and the Inter-American Development Bank (IDB). IDB touts itself as a multilateral source of financing for development in the Latin America and the Caribbean regions. Essentially, it convinces private investors and brokers partnership agreements that facilitate private investment in countries throughout those regions. Thus, when IDB promises funds to an initiative in developing countries, regardless the nature of the initiative, such funds are typically raised from private donors and investors who will most likely require a stake in that initiative. The stake could be financial or ideological.

For instance, educational projects, which IDB has been supporting, will receive financing from Happy Hearts Fund. According to a statement on its website, Happy Hearts Fund is:

> A non-profit foundation dedicated to improving children's lives through educational and sustainable programs in natural disaster areas. Globally, HHF has an active portfolio of operations in nine countries, including Haiti, benefiting more than 34,330 children and 337,450 community members.

There are many such organizations that partner up with IDB on these educational initiatives in the developing world and, as the ensuing discussion will show, the funds, which IDB has pledged or committed to for the projects in question, will come from likeminded organizations from various countries. On the other hand, Hagopian points out that:

> The IDB's proposed five-year, $4.2 billion plan for the remaking of the Haitian education system could be described as the "Trojan school", using the promise of the day when there is reduced tuition in the bulk of Haitian schools as a means to permanently enshrine a private schooling system

subsidized by the government. As the IDB explains of its proposal:

Under the reform, most Haitian schools will become publicly funded institutions, foregoing or drastically reducing tuition charges. The government will pay teacher salaries for schools participating in the plan.

But here's the catch:

To remain in the new system, schools will have to adopt a national education curriculum.[13]

This information raises the question of whether the schools will be "public" in name only. Like the "public" New Orleans school system where common curriculums are adopted, the actual schools are increasingly funded *and* managed by effectively private entities.

So far as this agreement between IDB and the Haitian government is concerned, primary education in Haiti will remain a public service (with the involvement of public teachers and the Ministry of Education supervising), but that veneer may change in 2015, the date in which this reform agenda sunsets.

While these new educational reforms in Haiti seem different from neoliberal reforms undertaken in the U.S., they nonetheless mirror a larger neoliberal apparatus aimed at norming, commodifying, and socializing children to standards that are consistent with creating a pool of workers, and a small coterie of managers to run the "new" economy. Essentially, the reforms aim at harnessing "social capital." Fittingly, the World Bank, which works in concert with IDB, refers to social capital as:

. . . the internal social and cultural coherence of society, the norms and values that govern interactions among people, and the institutions in which they are imbedded. Social capital is the glue that holds societies together and without which there can be no economic growth and human well-being. Without social capital, society will collapse, and today's world represents some very sad examples of this.[14]

Social capital embodies what neoliberalism considers most vital for success at both the personal and professional level in a given society, and as such, remains a core objective in the neoliberal agenda. Essentially, social capital is requisite for economic success in any capitalist society. Unfortunately, Haiti is extremely deficient as far as social capital is concerned. Establishing that base of social capital in Haiti, a newly minted initiate, must be one of the top priorities for the people at the helm of neoliberal endeavors in Haiti. Hence, neoliberal educational reforms in Haiti should not be surprising, neoliberalism prizes as well as touts education as the primary conduit to develop social capital.

The Looming Marketization of Haitian Education

In the article *Ideological Success, Educational Failure? On the Politics of No Child Left Behind,* Michael Apple offers a thorough but insightfully scathing analysis of how the neoliberal apparatus engages nation-states, particularly educational systems in those nation-states. Apple's analysis might help connect the dots between current educational initiatives in Haiti and the global neoliberal apparatus. We have seen the reliance of standardized tests, and a lauding of free market reforms (including supplemental education services and charter schools) that have flourished under NCLB. Where will this effort be under Race to the Top in New Orleans, Louisiana, or in its corollary, Port-au-Prince, Haiti?

The heart of Apple's analysis is conceptualized as a "marketization of education." Apple aptly describes this marketization process of education saying:

> The movement toward marketization and "choice" requires the production of standardized data based on standardized processes and "products" so that comparisons can be made and so that "consumers" have relevant information to make choices on a market.[15]

Having described this marketization process of education, Apple proceeds to demonstrate the ubiquity of such process in the U.S. education system as well as other areas around the globe. By way of example, the No Child Left Behind Law, Apple theorizes, adheres to this marketization process, along with an impetus of efficiency which manifests in business-like operations. A key practice of this business-like operation in neoliberalism is *audit culture.* Drawing from Leys, Apple suggests that this auditing culture is similar to current business practices related to the *measuring, as well as the evaluation, of performance.*[16]

This type of auditing aims in its imposed and ubiquitous mandated reporting of testing data to show inefficiency. When implemented in the public sector, it seeks to rigidly and persistently monitor educational services, as well as presents the private sector as a necessary condition for transformation of public education, resulting in a new standard of success and efficiency absent in publicly owned and operated schools. Thus, Apple writes:

> A key to all of this is the devaluing of public goods and services. It takes long-term and creative ideological work; however, people must be made to see anything that is public as "bad" and anything that is private as "good," a very real cause and effect of NCLB's emphasis on failure.[17]

If public services are proven inefficient, then resistance to the private sector intervening as a "salutary" agent is greatly diminished. According to Apple, this auditing is not value-free. Such auditing represents the outworking of ideology itself—not just any ideology, but the neoliberal ideology. In an interview with Richard Flesher who has spent time in Haiti supporting the rebuilding of schools, Flesher states:

> The ultimate result of an auditing culture of this kind is not only the promised decentralization that plays such a significant role rhetorically in most neo-liberal self-understandings but also what seems to be a massive recentralization and what is best seen as a process of de-democratization.[18]

Apple's analysis helps connect education to the neoliberal apparatus. In addition, it provides a basis to accurately interpret and understand the link between current educational initiatives in Haiti and the global neoliberal apparatus. Haiti shows patterns that are very similar to auditing culture and restructuring for efficiency. In addition, the objectives of these educational initiatives in Haiti are consistent with neoliberal standards of centralizing, norming, socializing, and standardizing. In Haiti, under the reorganization and promised, but largely undelivered public and private money for the creation of hundreds of new public schools, appears to run counter to neoliberalism, while the current efforts to create an expanded public education system appear to challenge neo-liberalism's privatization efforts. However, a careful look at what is actually happening in this new public school system shows us a different picture.

A Different Picture

Richard Flesher, an educator who has worked to rebuild Haiti's schools as well as monitored the neoliberal conditions in Haiti, provides an intimate but disturbing portrait of the outworking of neoliberalism in post-earthquake Haiti. Flesher's refreshingly different perspective:

> Allow me to offer a perspective on Haitian education that is rooted in both observation and communication with Institute Mixte Nao (IMN) in Darbonne, Haiti and Haiti Partners. The charity, Schools Count Corp., of which I am president, made significant monetary contributions to the rebuilding of IMN. I attended the rededication of the school in April 2010 and receive updates on the unfolding situation with the school on a fairly regular basis.[19]

Flesher's keen insights embody a panoramic picture connecting the dots between neoliberal marketization of education from NCLB past to Race to the Top present, and from New Orleans to Haiti. Flesher, a long-term educator, has a bird's eye view of the New Orleans to Haiti Diaspora, at least as it concerns education. In assessing the opportunity for Haiti to move forward educationally at this time, Flesher's words are both revealing and sobering:

> As most people are aware, the January 2010 earthquake did much harm to the country. Lives were lost, homes destroyed, families were ripped apart,

dreams forgotten and the nation imperiled for years to come. A tragedy is a word that doesn't suffice. Beyond the human toll, much of the devastation exists to this day that continues to adversely affect the delivery of education to the youth of the country.

This point can't be underscored enough. One can't expect, in less than two years, for thousands of children to forget the life altering agony of losing a parent, sister, grandparent, friend or neighbor. No child or adult, for that matter, can really move on with the everyday rhythm of life's events without suffering from the effects of such a cataclysmic event.[20]

This story is remarkably similar to the trauma, if on a lesser scale, experienced by citizens and families in New Orleans, as described briefly in Karen Roth's chapter. Flesher argues that while non-profits play a role, a much greater role needs to be made by government:

I have often been told by Haitian educators that the Ministry of Education is of no aid to them. Directives may come by way of the ministry but funding, in-service programs for teachers, assistance with making clean water and food available to students and teachers, and other necessary aid that could be provided by the ministry has not shown itself to be evident.

This point must be driven home because many of the educators don't believe that promises being made at the current time will come true. There is hope that President Michele Martelly will make good on his promise of free education, but it is tempered with the reality that schools are too often left to fend for themselves and will have to do the same in the years to come.

The idea of public schools under conditions of concentrated poverty and recent demolition of the landscape is a daunting challenge indeed. Flesher points out with lucidity that much of the vacuum of a functioning public sector is being filled by non-profits:

Allow me to make a comment about one government agency, the Ministry of Education, which will certainly bear the brunt of forging educational change in the Haitian school system. I am aware of the fact that the non-profit agency Haiti Partners actually trains leaders, in various educational organizations, through their 'Circles of Change' program (which deals with teaching methods adapted from Touchstones Discussions and Open Space). A number of people in the Ministry of Education have been a part of this training.

This is not to make any statement about the quality of training offered by Haiti Partners. I happen to think that Haiti Partners has done much good in the country. My point is this, it isn't the Ministry of Education doing the training; rather, it's an NGO that is educating the ministry!

Again, these developments are remarkably similar to New Orleans. While the current Haiti educational initiatives are a move in the right direction (free education for the poor), they are part of a larger neoliberal agenda.

The Role of the IDB

Consider for instance the details of the aforementioned educational initiatives sponsored by IDB. According to the agreement among the parties involved, the project named "Support for Educational Reform in Haiti II" or "SERIH II" aims to implement a set of structural reforms in the Haitian education system in order to remedy issues related to access and quality.

As of November 27, 2011, the Inter-American Development Bank posted on its website a detailed outline of the project's objectives:

> This operation will contribute to the bank's five-year program supporting the following objectives of the Haitian Education Plan: (i) improving access to education; (ii) improving the quality of education; (iii) improving TVET opportunities; and (iv) strengthening MENFP institutional capacities and governance. More specifically, HA-L1060 objectives are to: (i) increase the public supply of education benefitting 15,000 children annually; (ii) reduce education costs for 75,000 primary students; (iii) improve education quality through educational and technological innovations benefitting 13,500 children; (iv) improve TVET opportunities through a sustained investment effort and innovations in managing the sector and training centers benefitting at least 600 youth annually; and (v) increase MENFP's capacity to implement the Education Plan and regulate the education sector.[21]

This project was commissioned in May 2010 by the then-President Preval and was approved on November 21, 2011. Indeed, this project represents a comprehensive and ambitious initiative. Worth noting is that although the project is being funded by outside sources (*IDB, Haiti Reconstruction Fund, Trinidad and Tobago First Citizens Bank, and Agencia Española Cooperación Internacional para el Desarollo*), the agencies overseeing and executing it are national *Fonds d'Assistance Economique et Sociale* (Foundation for Economic and Social Assistance) and *Ministère de l'Education Nationale et de la Formation Professionnelle* (Haiti's Ministry of National Education and Professional Formation).

In addition, while the project seeks to restructure and regulate Haiti's primary education system, its overarching objective, as it stands, revolves around the reduction of cost for education through a more effective, publically funded, education system. In fact, according to component #2 of the plan's outline, the ultimate objective is to provide "universal, tuition-free and quality education to children in grades 1-6 by 2015."[22] Based on the details of current Haiti educational initiatives, along with the successful privatization of Haiti's public services such as telecommunications, cement factory, and many others, it might be accurate to conclude that Haiti's education system, at least primary education, may not be privatized right away. Still, developments in Haiti mirror how neoliberalism works to transform public services into efficient, privately run entities.

Neoliberalism Perpetrates Inequities and Inequalities

Inherent in the notion of free market, as formulated within the economic ideology of neoliberalism, is a specific view of the role that government should play. Particularly, this view maintains that the government should be involved as minimally as possible, which in most cases means the government must create laws that prevent interference with the market mechanism and laws that protect it. According to exponents of liberalism, this represents the only instance where the government may be involved, and even that involvement restricts the government as well. The practices of liberalism from a political standpoint have not been consistent or homogeneous, but ideologies such as individuality, free market, and the freedom to buy and sell at will remain virtually unchanged elements of liberalism. Now, these elements belong to a broader economic paradigm known as neoliberalism.

This neoliberal apparatus, which is characterized by a lack of evenhandedness, inequities, and inequalities, is not an abstract, apolitical force operating on its own. Indeed, a few of the most powerful international financial institutions such as the International Monetary Fund and the World Bank are orchestrating, selling, and enforcing it across the globe through both persuasive and coercive methods.[23] In addition, institutions such as the Organization for Economic Co-operation and Development (OECD) and the United Nations Educational, Scientific and Cultural Organization (UNESCO) are assisting its propagation through auxiliary initiatives such as education, microfinance, and publication. The collective activities of these institutions ensure the unfettered spread of neoliberalism as well as the plethora of issues—deterrence of freedom, inequities, inequalities, and exploitation—associated with neoliberal discourses.

Evidently, inequalities and inequities have no boundaries, and as such, they run amok in any context that harbors them. They pervade social and economic spheres within national context, and they are glaringly evident among nations at the global level. Haiti is no exception, and its social system has historically been very inequitable. In addition, inequities in Haiti run deep across racial lines, which one might say are rooted in the legacies of French colonialism. Girard reminds us that:

> White Frenchmen established a three-tiered colonial society organized along racial lines, which sparked a long and costly racial war that consumed half of Haiti's black and mulatto population and resulted in the death or exile of virtually all white planters. Mulattos have expressed racism of their own, leading them to look down on their black compatriots as uncouth.[24]

These 'three-tiered colonial' legacies as well as prevalent racism continue to drive the injustices in Haiti. As it is, Haitians with lighter skin already hold a majority of the economic capital in Haiti, as they are the business owners and bankers. As such, they represent the private sector, holding sufficient capital to buy off public assets and entities. Given these light-skinned Haitians have historically disliked and looked down on Haitians with dark skin, it is highly unlikely that the light-skinned Haitians will want to support a system that mitigates inequalities and benefits all Haitians, particularly their black counterparts.

With the implementation of neoliberal apparatus in Haiti, it is unlikely the disparities will vanish soon. Implementing neoliberalism in Haiti could result in more efficient services for Haitians, but this might as well come at the expense of reinforcing existing inequalities and inequities, for neoliberalism tends to concentrate power in the hands of the few who already hold the upper hand. One of neoliberalism's main tasks is to concentrate power within elites, resulting in global economic disparities. Not only has neoliberalism been blamed for the disparities that exist internationally, it has also been viewed as largely responsible for the social inequalities and economic inequities that exist in national contexts. From an educational standpoint, those with limited financial capital will inevitably be limited in terms of the quality of education. Moreover, with neoliberalism's emphasis on standardized tests, which lead to inequalities, the gap between the haves and have-nots in Haiti will very likely widen. In this regard, and many others, New Orleans and Port-Au-Prince school reform is cut from the same cloth.

Inherent in the U.S. educational system is a history of allocating opportunities to citizens based on race and economic status At issue is a systemic lack of equity grounded in a historical racial divide and segregation, a chasm that continues both in advanced modern societies like the U.S. and in neo-colonial states like Haiti. Inequity and the expansion of racial segregation in U.S. schools have been well documented, researched, and challenged, but they continue to exist and have been exacerbated by neoliberal school reform in the U.S., contributing to persistent and widening social, economic, and educational gaps.

Conclusion

Throughout this chapter, I have analyzed education in Haiti and the U.S., focusing primarily on the premises of neoliberalism. Though I highly doubt neoliberal educational initiatives, with their emphasis on standardized tests, will mitigate economic inequities in Haiti, I retain a modicum of sympathy and positive outlook, believing that the dilapidated Haitian educational infrastructure might benefit from an infusion of foreign investment, even if such infusion would mean a full-fledged neoliberal privatization of Haitian schools at a later stage.

From the standpoint of development economics, I have no objection to a potential neoliberal educational agenda that seeks to prepare Haitians to enter the workplace and produce, assuming that such preparation, along with its eventual economic output, means immediate and unlimited access to social, economic, and political capital that translates into sustainable and equitable integration into the Haitian society.

Traditionally, Haitian students, particularly the poor, have had limited educational and economic opportunities, and this limited access to education and economic opportunities has kept that Haitian majority sadly and unjustly on the fringe of society. Hence, for that majority to have educational opportunities, which are imbued with the prospect of greater economic success, along with a potential civic voice in the political process, represents an overdue game-changer. However, I would be wary of any educational initiative in Haiti that provides an apolitical and ahistorical bottom-line education to these students. A national curriculum that fails to factor in Haiti's historical and political narratives risks a revisionist enactment for Haiti where the present is stripped off its relevant past and built on a utopian future devoid of critical consciousness.

In the long haul, such an ahistorical and apolitical aspect of education would end up *manufacturing* (a metaphor for the capitalist production apparatus) a generation of Haitians whose collective immanent identity is confounded, if not forlorn, because of the omnipresent imprint of global corporate interest groups in shaping a national curriculum. U.S. educators ought to be similarly concerned, if such an outcome were to become imminent in their educational system.

Notes

1. Michael Apple, "Ideological Success, Educational Failure?" (*Journal of Teacher Education,* 2007) 58 (2): 108-116. p. 112.

2. Friedman, Milton, and Rose D. Friedman. *Capitalism and freedom.* (Chicago: University of Chicago Press, 2002).

3. See Jesse Hagopian, "Shock-Doctrine Schooling in Haiti: Neoliberalism Off the Richter Scale" (*CommonDreams.org* September 9, 2011)

4. Hagopian, September 9, 2011.

5. Philippe Girard, *Paradise lost: Haiti's tumultuous journey from pearl of the Caribbean to third world hotspot.* (New York: Palgrave Macmillan, 2005)

6. Naomi Klein, Aristide in Exile. *Nation,* 2005, *281*(4), 14.

7. Girard, 2005, p. 172.

8. J. Sprague and W. Pierre, *Haiti: Workers protest privatization layoffs.* (Interpress Service News, July, 2009) Retrieved on December 31, 2009 from http://ipsnews.net/news.asp?idnews=38646

9. See the Inter-American Development Bank. Accessed 12/9/11 http://www.iadb.org/en/countries/haiti/haiti-and-the-idb,1008.html. Accessed on November 22, 2010.

10. See International Finance Organization, World Bank Group. http://www1.ifc.org/wps/wcm/connect/corp_ext_content/ifc_external_corporate_site /home Accessed 12/9/11

11. Isabel MacDonald, Same Old Interest; New Plan for Haiti. 2010. From http://www.indypendent.org/2010/01/29/plan-for-new-haiti/

12. See *Haiti: World Bank Approves US$25 Million Grant to Support*

Education For All Program, Washington, April 26, 2007. Accessed 12/9/11 http://web.worldbank.org/WBSITE/EXTERNAL/COUNTRIES/LACEXT/HAITIE XTN/0,,contentMDK:21315053~pagePK:1497618~piPK:217854~theSitePK:33816 5,00.html

13. See the Inter-American Development Bank. Accessed 12/9/11.

14. B. Fine, *Social capital versus social theory: Political economy and social science at the turn of the millennium.* (London: Routledge. 2001) p. 158.

15. Apple, p. 111.

16. Colin Leys, *Market-driven politics: neoliberal democracy and the public interest.* (London; New York: Verso, 2003).

17. Ibid., p. 112.

18. Ibid., p. 113.

19. Interview with Richard Flesher on education in Haiti, 2011.

20. Ibid., Interview with Flesher.

21. See the Inter-American Development Bank. Accessed 12/9/11

22. Inter-American Development Bank; Accessed November 27, 2011. http://idbdocs.iadb.org/wsdocs/getdocument.aspx?docnum=36278811

23. N. Woods, *The Globalizers: The IMF, the World Bank, and their Borrowers,* (Ithaca, NY: Cornell University Press, 2006).

24. Girard, p. 205.

Part IV
Reclaiming Education for the Public

Chapter 14 "Corporate Siege and the Growing Resistance" by Todd Alan Price and John Duffy, picks up where the previous two chapters left off. In the first place this is accomplished by documenting the increasingly tense standoff between the Chicago Public Schools CEOs and the new CTU leadership. Secondly, the drama continues by reporting on—and foreshadowing the crises to come—the impact of budget cuts on teachers, students, and school districts. Lastly, Price personally and passionately describes the resistance and the massive outpouring of Wisconsinites and allies in the form of "the first responders" who drew national attention to the popular democratic struggle in Madison, Wisconsin that would set the stage for the soon to be born Occupy rebellion across the nation.

Chapter 15, "This *is* What Democracy Looks Like" by T.J. Mertz, describes in a compact and on-the-spot narrative what the victory of Governor Scott Walker meant for the state through the eyes of a staunch and unflinching defender of public education. It also demonstrates that public education's defenders will not stand aside.

The book concludes where we began, with the Commercial Club of Chicago: "Turning the Tide on Commercial Club "School Reform." Commercial Club Curriculum is being challenged in every respect today by the same parties—working class parents, teachers and students—who fought back one hundred years ago. John Duffy and Todd Alan Price write this narrative about the skirmishes at the end of 2011, "the year of protest," with an eye to the future of public education amidst Occupy Chicago and looming protests against unjust global economic forces in the "Global City."

Chapter 14
Corporate Siege and the Growing Resistance
Todd Alan Price

The first term of the Obama administration can be characterized as a series of colliding events that have severely altered the American public education   and the greater society. To relay the meaning of these cacophonous events beneath the banner Race to the Top (RTT) is the purpose of this chapter.

The following sections attempt to capture a whirlwind of events across the nation as they occurred. These developments include: the election of Barack Hussein Obama to the White House; the gridlock and collapse of the economy which prompted the emergency ARRA bill to save public sector teachers jobs; the disappointing appointment of Arne Duncan to the Secretary of Education post; Duncan's destructive RTT promotion "tour" which was rebuffed in Ohio and warmly embraced—behind the scenes—by top Wisconsin Democratic Party officials in Wisconsin; the subsequent defeat of the "Mayoral Takeover" bid in Milwaukee with the subsequent collapse of the Wisconsin Democratic Party; the national school policy shock reverberating from the Rhode Island Central Falls High School closing; threats made by Chicago CEO Ron Huberman to do the same in Illinois; the mobilization of Chicago and Illinois Teachers to fight back against corporate inspired policies; and, finally, the uprising of Wisconsin citizens and union members to save their schools in the face of expected budget cuts . . . only to be hit by an anti-public education tsunami orchestrated by incoming Governor Scott Walker.

Hope, Change and Reform

I was there that unforgettable warm autumn night back in November of 2008. I walked out of my office, down the stairs of my university's Michigan Avenue building onto the politically buzzing street. Amidst departing students a small cadre of our university's administrators uncharacteristically smiled and made small talk outside the main entrance. Then, I was literally swept up by one of the feeder crowds flowing into Chicago's Grant Park for an anticipated celebration of an unprecedented event in the grand political narrative of the United States.

In this, one of the largest crowds I had ever seen, there were vendors selling American flags, Obama t-shirts, flutes, drums and maracas. The omnipotent "O" coupled with the campaign slogans littered the sidewalks. Tens of thousands of parents, babies, children, teenagers, young professionals and members of the older generations triumphantly swarmed the streets slowly making their way to the massive open air party.

The check in point for the celebration was a short city block in length, nothing as personally intrusive as boarding a passenger jet at the airport. This evening would be the last time everyday citizens would have free and open access to Mr. Obama. As I entered the vast field just south of the grand but now dormant Buckingham Fountain, the air was sweet. Gone were the usual smells and sounds of food fests and music fests and the raucous, unpredictable atmosphere of historic political protests in Chicago. I could have been at a Fourth of July fireworks show, yet this was November in the windy city. We should have been cold, wet, and windswept. We should have been indoors, but clearly the weather gods had smiled on this historic gathering as the crowd grew to hundreds of thousands.

What seemed to characterize this event was neither titillation nor vindication of an impending victory. Rather, the mood ran cool; it was serene, almost surreal. It was filled with, in a word, hope. That a black man with such a name as Barack Hussein Obama was actually going to win the election and become *this* nation's president . . . well this was indeed a script for a movie. This group, to which I was now a part, was cut off and outside the orbit of parties in homes and apartments with loved ones or in neighborhood gatherings in bars with friends. We all shared a common nervous anticipation, all there waiting to catch a glimpse of our new President, to hear the "results" from the orator himself.

It wasn't quite to be; the televisions, huge electronic bulbs positioned around the park blurted out the secret; candidate Obama was mathematically over the top and "declared" to be the winner. Spoil the moment it didn't as folks, many still finding it hard to believe, grabbed and hugged each other. A din picked up, yet, unlike at a sporting match, the voice of one man in the crowd, one seated senior citizen, an African-American man, cried "Obama!!!"

Finally, President-elect Barack Obama with his characteristic soft-pedal emerged onto the stage with his beautiful family to address the world. But here in Chicago it was just like a pep rally for a familiar friend.

That changed as the president-elect with his customary patience, temperance and disciplined approach rose to the moment. Then with a steely, intense swagger, President-elect Barack Obama stepped before the microphone as his family was ushered off and with perfect timing began to speak:

"With this moment, change has come to America!"

Obama the Change Agent

Shortly after the party for the new president came the hangover from the outgoing gang, the Bush administration. Left with an economy in free fall, the Obama administration inherited the grim reality of some 700,000 jobs being lost per month and home foreclosures growing exponentially--the swindle brought about by the disappearance of securitized and bundled mortgage loans disappearing. Two wars, neither popular with the American people continued, claiming dozens of U.S. military each week and crushing the spirit of families who would suffer through the sea of grief such loss inflicted. There was a general sense that the nation was on the brink of something all but a small part of the population had ever experienced. The response of the new president was to provide a bailout, not for the people, but for the banks and the companies that were "too big to fail." The new administration did provide a stimulus, but one too small to matter for the millions devastated by the maelstrom. While the American Recovery and Reinvestment Act (ARRA) did at first in 2009 save thousands of teaching jobs, the economy would continue to fail and school districts—strapped by decreasing state revenues—were forced to make tough decisions concerning personnel.

Obama's detractors from the right included the so-called *Tea Party* which painted the president as a socialist for launching the ARRA and for trying to fix the healthcare system. On the other side of the political spectrum, progressive democrats criticized his administration for bailing out the banks and selling out their beloved single-payer healthcare initiative to the pharmaceutical industry and the insurance companies. During the rest of 2009-2010 the president had to contend with gridlock and a "do-nothing" congress. The Democrats who held power in Congress seemed quite ineffectual. When the Republicans took over the reins in the fall of 2010, the president's party went from ineffectual to utterly stymied. Lost in the corporate media newspaper pages and television spin was the fact that Obama himself would frequently cave to the Republicans on signature issues like the deficit and/or Bush era tax breaks for the wealthy. He catered to the Wall Street interests by bailing out the "too big to fail" banks that he would only later castigate, long after the infamous bonuses had been distributed and the thievery had been complete.

His selection of Arne Duncan for Secretary of Education, instead of Linda Darling-Hammond (many educators candidate of choice) indicated that the president, similar to his other appointments, mirrored Wall Street interests and less that of the teachers themselves. For anyone who had examined his education platform during the campaign—charter school enthusiasm, teacher pay-for-performance, and a "no excuses" signature strategy—the selection of Duncan was of little surprise. Then, Arne Duncan, proudly carrying the legacy of Chicago Commercial Club Curriculum reform, moved to Washington, D.C.

Duncan the Reformer

Who was Arne Duncan? Among other things he was a former professional basketball player and a sociology graduate from Harvard who grew up in Hyde Park neighborhood of Chicago and spent his youth schools days in the elite private setting of the University of Chicago laboratory school. He joined the Chicago school system under Paul Vallas in 1998 and was appointed CEO in 2001. It was immediately apparent that his vision for Chicago school reform represented the policy embodiment of the school restructuring designs advocated by the Commercial Club of Chicago and their elite allies among the national and global corporate community based in Chicago.

On July 17, 2008 Arne Duncan, CEO of Chicago Public Schools, testified at an Education and Labor Committee hearing concerning mayor and superintendent partnerships in education. When Representative Danny Davis, chair of that committee introduced Arne Duncan, he did so reading Duncan's portfolio and describing him as the person who directed the "Ariel Education Initiative" under "Ariel Capital" CEO John Rogers. It was telling that the hoopster's main experience in education was as a venture capitalist for Rogers and as a tutor at a business run school contracted under provisions of NCLB to help remediate struggling students. It was even more revealing that the Ariel Education Initiative/tutoring school would be closed and then reopened as a charter.

At the hearing of a committee convened to reauthorize the *No Child Left Behind* law,[1] Duncan touted the five successes of his Chicago tenure:

1) Ending social promotion: Chicago held students accountable to annual state assessments; requiring interventions of mandatory after school programs, summer schools and alternative schools, smaller class sizes and extended day programs

2) Implementing a back to the basics curriculum which provided great emphasis on literacy and placed hundreds of coaches in the schools, creating a requirement of 2 hours of reading every day in every grade, for every school and child. "We've expanded math" and now are looking at the social sciences

3) Opening an array of schools through R2010 initiative; 75 charter schools operating in Chicago; some are single sex schools, military academies and residential schools. Duncan would repeatedly claim that almost all are succeeding, and there was a waiting list. Duncan: "I see myself as a portfolio manager" who wants to open 35 schools in the fall but also close down schools that are failing. We are one of the few districts in the country that shuts down under performing schools and replaces the entire school staff. This turnaround strategy has taken an entire school and doubled or tripled school performance. Same children, same families, same socio-economic challenges, same neighborhood, same school building. But different teachers, different leaders and new educational approach. Puts the lie to the idea of what poor children can or cannot do. Buck stops with the mayor, pushing the envelope and driving change (his advocacy for mayoral takeover).

4) Dramatically expanding learning opportunities for pre-school, after school, Saturday school, and summer school; putting students to work more hours . . . presaging the longer school day.

5) Raising the quality of principals and teachers talent, getting the best and brightest working with our children every single day; which cut in half the number of persons eligible to become principals[2]

Duncan was throughout his professional career at the right place at the right time. He clearly had an inside track for upward appointments every step of the

way. And as Chicago school reform's favorite son, he was comfortable in the role of being feted by the Commercial Club of Chicago.

Nonetheless, Duncan's appointment did not go unnoticed by critical educators who raised the obvious question of whether his slim education credentials and close ties to the financial sector qualified him to make decisions affecting the lives of millions of children and adults in the public sector. One article by Giroux and Saltman immediately called out the president for betraying public education by appointing Duncan.[3] Another article by Ayers and Klonsky pointed out with alarming accuracy how the language of reform, small schools and even "social justice" had been co-opted by the *Renaissance 2010* resulting in a massive privatization of social space.[4] Yet another observer criticized the Duncan selection, going after the key issue: the lack of local control, democratic process, and shared decision making in the third largest school district in the country:

> . . . Chicago Public Schools (CPS) policies are not really about Duncan or his successor. The biggest threat to finally achieving equitable and quality education in Chicago's low-income African American and Latino/schools is not the individual who carries out the policy but a system of mayoral control and corporate power that locks out democracy. The impact of those policies includes thousands of children displaced by school closings, spiked violence as they transferred to other schools and the deterioration of public education in many neighborhoods into a crisis situation.[5]

Duncan was even criticized by the Commercial Club of Chicago's Civic Committee through the report *Still Left Behind*. When it came out in 2009, it created a stir because this group, previously seen to be quite supportive of the former CEO's reform, now unequivocally attacked and disparaged what they saw as Chicago's overall flat test scores![6] However, the most damning evidence of Duncan's tenure—and what was in store for the rest of the country under his tutelage—was his penchant to close Chicago city schools:

> Arne Duncan has overseen the beginning destruction of neighborhood schools with neighborhood students. Schools are no longer community pillars because many students no longer live in the area. When CPS closes schools and reopens them as Renaissance 2010 charter or contract schools, there is no guarantee or requirement that students who attended the old schools will go to the new ones—and many don't. For example, not all new schools are the same grade level as the old schools. There are complicated applications and deadlines, limits on enrollment, requirements of families and informal selection processes that may disadvantage some students.[7]

So there was great concern and trepidation among the defenders of public, democratically controlled schools when Duncan, as U.S. Secretary of Education, took his education reform agenda nation-wide aiming to do to Ohio, then Milwaukee, Wisconsin what he had done in Chicago.

Opening Salvos Fired on Public Education[8]

In February of 2010, a round of attacks on public education exploded, making the mainstream media pay notice. The shot heard around the country was the dismissal of the entire staff, 93—including the principal, three assistant principals and 77 teachers—at Central Falls High School in Rhode Island.[9] The Obama-Duncan administrations' enthusiastic endorsement of the Rhode Island school district's decision was noted by education reporter Valerie Strauss:

> Duncan said the district officials were "showing courage and doing the right thing for kids." And then Obama spoke out, saying in part, "If a school continues to fail its students year after year after year, if it doesn't show signs of improvement, then there's got to be a sense of accountability."[10]

In fact, as noted by many, the school had been improving, despite having extreme problems ranging from being one of the smallest and poorest in the state and serving a large population of transient, non-English speaking students.

Following this was the threatened layoffs of tens of thousands of teachers across the country. Chicago Public Schools CEO Ron Huberman struck fear in the hearts of many CPS teachers by stating in that thousands could be cut:

> Chicago Public Schools is facing a deficit of up to $1 billion next year that can be reduced only through a combination of pension reform, union concessions and job cuts, schools chief Ron Huberman said Thursday. Without all three measures in conjunction, Huberman said, teacher layoffs, increased class sizes and cuts to important programs are distinct possibilities.[11]

Chop the Top[12]

Subsequently, the entire school community started to mobilize against the CEO's calls for more cuts and austerity. On the corner of Washington and Clark, a throng of teachers, principals, parents, children, and others marched together, shutting down an entire Chicago city block during rush hour, and sending a clear message to then Mayor Daley about his political appointee Ron Huberman, the CEO. Their demand: "Save our schools and chop the top." One of the teams of veteran teachers on the march described the tension of this sprawling rally on May 25th, 2010 succinctly: "Save our schools, too many cuts. Huberman needs to go. He wants to cut everyone from the bottom."

Many onlookers honked in support as yellow school busses dropped off streams of supporters in front of city hall. One pedestrian, however, exchanged words, with a CPS student, asserting the rally was just a big show. The student explained that these weren't just teachers, but parents of CPS students, to which the "man in the suit" (as the student referred to him) became irate: "All of the people earning a paycheck from the private sector, they got to pay for all this stuff." Someone from the crowd joined in: "We all pay taxes!" Another cried: "Tax the corporations!"[13]

A union representative spoke about who would really be hurt given the budget cuts: "It directly affects the kids. We need to work together to really fund human capital and the kids who go along with it." And hearing from the parents, the concerns mirrored one another. This from one parent, hoisting her child on her shoulders above the crowd: "We don't want to see a 37 to 1 ratio. Teachers do a great job and we support them!" And from another parent: "We're from East School. The children should be the priority in this country . . . they're trying to put 35 students per classroom!"[14]

Chicago Teachers Union (CTU) President, Marilyn Stewart provided the union's position on Huberman's plan:

> Small class sizes are better for students, especially minority students. When you have larger class sizes, teachers cannot give students the individualized attention. Our schools need smaller class sizes to be effective.[15]

Stewart took a shot at the CPS leadership: "They have administrators who aren't even educators running our schools, it's absurd." She was followed by Leroy Smith, Chicago full time bus driver, representing dismissed Chicago Transit Authority workers (CTA), who joined the march, shouting "Save our ride, save our schools!" Smith made these observations:

> We are laid off CTA workers. We're out here joining forces with teachers and fighting their fight. First we lost parking, and then we lost meters. Now you take the rides from us, now you take the kids' teachers from us. You are tearing the city down. Ron Huberman cut and changed the routes, now instead of doing one street, you're doing two or three streets. He came in and turned around just like he did with the Chicago public schools. From CTA to CPS![16]

Stewart returned with: "I have this button that says Chop the Top . . . it's from 1987! And it's still appropriate today?!"[17]

Race to the Top? It's a Marathon, not a Sprint![18]

Later that summer in 2010 on a rainy afternoon in Milwaukee, a "SOS" Save our Schools Million Teacher March occurred. Milwaukee Public School students there performed a skit, depicting the impact of budget cuts on teacher layoffs and the resulting overcrowding of classrooms.[19] The point made during protest was that too many students with too few teachers would result in students getting less attention, fewer books and deadening curriculum. The students were well aware that a substandard simulation of what public education would be if the budget cuts proposed by Governor Doyle and the legislature would go through. The words of one of the teachers and one of the school board members followed the skit; they knew that public education was being made the fall guy for the thievery of Wall Street. They were sensitive to how the working people of Wisconsin were being laid off and made to pinch pennies while the corporations, after being bailed out by the state, were posting record profits.

Tina Owen, an English teacher, described the dire situation this way:

I've been to budget decision gatherings where we've gone line through line to figure out what can be cut and there was nothing there. What it really comes down to is this: The funding formula is broken. We're getting less money from the state. We're getting less money from the federal government . . . And we're not putting money into schools where it really needs to be![20]

Terry Falk, an MPS School Board Director explained the pickle they [Milwaukee] were in as follows:

Our school board [MPS] didn't like the cuts they made, but I want you to understand we were cut funding by the state of Wisconsin. And we're limited by law how much we can raise taxes. We see people saying 'we're leaving our children a huge debt' and calling it 'immoral'. But what is 'moral' about cutting classes and putting kids in [overcrowded schools]? We need to get a conversation in this country about what it means to have educated children, and how we're going to sustain that education, for the long haul.[21]

Falk ended by urging to, "Run the race, run the marathon, it's not a sprint."

Stopping Mayoral Takeover

As documented in Chapter 9, Secretary of Education Arne Duncan tried to launch the Race to the Top, in the heartland of the country, Ohio. But when faced with a strong showing of teachers and their union, and a true education reformer in the visage of Governor Ted Strickland, Duncan's message of competition and "no excuses" flopped. Duncan moved on shortly thereafter to Milwaukee, where—meeting behind the scenes instead of in front of a throng of public school teachers and their supporters—he found a smaller cadre of Race to the Top supporters in the visage of the Wisconsin Governor, the Milwaukee Mayor, and the State Superintendent of Public Instruction (see Chapter 7).

And so it was against this backdrop that in the March 2010 edition of *The People's Tribune* I reported on the successful setback to the forces of privatization of education, represented by the Obama-Duncan team, and the subsequent attempt at disenfranchisement of the citizen voter (represented by Mayoral takeovers of school boards).

I described at great detail the scenario: the literal soap opera where the Wisconsin Democratic Party and their officials switched sides in the struggle to save public education.

Literally, on the one hand was the lame duck Governor, James Doyle. Doyle as Wisconsin's Attorney General—during much of the 1990s—had fought vouchers, the Milwaukee Parental Choice Plan to be specific, in court . . . and largely won. Only years later as Governor (2002 to 2010) did he start to do a "turnaround," raising the caps on these voucher/public taxpayer-sponsored private schools . . . and enthusiastically supporting charter schools as well.

On the other hand, was enigmatic State Representative Annette "Polly" Williams, for many years the darling of the free market loving, public education hating crowd. Williams, a liberal Democrat and mother who was at one point reliant on public assistance, was the ideal figure for advancing the Republican agenda of "School Choice" . . . of vouchers for Milwaukee and beyond. Now having largely recognized how the voucher program had been hijacked by the rich (she had always maintained that vouchers would help poor Black children) Williams disavowed herself from that history. She opted in her public hearings—the final scene of this political soap opera—to oppose her Democratic colleagues, the Governor and Mayor[22] combined who sought to take over the Milwaukee Public School District with a hostile and largely unpopular dismantling of an elected school board and the placing of all executive appointment power in the hands of the mayor who would then personally select the school board.

One needed to keep a scorecard as the leaders of the Wisconsin Democratic Party shifted principles and loyalties like free agents switching teams in professional baseball. Next, Governor Doyle gave the green light for mayoral takeover after meeting with U.S. Education Secretary Arne Duncan. Then Doyle in a surprising plot twist opted to pull out of the Wisconsin governor's race entirely. Following this change of course Milwaukee Mayor Tom Barrett threw his support in for the mayoral takeover, only to affirm (not in so many words of course) that any such a takeover would likely happen on someone else's watch because he anticipated becoming Wisconsin's next governor!

But there was more.

The Governor and Mayor's efforts in securing the needed legislation for a Milwaukee mayoral takeover was buttressed with lobbying by a Wall Street friendly, hedge fund-sponsored, charter school advocate organization. Members of the Wisconsin Democratic Party quickly split into two camps. One camp was in support of public education and saw teachers unions as critical to protecting teachers' job and essential for safeguarding the overall conditions of the schools. Another camp aligned with Democrats for Education Reform, the anti-teacher union, corporate school reform faction of the Democratic National Committee. This split had significance beyond fomenting the battle for Milwaukee public schools. It represented a Wisconsin Democratic party at war with itself. The result was that in Milwaukee Mayor Tom Barrett's run for governor, his endorsement of the mayoral takeover certainly hurt him at the polls. On November 2010, Barrett and the Democratic Party across the country lost. This fallout among Democrats effectively opened the way for radical Republicans, none more so than County Executive Scott Walker, the "backwards Walkerman" as he despicably came to be called, to enter the front door of the Wisconsin Governor's mansion.

The Battle over the Wisconsin "Budget Repair Bill"[23]

With the passing of this statute in 1959,

CHAPTER III EMPLOYMENT RELATIONS SUBCHAPTER IV
Rights of Employees to Organize or Join Labor Organizations and Relating to Bargaining in Municipal Employment
2) Rights of Municipal Employees. Municipal employees shall have the right of self-organization, to affiliate with labor organizations of their own choosing

and the right to be represented by labor organizations of their own choice in conferences and negotiations with their municipal employers or their representatives on questions of wages, hours and conditions of employment, and such employees shall have the right to refrain from any and all such activities.[24]

. . . Wisconsin became the first state in the nation to recognize the right of all municipal employees to be represented through "meaningful collective negotiations between teacher organizations and boards of education."[25] Fifty years later, a firestorm was created when newly elected Governor Scott Walker in February of 2011 went after public sector employee's rights. The "Budget Repair Bill" was a reactionary reversal of the 1951 act. The proposed legislation included the following provisions:

STATE AND LOCAL GOVERNMENT AND SCHOOL DISTRICT LABOR RELATIONS
Collective bargaining
The bill would make various changes to limit collective bargaining for most public employees to wages. Total wage increases could not exceed a cap based on the consumer price index (CPI) unless approved by referendum.

Contracts would be limited to one year and wages would be frozen until the new contract is settled. Collective bargaining units are required to take annual votes to maintain certification as a union.

Employers would be prohibited from collecting union dues and members of collective bargaining units would not be required to pay dues. These changes take effect upon the expiration of existing contracts.

Local law enforcement and fire employees, and state troopers and inspectors would be exempt from these changes.[26]

The Governor rejected any overtures—concessions that had already been made by Wisconsin's American Federation of State, Council, and Municipal Employees (AFSCME) to pay for more of their benefits—and instead, immediately set about to balance the entire budget on the backs of working people. Following his announcement to strip away collective bargaining— effectively slashing not only benefits to all public sector workers[27]—the streets around the Madison, Wisconsin state capitol filled up with citizens from every walk of life standing up for their public sector coworkers . . . families, friends, brothers and sisters.

It's hard to express in words the pace of the breathtaking events, the worst for teachers being the plan in the "Budget Repair Bill" to cut $1.6 billion from the schools. Governor Walker was joined by the Fitzgerald team—two brothers who controlled the entire legislature—one as the Assembly Speaker, the other as the Senate President. The Fitzgerald brothers immediately followed the Governor with an aggressive legislative agenda that set the normally civil chambers and conference rooms on fire as lawmakers; both parties went into a tailspin. The proposed cuts to the public education budget, as steep as they were, paled in comparison to the hastily assembled legislation that—had it passed—might have killed public education in the state that had in many ways participated in its birth. Assembly Bill 92 was proposed, for example, to expand the Milwaukee Parental Choice Program—vouchers/public funds for private schools—beyond the city of Milwaukee to the county so that wealthy private schools and their constituents could also gain extra funding from the public's general revenues. Another piece of legislation, Senate Bill 22, proposed to institute a newly *unelected* charter school "accountability" board with members *appointed* by Governor Walker and the Fitzgerald brothers. The creation of a Walker's executive-appointed charter board would be able to supersede local authorization of charter schools, jettisoning democratic decision-making at the school board level and overturning what had been local jurisdiction over local school matters, which has been in place, since the early Puritans had called for a local tithe (tax) to support the education of the communities children.[28] This private board would also have created yet another drain on the public school coffers, beyond destroying the entire edifice upon which public schools currently reside, namely, being constituted by and democratically representing the local community.

The disastrous impact of Walker's proposed budget cuts on all aspects of life in Wisconsin were well understood by the citizens protesting on the street, but no more so than by the teachers and the students. They accurately foresaw what loomed for public education, and the results have only recently become fully apparent. The comprehensive and richly documented study "D is for Dismantling" provides us with substantial evidence from international, national and state reports that totally debunk the repeated claims Walker and his cabal used to defend their massive cuts to public schools and their attacks on teacher unions.[29] Public education in Wisconsin—despite being touted as over-priced and ineffective by Walker and other privatizers—fared very well overall in both national and international comparisons.

A close analysis of Wisconsin high school graduation rates with international comparisons placed the state in a tie at 6th place with Korea, a ranking only preceded by Germany, Finland, Greece, Japan and Norway. The Wisconsin Department of Public Instruction reports—required by the federal government under NCLB—show that 75% of Wisconsin students scored in the advanced or proficient range in reading, math and science on the 2010 Wisconsin Knowledge and Concepts Examination (WKCE). In comparison with other states reporting—in states where at least 70% of high school students take the ACT examination according to the American College Testing Service—Wisconsin ranks third in the nation with an average student score of 22.1 just behind first place Minnesota with average scores of 22.9 and second place Iowa with average scores of 22.3. And in an area deemed so vital to future school success, Wisconsin is one of only a handful of states where over one half of all four year olds are enrolled in four-year old kindergarten.[30]

Walker's claim that Wisconsin schools were in a disastrous condition was simply part of his campaign strategy, *Wisconsin Open for Business*. This effort aimed to and apparently succeeded in distracting many citizens from noticing the corporate tax breaks provided to his campaign sponsors as Walker launched an ideological attack to weaken and eventually destroy the public school system. The budget cuts to school funding provide more evidence to support this disturbing reality.

The dire financial situation Wisconsin schools are in as the 2011-2012 school year came to an end (and after Walker faced and proved victorious in a massive recall election) are the results of the deepest cuts to state school funding since the Great Depression of the 1930s. What compounds this dire situation is the fact that the Walker Administration's "Budget Repair Bill" has impacted not only inner city districts already struggling to provide adequate resources, but all of the districts, even those that were otherwise flush with resources.

Overall, the total loss in school funding amounts to $1.6 billion for this past school year (2011-2012). This total includes direct cuts to school districts of $749 million and an additional diversion of $37 million from public schools to new voucher and charter programs. Adding to the staggering total was the mandate for local districts to cut their property taxes by $326 million. These numbers equate to an average 9.98% cut in funding for all districts. As a consequence of these draconian measures, districts have had to make reductions to essential programs including media services, libraries, counseling, the arts, drug prevention, reading and early childhood education and special assistance to students with disabilities and English language learners. With over 8000 fewer teachers in the state this year, class sizes are up in 60% of the all districts.[31] Adding to all of these reductions is the more disturbing fact that the burden on districts and children has not been equally shared. The average reductions in general state aid per pupil has fallen hardest on districts with greater percentages of student(s) on free or reduced lunch, the figure that corresponds roughly to family poverty rates. Using this measure, state reductions vary from $294 per student in wealthier districts, those with less than 10% of students eligible for free and reduced lunch to $558 per student(s) in districts with over 60% of students receiving free and reduced lunch.[32]

It has become apparent to millions of other Wisconsin citizens that the national Republican plan to make the poor pay more and reduce taxes on wealthier citizens is playing out in the Walker design for undermining public school financial stability. This pattern replicates the impacts that inequitable tax cuts—which favor upper income tax payers—are having nationally. It is just the latest imposition of the infamous and failed "trickle down" theory which has failed in the past and repeats it failure in Wisconsin today. In the wake of Walker's $2 billion tax breaks for the business community, according to Bureau of Labor statistics numbers released in October of 2011, Wisconsin led the nation in job losses over the past year.[33]

First Responders to the Fire

Thus, to say Walker set the state on fire is an understatement. The protests put hundreds of thousands on the streets, and the recall movement that followed, though unsuccessful, mobilized even more. The outcome has been devastation for public education.

However, the embers of the growing resistance to corporate siege burnt early and have not been extinguished. It was in the first week of the outpouring of support for the public sector workers that citizens stood up and spoke out. Called upon to put out the fire set by Wisconsin Governor Scott Walker, a male teacher from Sun Prairie, a bit nervous, stepped to the microphone and laid it on the line during the third day of that Madison, Wisconsin rally:

> I want to let you know my wife is also a teacher . . . this "repair bill" the governor has so politely sent to the gentleman in [the capitol] behind us will double the impact on our household!!

> I have an eight year-old daughter and a ten year-old son who are going to be victimized by this bill! How many of you share that story? This is an attack on the middle class, it's an attempt to break our unions, and I say kill the bill![34]

Much to the surprise of the Governor (who had been "ousted," in a stealth telephone call, as warm to the idea of planting provocateurs amongst the protestors in order to justify bringing in the police to make arrests), the firefighters—public sector employees who would have been exempt from the law—also stepped up, and in a most inspiring manner, stood shoulder to shoulder in solidarity with their union brothers and sisters, the public school teachers. In support of collective bargaining, the chief, a young African-American man, immaculately dressed in a business suit, stepped to the podium. Mahlon Mitchell bellowed:

> When firefighters and police see an emergency, what do we do? We respond. When firefighters see a burning building . . . when everyone is running out, where do we go? In! Well our house is burning down ladies and gentlemen. So we're here to go in, we're going to lead the charge and go in first.[35]

To a backdrop of pipes, horns, music and cacophony Mitchell and the firefighters did just that; leading tens of thousands of citizens into the burning building known as the people's house, the state capitol. In the days ahead in showing their support for the rights of working people everywhere, firefighters and then the police officers stepped forward to literally say "I've got your back" and supported teachers' right to have a say in their workplace.

A Modest Proposal

Wisconsin citizens did not hesitate; they made the decision to push back. They were the first responders, like the Sun Prairie teacher who took the microphone, the third day of the protest:

> Brothers and sisters . . . this is about the rich history of unionized employment and progressive democracy in the great state of Wisconsin. For well over 50 years the managers and workers of Wisconsin have sat side by side and worked together to solve problems together. In one fell swoop the Governor and men

and women inside the capitol are threatening to take that rich history and throw it aside.

The nurses, the day care providers, the police, the state employees, the fire fighters, the correctional officers, the educators and the education support professionals of this state, the private sector employees, the small business owners . . . not just in Wisconsin, folks, but in America . . . our freedoms are under attack. The freedoms that workers in our state have spent over fifty years fighting for . . .

We can't stand by and let this happen. We just want a voice, a chance to talk, and a chance to work together. A chance to negotiate; he wants to legislate. Say it again, negotiate not legislate![36]

Notes

1. See "Improving Public Schools Hearing: Arne Duncan Part 1" http://youtu.be/_5k_4yOMKrI
2. Ibid.
3. Henry A. Giroux and Kenneth Saltman, Obama's Betrayal of Public Education? Arne Duncan and the Corporate Model of Schooling. *Cultural Studies ↔ Critical Methodologies*, December 2009 9: 772-779.
4. William Ayers and Michael Klonsky, "Chicago's Renaissance 2010: The Small Schools Movement Meets the Ownership Society," *Phi Delta Kappan*, Vol. 87, No. 06, February 2006, pp. 453-457.
5. Jitu Brown, "Arne Duncan and the Chicago Success Story: Myth or Reality?" (Rethinkingschools.org. Spring, 2009) Retrieved 2011 06-13.
6. *Still Left Behind: Student Learning in Chicago's Public Schools.* Civic Committee of the Commercial Club of Chicago. June 2009.
7. Op. Cit. Brown, 2009.
8. This excerpt is drawn from an article in the April 2010 edition of *The People's Tribune* P.O. Box 3524, Chicago, IL 60654, 800-691-6888 info@peoplestribune.org
9. Randi Kaye, "All teachers fired at Rhode Island school" CNN's AC360° February 24, 2010.
10. Valerie Strauss, "Why Obama, Duncan should have kept quiet about Rhode Island teachers." Posted at 6:30 AM ET, 05/17/2010
11. Azam Ahmed, "CPS faces $1 billion deficit, Huberman says Only pension reform, union concessions and layoffs can stave off crisis," Tribune, February 25, 2010.
12. This excerpt is drawn from an article in the June 2010 edition of *The People's Tribune* P.O. Box 3524, Chicago, IL 60654, 800-691-6888 info@peoplestribune.org
13. See "Chicago Teachers Union Rally" http://youtu.be/JzyM8q9zoaA
14. Ibid.
15. Ibid.
16. Ibid.
17. Ibid.
18. This excerpt is drawn from the September 2010 edition of *The People's Tribune* P.O. Box 3524, Chicago, IL 60654, 800-691-6888 info@peoplestribune.org
19. See "SOS Million Teachers March Part III" http://youtu.be/9I3zmemN2ew
20. See "SOS Million Teachers March Part IV" http://youtu.be/iX7-d4KYHSc
21. See "SOS Million Teachers March Part V" http://youtu.be/qO_93VQcHhw
22. See "Polly Williams" part 3 http://youtu.be/xcPqUbOvtiI

23. This excerpt is drawn from the March 2011 edition of *The People's Tribune* P.O. Box 3524, Chicago, IL 60654, 800-691-6888 info@peoplestribune.org

24. Myron Lieberman and Michael H. Moskow, *Collective Negotiations for Teachers: An Approach to School Administration.* (Chicago: Rand McNally, 1966) p. 53.

25. Ibid. p. 53.

26. Read summary of Gov. Scott Walker's budget repair bill. 8:27 AM, Feb. 16, 2011. See http://www.greenbaypressgazette.com/article/20110216/GPG0101/110216041/Read-summary-Gov-Scott-Walker-s-budget-repair-bill

27. Except police and firefighters, whom Governor Walker hoped would support his attack on the others; he was mistaken in this regard.

28. Spring, Joel H., and Joel H. Spring. 2008. *The American school: from the Puritans to no child left behind.* Boston: McGraw-Hill. Also, as Duffy notes, it is important to realize that the idea of the state chartering charter schools is not unique to Wisconsin; the commission in place in Illinois, it should be noted, is financed not with Illinois tax revenue, but with a million dollar plus gift from the Walton Family Foundation.

29. *The Institute for One Wisconsin Report: 'D is for Dismantle'.* Available at www.onewisconsinnow.org/press/institute-for-one-wisconsin-report-d-is-for-dismantle.html

30. Statistical data provided here on Wisconsin state test scores, education budget cuts, and comparisons of districts all come from studies found in *D is for Dismantle*. These studies include: National Center for Education Statistics (2011). NCES Public School Graduates and Dropouts from the Common Core of Data: School Year 2008-09 First Look (312), 6; The Organization for Economic Cooperation and Development (2009). Education at a Glance 2009, Excel Spreadsheet Table A2.1 Upper secondary graduation rates; Wisconsin Department of Public Instruction, 2010---11 WKCE Test Results; 2011 ACT National and State Scores, Average Scores by State; National Center for Education Statistics (NCES) Freshman graduation rates, 2008-09 (released in 2011); Trends in 4-Year-Old Kindergarten. Wisconsin Department of Public Instruction.

31. Andrew Reschovsky, Update to La Follette School Working Paper No. 2011-012: "The Impact on Property Taxes of the Governor's 2011-12 School Funding Proposals," July 3, 2011. Retrieved from: https://www.wasbmemberservices.org/campaigns/CMPART/ACC1/CMPART210/File/update_lafollette_sch_working_paper_.pdf

32. Bob Lang, *Property Tax Estimates of Senate Bill 27 and Assembly Bill 40.* Legislative Fiscal Bureau Memo; *Wisconsin Association of School District Administrators.* Wisconsin Department of Public Instruction Budget Survey Analysis. November 10, 2011. Retrieved from: http://dpi.wi.gov/eis/pdf/wasdasurveyresults.pdf; Richards, Erin. How Much Could Your District Lose Under Walker's Budget, *Milwaukee Journal Sentinel*, February 28, 2011. Retrieved from: http://www.jsonline.com/blogs/news/117096253.html.

33. See John Nichols, Under Walker: Wisconsin is No. 1 job loser, Cap Times available at http://host.madison.com/ct/news/opinion/column/john_nichols/john-nichols-under-walker-wisconsin-is-no-job-loser/article_e8984ba1-f2c5-5f5a-bc96-943cf53e8fd8.html

34. See "A teachers message" http://youtu.be/2T8AX87tNZM

35. See "First Responders" http://youtu.be/QZ5CqhL5X4o

36. Op. cit.

Chapter 15
This *is* What Democracy Looks Like!
T.J. Mertz

In late January, 2012 as I write this review and reflection of the extraordinary and nationally watched political developments of the past year in the state of Wisconsin, Government Accountability Board employees in Wisconsin are processing the over one million signatures gathered to recall Governor Scott Walker and tens of thousands of signatures collected for the second round of recalls directed at Republic State Senators. It has been barely a year since Walker took office and then along with new Republican majorities in the State Senate and Assembly began a series of systematic attacks on public employees and the public sector. Public education, teachers and teacher unions were among the most prominent targets of these attacks. They have also been at the center of the resistance that among other things resulted in one million Wisconsinites expressing their desire to see Governor Walker's term cut short. A full discussion of the roles of public education in the recent events in Wisconsin is beyond the scope of this chapter. Instead, I will provide a description and analysis of the political context and background for what has transpired by sketching a few of the key education-related aspects while concentrating primarily on the story of Senate Bill 22 (SB 22)—the currently stalled attempt to create a state charter school authorizing board, and make Wisconsin more welcome for Charter Management Organizations (CMOs) and virtual schools. Compared to Act 10, which stripped collective bargaining rights and Act 32, the state budget, which cut almost $2 billion in state and local education funding over the biennium, SB 22 may seem like a minor issue, but it became the focus of widespread citizen organizing and that organizing contributed substantially to one of the few defeats for the Walker program. For this and other reasons, the story of SB 22 is one worth telling.

My training is as a historian of public education and my avocation is as a public education activist and advocate. Both those perspectives are present here, but more the latter than the former.

Education policy played direct and indirect roles in the Republican victories of 2010 which brought Walker into office with new majorities in both houses.

Directly, in that teachers, teacher unions and public schools in general had long been favorite targets of ant-government and privatization activists like those funded by the Milwaukee based Bradley Foundation and the now infamous Koch Brothers. Through foundation "think tanks," AstroTurf organizations and independent advertising expenditures, the groundwork for Walker's election and program were laid. Indirectly education played a role in Walker's ascendency and the Republican attacks because over many years Democrats had often embraced bi-partisan compromises on issues like school vouchers, charter schools and virtual schools, while doing nothing to fix a state school finance system that most agreed was broken. During the two years immediately preceding Walker's election Democrats in control of state government had failed to advance the kind of progressive education policies that would have excited their base. Instead, key players like Governor Jim Doyle and Milwaukee Mayor (and Democratic nominee for Governor against Walker) alienated many educators and public school supporters with rushed legislation passed in pursuit of securing Race to the Top Funds and an attempt encouraged and supported by U.S. Secretary of Education Arne Duncan to establish Mayoral control of Milwaukee's schools. Wisconsin is a swing state nationally and fairly evenly divided between Republicans and Democrats, so voter turnout matters. At this time in Wisconsin education issues stimulated turnout among Republicans and depressed turnout among Democrats, creating the perfect formula for Walker's election.

The Walker campaign had been clear in its desire to cut educational spending and compensation for educators and other public employees, but had not previewed the dismantling of collective bargaining it would later unveil as part of the so-called Budget Repair Bill (what would eventually become Act 10) on Friday February 11, 2011. This lengthy bill ranged widely, touching on things as disparate as the sale of power plants and stripping affirmative action requirements for contracting. At the heart of the legislation were new rules for public employee unions that required annual recertification, new employee contributions to healthcare and pensions and limited collective bargaining to wages tied to and limited by the rate of inflation. In theory unions could still exist, but in practice this was a death sentence.

The reaction was swift and much of it came from educators. As many observed, a sleeping giant had awoken. Serendipitously, in anticipation of cuts to higher education, the Teaching Assistants Association (one of the oldest and strongest Graduate Employee unions) and other University of Wisconsin organizations had already organized a mass delivery of Valentine cards with the message "I (heart) UW, Governor Walker Don't Break My Heart." Thousands participated and the Budget Repair bill became part of the message.

The following day, teachers, staff and students from Madison schools, with the support of the local union Madison Teachers Incorporated (MTI), joined the protests and the numbers swelled to above 10,000. Madison schools were forced to close and would remain closed the rest of the week and the following Monday. The statewide teacher union, the Wisconsin Education Association Council (WEAC), followed MTI's lead in encouraging members to come to

Madison and join the protests. As a result schools were shut down in many locales. Although reaction was mixed, many parents and students supported the actions of the teachers. In Milwaukee an "I Love (heart) My Public School" group formed to organize against the Walker education agenda. Madison's Community and Schools Together (CAST)—I'm a member of CAST—issued a statement that read in part:

> Making public education work relies on trust and partnership. Despite Wisconsin's strong record on public education and despite all the benefits our communities receive from public education, Gov. Walker has decided to break trust and partnership with WEAC and other unions. In so doing, he has unnecessarily broken the state's relationship with teachers. The outcry has been mobilized by the broad assaults to organized labor, but they are marked most visibly by the many teachers, parents, and students who have provided the core and bulk numbers to the strong protests.

With lines being drawn and education issues defining where many stood, the next weeks were eventful and heady. Protests continued daily, with weekend crowds growing to 30,000, then 70,000 and finally over 100,000 people in the streets. Democrats held around the clock hearings where opponents of the bill gave voice to their objections. Celebrities such as Michael Moore and Jesse Jackson came to Madison to lend support. The rotunda of the Capital was occupied. Then the building was cleared as the mass public was locked at and those allowed to enter were limited and subjected to security checks. There was talk of a general strike. 14 State Senators fled to Illinois to deny the quorum required to pass the bill, and then the Republican majority decided that the requirement did not apply and acted with none of the opposition present.

Almost all who mobilized in resistance understood that the battle over the Budget Repair Bill would be lost (as it was on March 10), but the acts of mobilization and resistance nevertheless resulted in a sense of empowerment. It was exhilarating and transformative for many. Creativity blossomed via costumes; homemade signs and slogans; songs and chants, old, new and rewritten. The most prominent slogan "This is what democracy looks like" captured the spirit and reflected the idea that as Henry David Thoreau wrote, democracy "does not depend on what kind of paper you drop into the ballot-box once a year, but on what kind of man you drop from your chamber into the street every morning." Tens of thousands of people who never imagined themselves as activists came to understand the importance and power of activism. This new mass of mobilized citizens who in the past had paid little or no attention to legislative doings were now attending hearings or watching the live feeds. Thousands were pouring over analyses of bills; hundreds were producing and sharing their own analysis via the Internet or in spontaneous speeches to the gathered crowds at the Capital.

It was in this heightened atmosphere that SB 22 was introduced on February 23, 2011. After the Budget Repair Bill and the Budget itself (introduced on March 10th, after being delayed due to the protests), SB 22 was the first education related bill of the legislative session (Senate Bills 20 and 34, dealing with school properties in Milwaukee and residence requirements for Milwaukee Public School employees were introduced at approximately the same time) . Many other education initiatives would follow. These included Governor Walker's education "task forces" and "design teams" which were deliberately designed to be outside the legislative process and thus avoided public meeting notification and records requirements. Patricia Levesque of Jeb Bush's Foundation for Excellence in Education (who Walker brought in to present to his "Read to Lead Task Force), revealed the thinking behind the flurry of bills and actions at an October 2010 Gates Foundation funded conference. Lee Fang reported in *The Nation*:

> Next year, Levesque advised, reformers should "spread" the unions thin "by playing offense" with decoy legislation. Levesque said she planned to sponsor a series of statewide reforms, like allowing taxpayer dollars to go to religious schools by overturning the so-called Blaine Amendment, "even if it doesn't pass . . . to keep them busy on that front." She also advised paycheck protection, a union busting scheme, as well as a state-provided insurance program to encourage teachers to leave the union and a transparency law to force teachers unions to show additional information to the public. Needling the labor unions with all these bills, Levesque said, allows certain charter bills to fly "under the radar."[i]

In Wisconsin, to a great degree, this strategy backfired. Instead of distracting and overwhelming existing opposition, Walker's implementation created mass awareness and citizen activism.

The core of SB 22 was the creation of a politically appointed statewide Charter Authorizing Board, which would allow would-be school operators to bypass elected school boards and local opposition. Other provisions allowed for chains of charter schools to be authorized, opened attendance at independent charter schools to non-district residents, lifted the caps on virtual charter school enrollments, granted new civil and criminal immunities to charter operators, modified teacher licensure requirements for charter schools, prioritized funding for charter and created a mechanism whereby an entire district could be converted to charters. These Boards exist in a number of states and establishing them has been a priority for the American Legislative Exchange Council and the National Association of Charter School Authorizers. They have also been controversial, with reform efforts coming in Minnesota and New Jersey and the Georgia State Supreme Court ruling that state's Board unconstitutional. Still, in normal times it would have been probable that after some compromises legislation like SB 22, like earlier, charter, virtual school and voucher measures, would have passed with bi-partisan support.[1]

Even before the first Senate hearing was scheduled for March 23rd, a new kind of opposition began to coalesce. A group of University of Wisconsin education students and education professionals (including some involved with existing or proposed district charter schools) formed "Public Schools for the Public Good" to disseminate information and connect opponents. I formed a Facebook group "Stop the Charter School Bill" for similar purposes. The group quickly grew to almost 300 members and has continued as a statewide network for progressive education advocacy. Information about SB 22 also went out on many of the twitter, email, Facebook, blogs and Internet networks that had grown along with the resistance to the Walker agenda.

The March 23rd hearing was like nothing I had ever seen in years of attending legislative education committees.[3] In the past, hearings usually attracted only those with a direct professional interest, lobbyists for interested parties and on occasion choreographed attendance and testimony from interested members of the public. All these usual participants were present, but the overflow crowd was primarily made up of self-activated citizens, taking advantage of one of the first opportunities offered to bring the revitalized spirit of participatory democracy to bear on pending educational policies.

The hearing began with the usual suspects, 13 lobbyists and officials from charter schools, charter school organizations and "choice" advocacy groups testifying in favor of the bill. Groups represented included the Wisconsin Association of Charter Schools, the National Alliance for Public Schools, the National Association of Charter School Authorizers, and the Wisconsin Coalition of Virtual School Families. All of these organizations have strong ties to and receive funding from national education reform groups. Also testifying in favor was Kaleem Caire, formerly a leader of the Black Alliance for Educational Options, but the Director of the Urban League of Greater Madison. Caire would soon become embroiled in the deeply divisive controversy over a proposal to create the Madison Preparatory Academy Charter discussed in the concluding chapter of this book. 23 people, again dominated by representatives of charter schools, and right wing groups like the American Federation for Children, registered in favor of the legislation.

110 individuals testified against SB 22. In addition, nearly as many registered against the legislation. Many of these individuals including myself submitted written testimony because they had to leave before they were able to testify at the lengthy session. There were representatives from teacher unions, the Wisconsin Association of School District Administrators, the Wisconsin Association of School Boards, the Parent Teacher Association, the Department of Public Instruction and other old hands at legislative hearings. However, for the vast majority of opponents, this was their first experience testifying. People came from all over the state, and although teachers made up a sizable portion of the opposition, many parents, some grandparents and some with no direct connection to the schools offered their testimony. Their words ranged from heartfelt pleas on behalf of public education in general to focused critiques of the particulars of the bill. Three common themes emerged. The first was a broad protest against all of the attacks on and cuts to public schools and moves toward privatization. The second theme emphasized the loss of local control and asserted that the current charter school authorizing system was working. The last theme was the questioning of the wisdom and benefits of charter schools as a means of educational improvement and pointed to the lack of evidence in favor of market-based choice reforms. The citizens of Wisconsin were making their voices heard in the halls of power. It was amazing to witness and be part of.

By the end of the hearing, SB 22 was off the fast track. Seven days later, Republican Senator Dan Kapanke withdrew his name as a co-sponsor. Then things went on hold. In June, the Republicans offered a series of amendments which dealt with technical issues and tweaked two of the more offensive aspects of the proposal. The new version of the Board was designed to be less partisan and include two appointees of the State Superintendent of Public instruction. The other big change required charter petitioners going before the Board to concurrently apply to the district where they would be located. They could no longer by pass the district process, but groups applying to open charters could still win approval for a school turned down by the local district. On June 7th, at a sparsely attended executive session the Senate Education Committee approved the amendments and advanced the Bill to the Joint Committee on Finance.

The democratic energy manifested at the public hearing was still alive, but much of it was now directed towards efforts to recall eight Republican Senators (eight Democrats were also the targets of recall campaigns). These were massive undertakings; requiring approximately 20,000 signatures in each senatorial district, followed by hard fought and expensive campaigns. Sufficient signatures were gathered to force recall elections for six Republican and three Democrats. Ultimately two Republican and no Democratic Senators were removed from office. Senate Education Committee Chair Luther Olsen narrowly prevailed in his election. The Republicans now held a narrow 1-vote majority in the State Senate.

Some people in the Wisconsin resistance see the redirection of energy to electoral politics in support of Democratic candidates as a diversion from the work of building new structures and expanding direct participatory activities. I don't reject that view. However, in the case of SB 22 the electoral efforts worked in concert with the participation in the legislative process and the protests to keep the law from being enacted. In October, the Bill was again amended and approved, this time by the Joint Finance Committee. Since then, nothing has happened. A news report from November indicated that one Republican Senator was reluctant to support the Bill and one other was non-committal. After the recalls, this was enough to effectively kill the Bill.

When the news came that SB 22 was dead, I put up a blog post titled "People Have the Power" (complete with the Patti Smith song of the same title). In that post I wrote: "This is a huge victory for public education in the state, local control, and the Wisconsin people's mobilization." I stand by that, but I also understand that the Budget Repair Bill did become law, that the Budget itself accelerated the cuts to public schools, and that other legislation harmful to public education and many other things passed, although not without protest. As I write this chapter, in addition to the recalls of Governor Walker and more Republican Senators going forward, a new set of education legislation based on misguided standardized test based "accountability" is about to be introduced into the state assembly. As I closed my blogs on that development, I likewise now also remind all of us to ". . . remember that progress may start with getting better people in office, but it isn't going to get very far if we don't remain mobilized, remain powerful."

Notes

i. Lee Fang, "Selling Schools Out." *The Investigative Fund a Project of the Nation Institute*, November 17, 2011. Accessed at August 23, 2012. See http://www.theinvestigativefund.org/investigations/corporateaccountability/1580/?page=entire

2. One manifestation of this bi-partisanship was that Sara Archibald who had headed Democrat Jim Doyle's Race to the Top team now staffed the Senate Education Committee for the Republicans and was in charge of shepherding SB 22 and other initiatives through the legislature.

3. Rebecca Kemble's report here: http://www.progressive.org/conniff0511.html

Conclusion
Turning the Tide on Commercial Club "School Reform"
John Duffy and Todd Alan Price

The struggle to preserve public education today, as we have shown throughout this book, needs to be nestled in local democracy which honors and sponsors the rights of diverse communities and the teachers who serve these communities to control and shape their schools as the key foundational institutions for imagining our greatest ideals as a society. In taking up this challenge today, just as citizens did at the beginning of the 20th century, the resistance to what we have called Commercial Club Curriculum has been renewed with full vigor on many fronts. It is a fight today for building public schools that are democratic, racially and ethnically inclusive, gender equitable, funded adequately and fairly. Schools like these do exist and can become the norm, serving as laboratories for critical democratic learning that prepares children not just for a life of work, but for a thoughtful civic engagement, respect for our shared right to equality and fulfillment of the opportunity for *all* of our children to nurture their individual human potential.

The hard work to achieve this vision of democratic public education is not only taking place in Ohio, Illinois, Wisconsin and California, it is happening across the American landscape. It is a fight that, like all past efforts to preserve and expand democratic institutions, is complicated by other social divisions, but especially by race and class. The penalties, impositions and outright destruction of public schools are targeted first at those communities that have historically confronted chronic inequities that mirror persistent and pronounced social and economic inequality in America. On one hand public schools offer extraordinary opportunity for most American children while at the same time failing to provide comparable educational resources and opportunities to tens of millions of other students, especially the urban and rural and students of color.

Public Schools and Growing Inequality in the United States

In a recent compelling essay Linda Darling-Hammond, the director of the Stanford University Center for Opportunity Policy in Education and founding director of the National Commission on Teaching and America's Future (NCTAF) offered a brisk, but painful description of the social and economic inequalities which place serious limitations on the opportunity for schools to provide children with equitable learning opportunities.

Darling-Hammond argues, and we concur, that while RTT abandons the impositions and penalties of making AYP, it continues to impose radical turnaround models on the bottom 5 percent of American public schools—schools where the overwhelming majority of students are poor, African American, Latino and include the greatest numbers of immigrant children. Unfortunately, there is national bi-partisan political agreement on not recognizing or responding to the historic relationship between poverty and school achievement. This was not the case during an earlier era in modern American history. With the support of concerted federal financial intervention in the late 1960s through the early 1980s, historically underperforming schools and students experienced unprecedented progress in narrowing student achievement gaps in the United States. Yet, following significant educational gains in reading, math, high school graduation, and college attendance during these years, federal and state programs such as major initiatives to reduce poverty, increase employment, re-invigorate depressed communities, invest in pre-school and K-12 education, promote racial desegregation, and offer financial assistance and major resources for teacher training (major features of the Great Society vision of liberal Democrats led by President Johnson) were largely abandoned by the mid-1980s. The dismantling of these federal educational initiatives, coupled with the redistribution of wealth and income upwards has contributed to reversing education gains of the 70s and 80s.

Today in the era of RTT there is a general refusal by corporate and federal policy leaders in the Obama administration to note the common socio-economic contexts that historically surrounds our most struggling schools. The Obama administrations' *A Blueprint for Reform* adopts the "no excuses" mantra so popular with corporate promoters of school restructuring. In doing so federal policies fail to address in any substantial way the social conditions that correlate most significantly with the lives of struggling students—high rates of poverty, homelessness, inadequate nutrition, and gross funding inequities from one school district to another with the greatest disparities occurring between large urban school systems and strongly resourced, suburban school districts. Even as the essential importance of early childhood education becomes more and more accepted as indispensable for ongoing school success, the current iteration of RTT provides only modest increases in pre-school funding, which as Darling-Hammond points out, remains grossly inadequate given the large cuts in these programs because of the current fiscal crisis states face . . . $7.5 billion in cuts this year on top of $3 billion in reductions last year.

Corporate backers of federal policies that blame teachers, close schools and move children around like widgets on an assembly line refuse to engage the connections between poverty, student achievement and school funding. Instead, they habitually manipulate and misuse international testing data such as the reports from the Organization for Economic Cooperation and Development's (OECD) PISA (Program for International Student Assessment) studies to show how American schools are failing. Then, they ignore other OECD data reporting that shows the U.S. with the highest rate of childhood poverty (25 percent) among modern industrialized nations and a ranking of second from the bottom of 25 monitored nations in funding equity for public education. Darling-Hammond reinforces this data, pointing out that in 2009 U.S. schools with fewer than 10 percent of the students in poverty ranked first among the nations compared in the PISA study. On the other end of the socio-economic continuum, schools with more than 75 percent students from poverty homes ranked 50th alongside nations like Serbia. Finally, as Darling-Hammond stresses, it is the nationally low performing schools, the bottom 5 percent, which serve students living in poverty, that have had the resources and programs so necessary for development cut. In the larger national picture the majority of school districts spend three times more in high income school districts than is spent in the poorest districts. It is within the context of this ever widening economic and racial divide that we must frame and challenge the punitive impact that RTT continues to have on our most under-resourced public schools.

The struggle for school equity and equal opportunity has been central to the process of creating a more democratic and fair society for much of the 19th and 20th centuries. It is a struggle which again today complicates conversations in our communities, and within and between diverse groups of people who share a common goal of wanting what is best for the education of *all* of our children. Two communities where we live work and participate politically as educators illustrate this point well in their most recent developments—the public schools of Wisconsin, specifically the schools of Madison, Wisconsin and the Chicago Public Schools.

A Tale of Two Cities

During the same month, December of 2011, as the year of protest drew to a close, two epic dramas around charter schools were unfolding.

While hundreds of parents, teachers and citizens in Chicago rallied outside the South Clark Street Board of Education building, challenging the latest proposed round of school closures and the expansion of charter schools, 150 miles to the Northwest hundreds of citizens wearing blue Madison Prep Academy t-shirts packed a special Madison Metropolitan School District school board hearing and rallied to support their charter school proposal. In Chicago citizens, teachers, parents and students would occupy the school board meeting, effectively shutting it down. In Madison a large crowd of several hundred, at least the majority who were in favor of the charter school proposal, whooped it up, led by Kaleem Caire, the charismatic Urban League president. These two starkly contrasting pictures portrayed an amazing point of view wherein race and class caravan together, run parallel, intersect and collide across school reform battle lines.

Occupy Chicago Slows the CPS Board of Education Train

In Chicago, December 13, 2011, a Mayoral appointed school board continued, with Commercial Club of Chicago sponsorship, yet another round of school closings. Allied with the Mayor and the corporate dominated charter sponsoring organizations and other privately funded agencies like the Chicago Public Education Fund, the board members sought to apply another rubber stamp to school closures and charter expansion.

As the Chicago school board was scheduled to meet to take the first moves in closing a new group of schools, parents, citizens, and teachers occupied the street in an all-night vigil prior to the meeting. Co-authors John Duffy, Todd Price and the *Labor Beat* videographer(s) were there in solidarity, serving to witness first-hand the display and describe the tenor of the moment. Here is the testimony of one worker who calls out the board for its entanglement with the Commercial club interests, and exploitation of city workers:

> I work in Hyatt Hotel of Chicago for 16 years. Many of the members of my union work in the school cafeteria; they work for the school board. Let me tell you we have been fighting the Hyatt for over two years. A few months ago we went on a one week strike to send the Hyatt a message to meet the same standard as union workers across the city. The owners of the Hyatt Corporation are billionaires . . . one of the Pritzker family members in Chicago, Penny Pritzker . . . she is on the Chicago school board.[1]

After packing as many people as possible into the meeting, opponents of Chicago's turnaround and chartering policies directly resisted the board by putting into action a 'mic check' action, created and popularized by the Occupy Movement. Speaker after speaker read and repeated the words of the speaker that preceded them in challenging the proposed school closings with key words and phrases such as "save our schools" and "no more turnarounds" echoing loudly through the packed meeting room. The latter phrase significantly resonates with the Civil Rights era song "Ain't Nobody Gonna Turn Me Round." As security guards removed one protesting person, a new person would continue the challenge to the board with the remaining crowd shouting the refrain in turn. This went on until all protesters had been removed from the room well after the school board had retreated to recess out of the sight and sound of the citizens they refused to hear.

In the face of this growing, militant alliance of citizens, parents, the Chicago Teachers Union and university academics—who have come together as community allies in a group called Chicagoland Researchers and Advocates for Transformative Education (CReATE)—the board of education opted to go behind closed doors to make its decisions. The deliberate and planned disruption of the CPS meeting by union teachers, parents, community leaders and their allies was a new tactic that the resistance to school closing has adopted in Chicago where just as in Wisconsin those funding the attack on public education operate behind the scenes. Leaders of the Commercial Club of Chicago have attempted to characterize Chicago school reform as a failure (which is ironic, we note, because much of the school reform is informed by their corporate sponsored efforts). At the same time they adopt carte blanche the Obama *A Blueprint for Reform* which calls for, among other things, doubling down on high stakes testing and relying ever more so on charter schools.

The resistance movement in Chicago has directly confronted the Commercial Club approaches to reform by calling public attention to major Chicago initiatives around school improvement that challenge school closures and the federal turnaround model. In their most recent opposition to CPS school closures, union teachers, led by Karen Lewis and the Caucus of Rank and File Educators (CORE) and community activists have called on the school board and the Chicago media to give full attention to what a large group of schools have done to improve their overall operation, teaching and student learning. A small but compelling set of studies finds patterns in these schools that both question and refute the logic, fairness and effectiveness of CPS school closure and turnaround policies. The common features these schools share are no surprise to anyone who has ever taught in, worked in, sent their children to or personally spent any time in such schools. They share these common features: 1) strong, responsive school leadership, 2) the necessary resources to support school innovation, 3) the full respect for, participation and collaboration of parents and community, 4) an ongoing professional development focused on improving instruction and curriculum, and perhaps most importantly, 5) the fostering of a school culture and school-community relationships characterized by a strong sense of mutual respect and trust. These schools and their communities across the city have all contributed vital evidence and lessons about what it takes to strengthen schools in affirmative, vibrant and democratic ways.[2] Unfortunately, the stories and supporting research of these schools gets ignored and then buried locally and nationally as Commercial Club corporate reformers push chartering, school closure and the RTTT turnaround formula as the only hope for Chicago schools.

Putting the Brakes on Non-Instrumental Charter schools in Madison, Wisconsin

Much of the crowd gathered there on that fateful night in December 19, 2011, in Madison, Wisconsin demanded a board "yes" vote for a plan they hoped would result in a more racially equitable school system through the creation of two new African American charters, gender segregated and taught largely by African American teachers. The publicly elected school board voted down the proposal. The 5-2 vote came after hours of emotional testimony by supportive witnesses representing a multi-racial coalition of parents, business groups and many teachers.

The opposition, which represented a similar cross section of Madison, minus the business community and with fewer people of color, framed their dissent around principles tied to equity, concerns about corporate elite sponsorship, and strong reservations about a governance design that removed most of the control of the new schools from elected representatives and planned to staff the schools with teachers who would be non-union.

As is often missing in such debates, but present in Madison opposition, were well articulated concerns as to just how responsive and inclusive the educational programming would be to the needs of the students currently struggling and being failed. One key objection centered on the International Baccalaureate curriculum that these schools planned to use and doubts that this would be effective in addressing the academic needs of the vast majority of African American students. School sponsors led by the Greater Madison Area Urban League claimed to want to help children, however, the students who would be eligible to attend this school could be no more than one year below grade level on basic math and literacy development.

While we attended and videotaped much of the Madison meeting, two themes stood out for us—one was dominant and apparent; the second was hidden and only brought up by key opponents among the teacher union leadership, community activists and policy experts from area colleges. As outsiders and as advocates racial equity in public schools, we were greatly impacted by the repeated and eloquent outrage of so many deeply caring people with the failures of Madison public schools to make significant differences in the lives of large numbers of poor, black and Latino(a) children. Yet, as advocates for public education, we understood fully that the alternatives being proposed had been sponsored and supported by corporate foes of public education in Wisconsin—the Bradley Foundation, The Gates Foundation and their Commercial Club allies in Chicago, New York, Milwaukee and across the country and globe. What they sought in Madison, was not just two new public charters, but charter schools that intentionally were designed to be outside the democratic traditions of public education—they would be deliberately race segregated, freed from control of public accountability, deliberately non-union, but still financed with tax payer money. But that was not to be, at least on that fateful day. It was a victory for the traditions of inclusive democratic education that ironically was perceived by many Madison citizens as a loss for empowerment and opportunity. The work of reconciling these tensions remains.

Public Education Under Audit

The lives of teachers and students are being impacted in major ways, frequently disconcerting and often misunderstood. Even in places once thought immune, turnarounds and charterization are becoming the norm, and no one will escape the new audit culture of evaluation. As the attack on the rights of all teachers unfolds, the imposition of high stakes testing linking students' scores to teacher evaluation now spreads across the entire nation (and not just in our inner cities). Now the entire public education system is feeling what once only inner city teachers and public employees would experience. Soon, any state (and all of its school districts) accepting federal education money will need to put in place teacher evaluation methods tied in a substantial way to student test scores; they will have to have expanded the number of charter schools, and they will be forced to close and turnaround all of their schools with the lowest test scores. Often they will be approached with the possibility of having to turn over the governance of their turnaround school or schools to an outside educational maintenance organization.

What many are now concluding, not only the authors of this text, is that much of the so-called school reform is a fairly overt, orchestrated attack on public education governance, a political agenda which is parallel and complimentary to an undermining of democratic governance across American political life, not seen prior to the last generation.

Attacks on teachers are also attacks on the ideas, not only symbolic ones, but literal ideas concerning the purpose of education in a pluralistic democracy. If schools are forced to compete for students, if students and families are forced to choose, and if teachers are forced to teach to the curriculum that is prescribed to them, not only will education suffer, but so in turn will ideas. Historically it is this social space that is provided in the public sphere, the location for idea generation that has moved mountains. Ideas, emergent in the public school, have been contested, struggled over, fought for, implemented and ultimately enacted upon.

Ideas are powerful things, and those developed in the miniature community (as Dewey was to characterize the school) often preface progressive change for here and around the world. The peace and the civil rights movement(s), the deliberate and engaged consideration of pressing issues such as these are frequently, if at times only, given their due in public school classrooms . . . it is this social space that is under assault given a school reform agenda that feeds an audit culture, and starves a culture of inquiry.

Critical democratic educators need to address, not only the damage done to the culture of education, but must not shirk from calling out the unconscionable and growing disparity in resources, and consider the redistribution of wealth if we as a nation are to expect all students to have fair opportunity. Likewise, an engaged citizenry, knowledgeable and informed, should not long tolerate the corrosion of our democracy posed by the *Citizens United Supreme Court Case* and the undermining of the Bill of Rights by way of the so-called "War on Terror". These are the educational issues of our time, and we dare not let them slip away unexamined and unchallenged.

Democratic Curriculum: Vehicle for Educational Transformation

Public schools in the U.S. will fail to become the transformative, miniature communities that John Dewey had originally envisioned without widespread community support. Current school reform depends on an "all hands on deck" approach as the Obama administration is quick to proclaim, but turning around schools requires resources and a critical amount of trust, but now that support seems lacking. Indeed, many of the neighborhood organizations we've encountered throughout this book are growing increasingly suspect of the intentions with federal policies and top down reform. The increasing reliance on rigid teacher evaluations will hardly support the aim of fostering collaboration between those entrusted with the greatest responsibility for turning around the school—the teachers themselves.

Just as in the past, public schools can bolster and reproduce the status quo or they can sponsor dialogue and learning that critically examines the status quo, in effect, a *democratic curriculum.* Such a curriculum for expanding popular democracy had been a vehicle, parallel to but in great contrast with Commercial Club Curriculum. It offers schools and communities an opportunity for envisioning schools as liberatory organizations for social life and learning. A curriculum like this has features that should be found in the study of the humanities as well as mathematics, science and technology. As our friend, research scholar and citizen teacher activist Pauline Lipman points out advocates for public schools must also be proponents of schools that educate for civic engagement and true equality of human opportunity for the entire community. We cite and quote Lipman one more time here, for she has articulated four common features that we as citizen teachers have worked over the years to make integral to our classrooms on all levels of education. Lipman says such a curriculum would include:

1. *Participatory democracy:* Schools should be space where children, youth, educators, parents and community members participate in democratic discussion about what goes on there and about school improvement.

2. *Education for full development*: All children should have an intellectually and socially rich, culturally relevant, hopeful and joyful education that develops their full potential through academic subjects, arts, athletics, and connections with the community and environment.

3. *Equitably funded free public education*: All children and adults should have equal access to richly funded and resourceful free public education, pre-K through higher education, with the first step being to redress the education debts owed African Americans, Native people, Latino/as and others historically denied equitable education.

4. *Education as a tool for liberation*: Public education should be antiracist, anti-sexist, anti-heterosexist, and fully inclusive of all people. It should teach oppressed people's true histories and draw on their communities' cultures, languages, experiences, and social contributions and support their self-determination. Education should develop critical consciousness that is global in scope and prepare students to participate in transforming injustice and defending the environment.[3]

Educators, citizen teachers as we call ourselves and others who have taken up the defense of public education are resilient. We have not become resigned given recent victories versus the forces that would undo the modest yet powerful gains and future possibilities of the venerable if not staggered common school. The shutdown of the CPS board of education and the board's subsequent retreat behind closed doors to do the "people's business" reaffirms that board member should be elected in order to better reflect the face of the community. As the board of education advances with its failed plans for school closings and turnarounds, parents, citizens and teachers now call for a new model of school reform—based on funding equity, democracy and true local initiative that challenges the turnaround model entirely. Indeed, the many schools creating proven, successful alternatives indicate that the citizens have taken school reform into their own hands.

The blocking of the Mayoral takeover effort in Milwaukee in 2010, and the stalling of the creation of an unaccountable charter school authorizing board in 2011, which would have effectively given chartering power to the governor in Wisconsin, also indicates local grass roots support for real change, not a dismantling of the local and statewide public school systems. Wisconsin's resistance, including a successful campaign/recall to force another vote for governor, provides a template for how to respond to the worse, most regressive legislation that the state has seen in years.

Furthermore, the defeat of the anti-union referendum in Ohio indicates that rejection of the most extreme measures across the country is a battle now being engaged by citizens everywhere. Yet this Ohio effort to restore collective bargaining rights to public service workers including teachers, and the Wisconsin and Chicago efforts at pushing back against the privatization train, are tempered by the reality that corporate school reform efforts continue to proceed, as if in a vacuum, not hearing or seeing the resistance from below.

Still there is reason to believe that there may yet be "light at the end of the tunnel." At risk of being overly optimistic about the movement(s) underfoot— and in spite of the thirty year war waged on public education's students, schools and teachers— parents, teachers and students, and administrators are clamoring to participate on the road to authentic school reform. A *real* struggle for democratic public education carries forth across the country.

But as a school board supervisor from Milwaukee maintains, the race on the road to change will be a marathon, not a sprint. As we all trudge forward, not run blindly along this well beaten and shared path, we take inspiration from Howard Zinn, the late peoples' movement sage and historian. Zinn counseled us well on embracing optimism and avoiding pessimism in these difficult times when he said:

> I can understand pessimism, but I don't believe in it. It's not simply a matter of faith, but of historical evidence. Not overwhelming evidence, just enough to give hope, because for hope we don't need certainty, only possibility.[4]

With this spirit we have gathered the voices and told the stories that strengthen the optimism and determination of all of us who believe in the vital need and ongoing but yet to be fully realized promise public education must play in sustaining democracy in the United States.

Notes

1. Recorded by Larry Duncan, *Labor Beat: Shutdown at CPS Board Meeting Chicago*, 2011. See http://youtu.be/FAiDwPf7G8E

2. See *Designs for Change. The Big picture: School-initiated Reforms, Centrally-initiated Reforms, and Elementary School Achievement in Chicago* (1990 to 2005). (Chicago: Designs for Change, 2005). Retrieved June 18, 2010, from http://www.designsforchange.org/pubs.html; P. Sebring, E. Allensworth, A. Bryk, J. Easton, & S. Luppescu, *The essential supports for school improvement.* (Chicago: Consortium on Chicago School Research, 2006). Retrieved June 18, 2010, from http://ccsr.uchicago.edu/content/publications.php?pub_id=86; John Simmons, *An Education Success Story: How Eight Failing Schools in Chicago Were Turned Around Within Three Years; Strategic Learning Initiatives*, Chicago, 2010; also see John Simmons Testimony on school renewal in Chicago before the U.S. House Labor and Education Committee available at http://strategiclearninginitiatives.org/index.html; and *Chicago School Reform: Myths, Realities, and New Visions,* prepared by Chicagoland Researchers and Advocates for Transformative Education, June 2011 (updated) at http://createchicago.blogspot.com/

3. See Pauline Lipman, *The New Political Economy of Urban Education: Neoliberalism, Race, and the Right to the City.* (New York: Routledge. 2011). p. 164-165. See http://site.ebrary.com/id/10462530.

4. Howard Zinn, "The Optimism of Uncertainty" November 8, 2004, available at www.commondreams.org

About the Authors

Todd Alan Price is a National Louis University Associate Professor with a Ph.D. from the University of Wisconsin-Madison in Curriculum and Instruction, specialization Education Communications Technology. His work includes the study of educational policy and the implications of corporate-sponsored education reform on curriculum and instruction, at all levels. His previous books include *Classrooms without Walls: An Exploration in the Management of Video Distance Learning (VDL)* (2010); *The Myth and Reality of No Child Left Behind: Public Education and High Stakes Testing* (2009); and a chapter "Wiring the World" in *Campus Inc. Corporate Power in the Ivory Tower* (2000). He has lectured in China, Great Britain, and Germany and has received a diploma from Cuba for his study *Las Etapas de la Educación y la Revolución* (1994). Dr. Price teaches educational foundations, qualitative research and curriculum theory courses. He frequently uses video documentation of policy maker interviews and K-12 classroom observations in his research. He has also presented at conferences in Canada, Vietnam, Brazil and has traveled to Nicaragua, Mexico and El Salvador.

John Duffy is a retired high school Social Studies and English teacher who has worked in teacher education at National College of Education in the Interdisciplinary Studies Department and National Board Certification Program. He now coaches administrators and classroom teachers at a small alternative Chicago charter high school and is currently involved in community based inquiry and advocacy addressing curriculum equity. His research interests include critical democratic multicultural teaching and curriculum history around how students, parents, teachers and community activists challenged racial inequities during the first generation of integrated schools in Maywood and Oak Park, Illinois.

Tania Giordani is an advocate for equal access to quality education for all children. As an educator, she has taught at public elementary schools, private colleges and is currently a professor of Adult Education at the College of Lake County. No matter her role, Dr. Giordani's passion for children, parents and education always shines. Dr. Giordani recently presented *Theatre of the Oppressed* concerning school closings at the *We the People Tour*. The *We the People Tour* seeks to inspire local communities to get a conversation moving among and across stakeholder groups in today's educational landscape, prioritizing the voices of students, parents and teachers in helping to initiate a national dialogue about high quality education as a Constitutional right. Using a variety of educational and social events, the Tour promotes local activism around quality education for every child.

Andrea Lee is a social worker at the Grand Boulevard Federation. Grand Boulevard Federation is a collaborative community based not for profit organization whose mission is to increase the quality of life for children, youth, families and residents of Bronzeville by advocating for, and influencing policies, funding, programs, and strategies that maximize the effectiveness of the delivery of human and educational services, and by increasing the coordination of and access to these services and resources. The goal of these activities is a reformed system for the delivery of community, health, human and educational services that will improve the lives of children and youth, strengthen families, and result in a spiritually, physically, economically and socially healthy community.

Theresa Robinson is an assistant professor of secondary education at National Louis University and serves as the secondary science program coordinator. She provides content area professional development to Chicago Public School teachers grades Pk through 5. She has taught middle school through high school general science, biology and environmental science. Robinson studied biological sciences and secondary education at Southern Illinois University in Carbondale, Illinois, where she graduated with a doctorate in curriculum and instruction with a specialization in science and environmental education. She specializes in science teacher preparation, assessment for student learning, and culturally relevant science teaching.

Karen Roth is an adjunct faculty with the Department of Early Childhood at National Louis University. A 1985 graduate of Mills College masters in Early Childhood program, Roth has taught preschool and Kindergarten in lab schools and private schools in Illinois and California. She has been acting Community Service Director for NLU's Civic Engagement Center and is the coordinator of the NLU's NOLA Schools Project. Her research is focused on the professional development of university students through engaged service-learning experiences. Roth was a member of the planning committee for the 11th Annual International Association on Research in Service Learning and Civic Engagement Conference, Nov. 3-5, 2011, Chicago.

Robert Miranda is a Latino community activist in Milwaukee, Wisconsin. He is Publisher/Editor of the Milwaukee Spanish Journal and the Executive Director of Esperanza Unida, Inc. Miranda is also a columnist for the Yeni Asya Newspaper based in Istanbul, Turkey. His column is published once a week and is read nationwide.

Jack Gerson taught math at Oakland's Castlemont High until his retirement in June 2010. He is a co-founder of the Oakland Education Association's campaign to Bail Out Schools and Services, Not Banks, and in the past served on the OEA Executive Board, Bargaining Team, and represented OEA on the State Council of the California Teachers Association. He was an anti-war and anti-draft activist in the 1960s, and remains active today in the fight against austerity and for social justice.

Terry Jo Smith is a professor in the Disability, Equity and Education Doctoral Program at National Louis University in Chicago. Her major areas of interest, research and teaching involve the intersection of disability and delinquency and the social, political and systemic forces that contribute to and maintain marginal identities and experiences for those so labeled. She is the author of three books, including "Teaching the Children We Fear; Stories from the Front" which is a critical auto-ethnographic rendering of a decade of teaching students labeled "severely emotionally disturbed" in the inner city. Her current research focuses on the ramifications of what gets designated as "data" in educational reform and the shifting locus of those decisions in the current "occupation" of the educational enterprise by government and business elites.

Geoff Berne is a former teacher of English literature at San Jose State College, California State College at Hayward, and UCLA who was a member of Ohio PTA/Citizens Against Vouchers in the 1990s. He was communications director for electoral opponents of State Representative and later Butler County Commissioner, Michael A. "Mike" Fox, the author of the law establishing Ohio's U.S. Supreme Court-tested vouchers experiment in Cleveland, and was an internet commentator and campus lecturer on the 1999 war in the Balkans. In between stints as university instructor and internet journalist, Berne founded and hosted a concert hall for bluegrass and other vintage music, the Englishtown Music Hall in Englishtown, New Jersey, and co-produced the series "Bluegrass At The Englishtown Music Hall" for New Jersey Public Television and "An Evening With Bill Monroe And Friends" for WXXI-TV, Rochester, New York, the latter broadcast on PBS. He produced an African-American jazz and lindy dance cabaret at New York's Village Gate and a total of nine bluegrass festivals at Lincoln Center in New York City, three in Avery Fisher Hall.

Thomas J. Mertz is a history instructor at Edgewood College and a co-chair of Community and Schools Together, which works to maintain strong education funding for Madison schools. Thomas "T.J." serves on the board of the Wisconsin Alliance for Excellent Schools and was a member of Madison's School District's Equity Task Force. His civic work has been about bringing together diverse people to improve our community, and to that end he is a relentless and insightful blogger/editor for the site Advocating on Madison Public Schools (AMPS).

Baudelaire K. Ulysse earned his B.A. in religions from Northwestern College, his M.Div. from Trinity International University, and his ED.D. in curriculum and social inquiry from National Louis University. He has taught at National-Louis University, Elgin Community College, and Waubonsee Community College. His research interests span across various topics such as globalization, educational economics, faculty development, neoliberalism, Haitian history and politics, philosophy, theology, and religions.